THE RELUCTANT AMBASSADOR

The Life and Times of Sir Thomas Chaloner,
Tudor Diplomat

THE RELUCTANT AMBASSADOR

The Life and Times of Sir Thomas Chaloner,
Tudor Diplomat

Dan O'Sullivan

First published 2016

Amberley Publishing
The Hill, Stroud
Gloucestershire, GL5 4EP

www.amberley-books.com

ISBN 978 1 4456 5164 4 (hardback)
ISBN 978 1 4456 5165 1 (ebook)

British Library Cataloguing in Publication Data.
A catalogue record for this book is available
from the British Library.

Typesetting and Origination by Amberley Publishing
Printed in the UK.

CONTENTS

FOREWORD BY LORD GISBOROUGH

I am delighted that Dan has produced this history of the only member of the Chaloner family, along with his son, to reach fame. It must have taken considerable thought and research, and has thrown up a quantity of information new to me. It is also nicely produced. I read it with the greatest interest and enjoyment from cover to cover.

Some years ago I was intrigued to find, when cycling in Wales, the house still standing where Sir Thomas Chaloner's father, Roger, was brought up, before emigrating to London in the second decade of the sixteenth century to make the fortune that enabled him to have his son educated. Roger, I imagine, must have been a second son since the first would have taken over the farm on his father's death. There are still many Chaloners in the area of Wrexham who probably derive from this older brother.

Richard Chaloner, 3rd Baron Gisborough

PREFACE

Sir Thomas Chaloner was an ambassador for Queen Elizabeth I and a prolific author whose life has not received from historians the attention it deserves. This book is an attempt to go some way to remedying this. The early chapters are about Chaloner's youth and rise to prominence as a courtier and diplomat. Of these, chapter 7, which contains extracts from his account book, made when he was in his early thirties, is the most personal, and perhaps gives the greatest insight into his character.

The second half of the book concerns Chaloner the ambassador. The main sources for this period are the hundreds of letters from and to him which he or his recipients presumably filed carefully, and which are today held in various archives. They are paraphrased and quoted in the volumes of state papers compiled and published over a century ago, but can today be most easily consulted on the internet. I have mainly quarried this invaluable source[1] but I have also tracked down a few of Chaloner's original letters in the British Library and the National Archives at Kew. This is why the majority of the letters I quote from seem relatively modern, though the ones taken directly from the archives revert back to the sixteenth century in their style.

In most cases the spelling has been modernised. I have tried to make references to my sources as full as possible for others who may want to follow up aspects of Chaloner's story.

Before I started this project I imagined state papers to be most likely boring and limited in scope, but I have been surprised how much information on various aspects of Chaloner's life can be gleaned from this source, including about his family, his literary output, his illnesses and even his shopping habits. We hear his opinion of Spain ('Spain, quoth he, nay rather Pain') and of his young niece and nephew ('my next brother's children are not such as he or I make great account upon'). Much is revealed in the state papers.

I am most grateful to the authors of two dissertations concerning Chaloner. Without them I very much doubt if I would have ever got started, and I owe a lot to all their insights and hard work. They are Professor Clarence Miller, who wrote a life of Chaloner as part of his Harvard PhD thesis on Chaloner's translation of Erasmus' *The Praise of Folly*, and Phyllis Gene Blazer, whose PhD thesis from Buffalo University, NY, was about Chaloner more generally. I also have a debt to Yvette Erskine, who, as a graduate student at the University of Tasmania, wrote four papers on Chaloner which she kindly showed me.

A Note on Dates

Under the Tudors, the year was reckoned as beginning on 25 March. This means that dates falling between 1 January and 24 March, which we see as towards the beginning of a new year, were considered by them as being towards the end of the old year. Therefore, when citing a date falling between 1 January and 24 March, I have modernised the dating, changing the year as though 1 January had been the beginning of that year. So, for instance, 14 February 1561 in a contemporary document becomes 14 February 1562, or occasionally, to avoid confusion, 14 February 1561/2.

FAMILY TREES

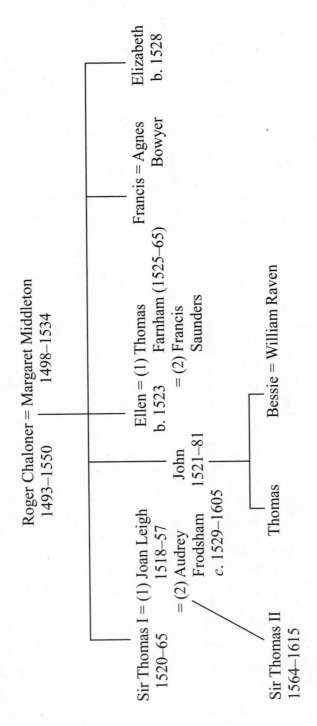

Sir Thomas Chaloner's immediate family.

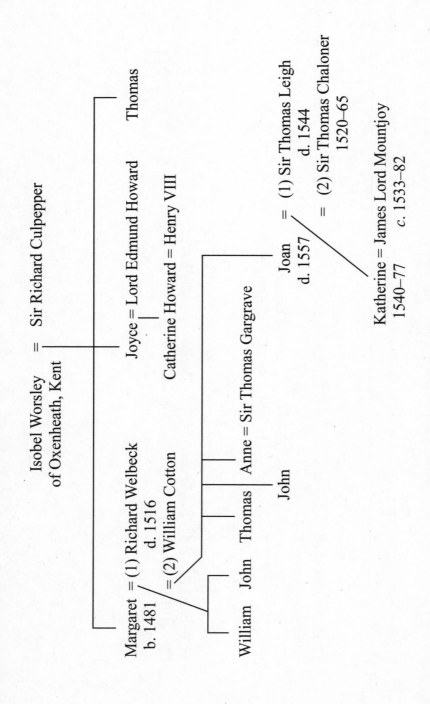

Family connections of Sir Thomas Chaloner's wife, Joan.

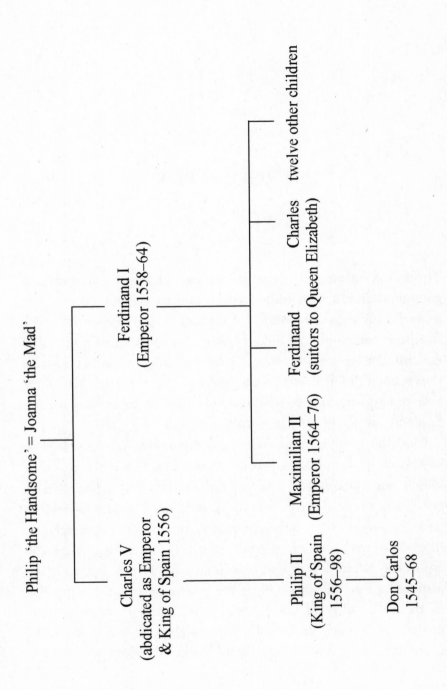

The Hapsburgs in Chaloner's time.

INTRODUCTION

Thomas Chaloner is an outstanding example of someone emerging from a mercantile background to achieve prominence in early Tudor government and diplomacy. He also personifies the close contemporary links between humanist scholarship and government service. However, his final posting, as ambassador to the court of Philip II at Madrid, also shows clearly the difficulties and dangers facing one whose job was to mediate between England and Spain early in Elizabeth's reign.

Chaloner grew up and started his diplomatic career at a time of relative peace and good order nationally. The efficiency with which both Henry VIII and his father before him managed to crush any opposition or discontent contrasted with the violence and anarchy of the previous century, and successful merchants like Chaloner's father, Roger, were able to profit from the country's internal stability. It was a time, too, when learning acquired a new prestige among the governing classes, partly due to the availability of the printed book, and the accompanying growth in literacy and readership. Intelligent young men like Chaloner, whose fathers had useful contacts and could afford to send their sons to the grammar school and then on to university, now had chances often denied to earlier generations. As lawyers, officials and courtiers they could rise through the Tudor hierarchy largely through hard work and their own talents rather than merely via aristocratic patronage. Yet this was still a violent age. When Sir Nicholas Throckmorton and Sir Thomas Smith, Elizabeth's two genteel ambassadors to France, had an argument, they both drew their daggers and had to be restrained. War and warlike skills continued to carry their age-old prestige – Chaloner received his knighthood on the field of battle, as did many of his colleagues – yet the appeal of humanism and scholarship was now a close rival. As a contemporary wrote:

> A knight hath received that honour not only to defend with the sword Christ's faith, and his proper country but also, and that most chiefly, he should effectually with his learning and wit assail vice and error, having thereunto for his sword and spear his tongue and pen.[1]

Chaloner was knighted after the Battle of Pinkie Cleugh against the Scots in 1547. A knighthood was, of course, a major step forward for an ambitious young courtier and diplomat. By this time he held the post of clerk to the Privy Council, and had established a reputation as a reliable and energetic official. He was also starting to achieve repute as an author, much increased two years later by his translation from Latin of *The Praise of Folly*, the well-known satire by Erasmus. He was a member of a coterie of young humanists, all involved in both politics and literature. In addition, he had managed to acquire some knowledge of both Italian and French. Undoubtedly, too, he could converse fluently in Latin with clerics and also with classically educated laymen from different nations.[2] But perhaps his most valuable asset was his cautious and apparently neutral attitude when it came to the various religious changes brought about

by the regimes of Edward VI, Mary and Elizabeth. As he once
wrote to his friend Sir John Mason, he knew how to keep his
opinions to himself. These qualities led to his almost continuous
employment by the state during the stormy period between
Henry's Dissolution of the Monasteries and Elizabeth's accession.

Chaloner's rapid rise to prominence as a trusted diplomat was
no doubt helped by his friendship with William Cecil, the future
secretary of state to Queen Elizabeth. His success culminated in a
promotion which might have seemed to many an agreeable and
prestigious prospect, but which to him soon proved the opposite.
He was appointed resident ambassador at the court of Philip II,
ruler of Spain, Flanders and the New World. In fact, he never
wanted to be sent to Spain and as soon as he arrived could not
wait to be allowed to leave. Today thousands of Britons rush
to Spain for sun, sea and the Mediterranean diet, but, as I shall
explain, poor Chaloner's case was very different. He once wrote
to Queen Elizabeth from Madrid, 'I have always had a zeal to
live at home, and do prefer my country before all others. Your
highness pleasure and service excepted, it is not large proffers
could make me continue here lengthier than to spur the horse
and away.'[3]

For two reasons this posting turned out to be particularly
awkward and demanding. Firstly, this was an age of warring
ideologies: Lutherans and Calvinists faced the Catholic powers
of Europe led by Philip, and neither side was prepared to
compromise. Unfortunately, the Elizabethan settlement of 1559,
the year of Chaloner's appointment, put England firmly in the
Protestant camp, which meant that Spain and England were now
ideological enemies. Secondly, the post of resident ambassador
was a fairly new one throughout Europe, and no one had quite
worked out how such an official ought to behave or be treated.
All this put a great burden on the ambassador himself, who was
expected to please simultaneously two governments with very

different laws and customs. Chaloner was perhaps the man to succeed here if anyone could, but nevertheless he felt a failure, and the strain of trying to fulfil his duty against all the obstacles put in his way no doubt contributed to his ill health and his death shortly after returning home from Spain.

We know quite a lot about two periods in Chaloner's life. One is the early 1550s, due to the survival of his personal accounts, and the other is his time as ambassador, dealt with in chapters 9 to 20. The rest of his life is not so well served, and there are gaps in the sources where assumptions have to be made. Chaloner died young – in his forty-fifth year – but I feel Clarence Miller was quite right in saying that he achieved more than most people who live their full three score years and ten. Miller also wonders whether 'like many (perhaps most) men he was too busy to be happy', but this to me seems more questionable since surely a full and busy life, and a consciousness of having done one's best, is a road to happiness, even for a reluctant ambassador.[4]

I

ROGER CHALONER
1493–1550

This first chapter is not about Sir Thomas, but rather his father, Roger, who was born in Denbighshire, Wales, in 1493. The Chaloner family was an old one with roots going back into the distant history of Wales, and allegedly there were princes and tribal leaders among their remote forebears. In the Revd John Graves's *History of Cleveland* (1808) there is a detailed family tree of Chaloner ancestors, said to be 'transcribed from a roll now in the possession of Robert Chaloner of Guisborough' who was a descendant.[1] It should be remembered, however, that the sixteenth century was an age when the upwardly mobile, often with the connivance of the College of Heralds, frequently tried to improve their status by inventing family trees stretching far back into the past. Similarly, we cannot be certain that the family derived their name from Châlons-sur-Marne, from where they were said to have originally migrated to this country.

Sometime between 1515 and 1520 Roger and his wife Margaret migrated to London, becoming two of the hundreds arriving to seek their fortune in the rapidly expanding capital. In 1520 Margaret gave birth to Thomas, the first of her five children. From what we can gather from scattered references, Roger now embarked on a successful business career, finally becoming a member of the prestigious Company of Mercers. It may be that his wife's father, Richard Middleton, who came from a well-off Welsh family and who was already settled in London, helped him make a start in his career as a merchant.

In 1522 Roger Chaloner was granted the office of gauger, or exciseman, for Bristol. It was apparently understood that the duties of this post need not involve residence in that city. A few years later we hear of him as an official in the London Custom-house, a place of opportunity and useful contacts for an up-and-coming merchant. In 1531 he was a member of a commission appointed to examine the accuracy of a list of commodities and the customs duties payable on them. There is a report about this time which reveals that among the goods he was himself dealing with on the European market was spermaceti, a substance derived from sperm whales and much used in the making of candles. Stephen Vaughan, the English ambassador at Antwerp, wrote to Thomas Cromwell to ask him whether or not he should now sell Cromwell's stock of spermaceti, remarking that 'the price is not likely to rise, as so much comes from England. Roger Challenger, late of the Custom-house, has much and always hearkens for the price in these parts'.[2]

This letter shows that Roger was already known to Vaughan, and probably also to Cromwell, who at this moment was riding high, having just been appointed to the Privy Council. Between now and 1536 it is clear that Roger Chaloner had a business relationship with Cromwell. He acted as a receiver of fees due to Cromwell from certain lands in Hertfordshire and Middlesex. Two years later, when he was granted the lease of a water mill in Ireland, he is described as 'a sewer of the Chamber'. The duties of a sewer were theoretically to seat the guests, and taste and serve the food at royal banquets, though by this date these tasks were mainly nominal. Then, in 1534, Roger and a colleague jointly obtained the lucrative position of teller of receipts in the Exchequer. Interestingly, he received this post not from Cromwell but from Henry Norris, a leading courtier and close friend of the king.

All these various offices accrued by Roger Chaloner – gauger, commissioner, teller, sewer – were part of the elaborate and unwieldy network of Tudor government. The Tudor court, and within it the royal household, was not merely concerned with the king's personal needs, but also in governing the whole country. Members of the household, down to and even including domestic servants, were being utilised to perform duties that were nothing to do with their official tasks. We might describe those like Roger, who existed on the periphery of the court, as civil servants, except that the term itself is quite anachronistic. There was no organised bureaucracy of responsible departments staffed by trained and salaried civil servants. If a salary was attached to a certain office it was often small and irregularly paid. The holder was expected to compensate for his time and effort through fees, expenses and gifts, not to say bribes. It was a time when the creaking machinery of central government was expanding fast, opening up new areas of possible advance to men of ability from the middle strata of society. But in this seemingly confused and casual system it was not enough to be hard-working; one also needed luck and, above all, patronage from those further up the ladder. From what we can deduce about Roger he possessed all three of these assets. Richard Middleton, Stephen Vaughan and Henry Norris – to say nothing of Thomas Cromwell himself – might all have had a hand in his rise to wealth and influence.

By 1537 Roger Chaloner had definitely arrived. He is listed as one of the fifty-three freemen householders of the Company of Mercers for that year.[3] The members of the twelve livery companies of London were among the wealthiest merchants in the country. Each company represented a trade, and of them all, the mercers held the highest status. They played a prominent part in public processions as well as supplying the luxury cloths, the silks and satins from abroad, which were necessary for such occasions. Naturally, by now Roger would have had accommodation suitable for his status, his family and his business. Various clues make it likely that he owned or leased a property on 'Marry's Key' in the parish of St Mary Hill in the ward of Billingsgate.[4] This comprised 'a messuage, a wharf and a jebitt', which must have been entirely consistent with the activities of a mercer.[5] It was a waterfront property in the wealthiest part of Billingsgate. The 1541 subsidy shows Roger Chaloner paying a tax of thirty shillings based on 'goods' valued at £60. The subsidy was a tax which applied only to the relatively rich, and was probably a considerable underestimate of real wealth. Goods deemed assessable included coin, plate, household items, stocks of merchandise, and any 'moveable' goods aside from clothing. Roger's assessment implies that his was certainly among the richest 5 per cent of London households in 1541.

Three years later Roger and his second wife were granted a much larger and more imposing property: the mansion known as 'Abbots Inn', or 'Waltham'.[6] This had once been the town house of the abbots of Waltham Abbey, one of the largest monasteries in London. It was in the same parish as Roger's wharf, but further up St Mary Hill from the river, and just to the south of the parish church on the western side of St Mary-at-Hill Street.[7] The house was destroyed in the Great Fire of 1666, but a few fragments of ancient wall have survived, and these were investigated in 1980 by archaeologists from the Museum of London.[8] On his death in 1550 Roger left this house, described as 'my great mansion in Saint Mary Hill parish called Waltham', to his widow, Isobel.

Roger had at least three wives, but we possess little information about any of them. When he first arrived in London he was already married to Margaret, by whom he then had three sons, including Thomas, and two daughters. She died in 1534. Ten years later, when Roger was granted a lease on Abbot's Inn, his wife was named as Dorothy. But when he died his widow was Isobel. So far as is known, neither Dorothy nor Isobel bore him any children.

What was Roger's attitude to the world – his politics, his religion? We know nothing whatsoever about them, but, as Michael Holroyd says, it is permissible for a biographer to speculate. During the thirty years or so that Roger lived in London, buying and selling goods and penetrating at least to the fringes of the court, momentous changes were taking place. It was a dangerous time to have personal views about these changes, or at least to express them in public. Roger would certainly have been aware of the massive propaganda put out by Henry's scholars, publicists and printers defending royal policies. To mention just one example, in early 1532 there was the public scattering in the streets of London of a pamphlet originally produced in 1529 by the lawyer Simon Fish which attacked papal authority and the pretensions of the English Church.[9]

From 1527 onwards the English had been confronted with a dangerous paradox. On the one hand, their ruler, Henry VIII, was determined to divorce his wife Catherine and marry Anne Boleyn. This was the king's 'Great Matter', and it eventually involved his repudiation of the pope, and his assuming headship of the Church in England, since there was no other way to achieve his aim. Opposition to these measures was made treason, and punished by execution. Shortly afterwards came attacks on the wealth of the Church, and in particular on the monasteries, all of which were dissolved between 1536 and 1540. It does seem unlikely that Roger was opposed to this particular policy, since he benefited directly from the dissolution of Waltham Abbey.

On the other hand, Henry was nothing if not conservative in his religious views. He in fact became a Catholic without the pope. It was heresy to express Lutheran views or to acquire the forbidden books of the reformers, even including English translations of the Bible. The path between treason and heresy was therefore not an easy one to follow for anyone with strong religious principles. Did Roger have such principles? As a mercer, he would no doubt have had dealings with merchants from the Continent, and hence would surely have known about the new ideas coming out of the Netherlands and Germany. He also might have had access to illegal books which were being smuggled from ships into English ports. Did he avail himself of such opportunities?

Roger would no doubt have been taken aback when Henry Norris, through whose patronage he had obtained an office in the Exchequer, was implicated in the fall of Anne Boleyn in 1536. Norris, one of those accused of adultery with Anne, was imprisoned in the Tower and subsequently executed. However, it seems that Roger had by this date formed a business connection with Thomas Cromwell, whose fall from power was still some way off.

All in all, we might conject from the few facts we know that whatever his personal views about what was happening to the country, Roger Chaloner kept them to himself, as did the vast majority of his contemporaries. Once Henry had decisively broken with the pope, England became somewhat isolated diplomatically, and there was no knowing how other Catholic powers, especially France and Spain, might react. Merchants who dealt with foreign countries valued peace and stability above all. With few exceptions they got on with their business affairs and left diplomatic and religious arguments to others.

Roger certainly played a crucial role in his eldest son Thomas's upbringing and early career. He must have hired tutors to teach the boy Latin in preparation for grammar school, and later on most likely hired other tutors to teach him French, Italian and possibly Spanish, not languages that figured in the curricula of either school or university. And later, following university, it was presumably Roger who somehow arranged that Thomas, aged seventeen, should join the household of Thomas Cromwell. It was also Roger who, in 1544, found Thomas his first position in government, as a petty official. This was the post of teller of receipts in the Exchequer, which had become vacant after the death of Roger's original colleague in that post. It was now to be shared between father and son. But Roger must surely have been delighted when, a year later, Thomas gained in addition a more important office, that of clerk to the Privy Council. The son had now progressed further than his father ever could, and the main reason for that was the education the father had obtained for the son.

In 1550 Roger died. According to Thomas, in a letter written thirteen years later, he died of 'calculus renium', or stones in the kidney.[10] In his will, while Thomas and his other children were granted shares in his estate, his widow Isobel was also well provided for. She was left considerable property: 'the great mansion in Saint Mary Hill parish', along with 'a dwelling mansion in Tower street' and 'the lease on a house in which Doctor Huych dwelleth on this side of Charing Cross'.[11] Servants and various relatives were also remembered with bequests ranging from 14s to £20, and ten gowns were to be made for ten poor women, to be delivered on the day of his burial. Consistent with Roger's character as a self-made man, his three sons were ordered to pay to his estate the debts they owed him 'or suffer to have the same amounts withdrawn or deducted from their portions'. Roger's recently knighted son Thomas was now the head of the family, with all the responsibilities that entailed.

2

EDUCATION
1527–1538

Thomas Chaloner, the oldest of Roger's five children, was born in about 1520, very likely in the parish of St Mary Hill, Billingsgate.[1] He almost certainly attended one of the nearby grammar schools at the usual age of seven or eight. Of these the strongest candidate is St Paul's School, partly because it was the nearest to the Chaloner home, but also because it was closely linked with the Company of Mercers. John Colet, who refounded the school in 1512, was himself the son of a master mercer. In the statutes which he composed for St Paul's, Colet ordained that the mercers should be responsible for governing the school, including the appointment of the headmaster (known as the high master):

The Mercers shall assemble together in the schoolhouse … they shall chose this master, and give him his charge, saying unto him in this wise: 'Sir, we have chosen you to be master and teacher of this school, to teach the children of the same not only all good literature, but also good manners, And every year at candlemass, when the Mercers be assembled in the schoolhouse, ye [the Master] shall submit to our examination, and found doing your duty according, ye shall continue; otherwise, reasonably warned, you shall content you to depart.[2]

Yet another reason why Roger Chaloner is likely to have chosen St Paul's for his no doubt precocious young son was that the school already had a reputation for turning out pupils well grounded in the Latin they would need to enter university, where even the lectures were given in that language. Colet himself was an eminent humanist, and both he and his friend Erasmus had written textbooks to be used in the school.

St Paul's was founded to provide a free education for 153 boys, which made it the largest grammar school in the country. Discipline was strict, and the hours long. Colet wrote, 'The children shall come into the school in the morning at seven of the clock, both winter and summer, and tarry there until eleven, and return again at one of the clock, and depart at five.' Although education was free, parents were expected to provide the required books for their children, as well as wax (not inferior tallow) candles in winter. More importantly, Colet specified that boys applying to enter the school must already be able to 'read and write Latin and English sufficiently'. This would imply that Thomas had been tutored privately at home from a very early age.

St Paul's School was situated on the east side of St Paul's churchyard, an important public space where crowds often gathered to witness civic or religious ceremonies. During his years as a schoolboy Thomas may have seen and noted many of the major events of the epoch, either when he was at school or from his home near the river. For instance, on Shrove Tuesday 1527 Cardinal Thomas Wolsey organised the formal burning of Luther's books in front of the cathedral. A procession involving six Lutherans in penitential dress carrying symbolic faggots and huge lighted tapers halted at the north door, where the prisoners repented their sins and were led around the fire three times before casting their faggots into it.

Then again, in 1533, when Thomas was thirteen, there took place the coronation of Anne Boleyn. This event lasted four days and has been called 'one of the best organised and best documented coronations in English history'.[3] It was designed by Henry partly as a test of the loyalty of the court and city, and of their support for his policies. The Company of Mercers played a major part in the ceremonies and their preparation. As mentioned above, it was their members who supplied the vast amounts of luxury cloth needed for the event. Some of the items required for just one of the many processions organised for this coronation are listed in the state papers. They included 'a kirtle and mantle of cloth of gold furred with ermines, a lace of silk and gold with tassels for the mantle, a litter timber covered with cloth of gold … the streets between the Tower and Westminster to be garnished with tapestry, arras, silk, &c … a canopy of gold with valance to be borne by 16 knights … six henchmen on palfreys harnessed with cloth of gold … a stage to be made latticed and covered with rich cloths'.[4]

Roger Chaloner may have played a role in all this because part of the coronation ceremonies involved forty-eight livery barges, 'all painted and gilded and hung with banners and tapestries', which set off from St Mary Hill, Billingsgate, for Westminster. He might have been on one of the barges, or perhaps he witnessed the event from outside his house together with his family. It may be, too, that the thirteen-year-old Thomas was one of the children who sang for Anne in St Paul's churchyard, or that he was among those who were placed on a platform at the east end of the cathedral to recite poetry for the king and queen.[5]

It is also possible that Thomas witnessed some of the executions of those who refused to swear agreement to Henry's headship of the English Church, although, since most of these took place in 1535, he might have already left London for Cambridge. It was, for example, the fate of several leading

Carthusians to be dragged across London from the Tower to Tyburn (now Marble Arch) where they were half-hanged, disembowelled, quartered and beheaded, as an example to others who might have been disposed to deny Henry's supremacy.

Such happenings no doubt had a powerful effect on the mind of a sensitive and intelligent boy growing up in the heart of the city. It must have been a confusing time – and not only for Thomas. A time when one was expected to reject the authority of the 'Bishop of Rome', but also to hate the teachings of that 'heretic' Martin Luther. The ageing and conservative English king was insistent that his people follow him along the narrow middle path that he had chosen. The lesson that Thomas was learning as he grew older was perhaps the same lesson that had been learnt by his father before him: to keep one's personal religious and political principles to oneself. Caution and flexibility were the keys to survival in a world that had been deposed of its certainties.[6]

In the mid-1530s, when he was about fourteen, the usual age for entry to university at that time, Thomas went up to Cambridge.[7] According to the Venns, the father-and-son authors of *Alumni Cantabrienses*, he may have gone to St John's College, and other historians have followed this lead.[8] Each college was a self-contained unit, much smaller than in subsequent centuries. For instance, in 1522, about fifteen years before Chaloner's arrival, St John's contained thirty-one fellows and rectors, nineteen scholars and forty-nine undergraduates.[9] It was at that time said to be the largest and most learned college in either Oxford or Cambridge. Whichever Cambridge college Chaloner did attend, discipline was harsh, and corporal punishment by no means exceptional. The working day seems to have been even longer than at grammar school. At St John's the statutes prescribed that the students should rise at 4 a.m., summer and winter. It was also laid down – whether universally obeyed or not, one doesn't know – that only Latin should be spoken throughout the college once they had left the confines of their rooms. Students had to attend a range of lectures, and be examined every day as to how much they had grasped of the content of these lectures. No doubt they were also expected to study in the college library, with its hard benches and chained books.

As in earlier centuries, the usual curriculum for an undergraduate was still the *trivium*, which consisted of grammar, logic and rhetoric; the word *trivium* itself is a Latin term meaning the three ways which lead to truth. It formed the foundation of a medieval education, but by Chaloner's time it had been considerably modified via the insights of Renaissance humanism. For instance, with rising standards Latin grammar was no longer regarded as a necessary part of the curriculum, since students were now assumed to have fully mastered this by the time they reached the university. But the other parts of the *trivium* were still considered important. Logic (or dialectic) was the process of analysing thought and learning to distinguish between good and false arguments. Rhetoric was the art of communicating ideas from one mind to another. All the teaching and the discussions between students and teachers were, of course, in Latin.

Apparently, Chaloner left Cambridge without taking a degree, as did many students, so we have no way of knowing how far his studies went. The *trivium* was a preparation for the *quadrivium*, which involved arithmetic (number), geometry (number in space), music (number in time) and astronomy (number in space and time). At St John's there was a particular emphasis on the two former subjects. This was due to John Fisher, Bishop of Rochester, a scholarly humanist who had helped to found the college in 1515.[10] Fisher allotted a special place to mathematics, funding lectureships out of his own pocket. As far as music is concerned, we do know that Chaloner was musical and played the lute, but of course this proves nothing about his university studies.

Another innovatory reform which Fisher had introduced to St John's was the study of Greek. It is debatable whether Chaloner, who in later life gained a reputation among scholars for the reams of Latin verse he produced, also knew Greek. Miller thinks probably not, arguing that if he had, he would certainly have translated something from Greek into Latin or English during his literary career. However, Roger Ascham, who taught at St John's in Chaloner's time, wrote to a friend that 'Aristotle and Plato are now read by the boys in the original language but that has been done among us at St John's for the last five years'.[11] It seems unlikely that Chaloner, no doubt one of the more linguistically gifted students in the college, did not do the same – he may even have started Greek at St Paul's. There is also other evidence. In 1553 John Withals, the author of *A shorte dictionarie for yonge begynners*, dedicated his book to Chaloner, humbly submitting himself 'to your mastership's correction, whom I know to be excellently well learned both in the Greek and in the Latin'.[12] Furthermore, one item in Chaloner's account book shows that a year after this dedication he bought himself a Greek lexicon.[13] All in all, it seems probable that he did have at least some Greek.

By examining events, national or local, that took place during Chaloner's time at university, one might make a guess at what he himself experienced and felt. The second half of the 1530s was a disruptive time for students at Cambridge. In 1535 royal injunctions were published which covered various aspects of university life, including the syllabus. The teaching of canon law, the medieval apparatus governing Church courts, was downgraded, new textbooks prescribed, and the 'frivolous questions and obscure glosses' of medieval schoolmen abandoned.[14] All scholars and fellows now had to swear the Oath of Supremacy, agreeing that the king, not the pope, was head of the English Church. For the members of St John's College the most terrible result of these measures was what happened to John Fisher, who had been the guiding star of the college ever since its foundation. Over the years he had produced no less than three sets of statutes governing the way the college was run, and his influence as a humanist and educationalist was widespread. For a long time Fisher had been a supporter of Catherine of Aragon, Henry's first wife, and he had opposed the royal divorce and Henry's marriage to Anne Boleyn. He had even gone so far as to enter into correspondence with Emperor Charles V's ambassador concerning a possible invasion by imperial forces to forcibly restore Catherine – who happened to be Charles's aunt – to the English throne. Now he refused the oath, was accused of treason, and beheaded on Tower Hill on 22 June 1535. Fisher was then sixty-nine, and his death must have been a major shock to all those whose lives he had touched.[15] It is not unreasonable to conclude that Thomas Chaloner was one of these. Very likely he was studying at St John's at the time Fisher was executed, or at least was there, or at another college, within six months of the event.

Between 1536 and 1540 all the monasteries in the kingdom were dissolved, and their extensive property passed on to others. The Dissolution provided an opportunity for profit to Cambridge colleges, which were able to make deals with abbots and priors who realised that their monastic houses and property were about to disappear and thought they might as well sell what they could before this happened. After the Dissolution it also became possible for colleges to pillage the numerous empty buildings for stone and tiles, or to negotiate favourable prices for all the lead suddenly available on the open market. The result of all this was a very visible building spree, but on the streets of Cambridge monks and friars in their various distinctive robes were no more to be seen. Was their passing regretted by the students? Probably we will never know.

As well as the disappearance of the monks, there was the psychological impact on ordinary citizens of Henry's treatment of the monasteries, which had played such an important role in urban life. As one historian explains, many ordinary people took the opportunity to acquire ex-monastic items. It is likely that in doing so the new owners changed their basic attitude towards things religious:

> People learned to devalue sacred properties and objects. The livery men whose cushions were made of altar cloths, the woman whose crystal perfume bottle once held the finger bone of a saint, the carpenter who made his living making and dismantling sacred objects, the yeoman whose doorstep had been an altar, and all the families whose fortunes were improved by the dissolutions had lost their fear of the sacred. They had lost some of their respect for the church, too, learning to see it as a source of wealth rather than a source of spiritual comfort.[16]

In 1536 the Pilgrimage of Grace, a revolt against Henry VIII's Dissolution of the Monasteries, flared up in Lincolnshire and then in Yorkshire. This traumatic event would certainly have had a major impact on Cambridge students, all the more so because troops under the Duke of Norfolk were stationed in the town for several weeks before being sent north to confront the rebels. This dangerous, though ultimately unsuccessful, rebellion of the common people very likely had the effect on someone like Chaloner of confirming his support of authority and his awareness of the ease with which law and order could be disrupted at a time of popular unrest. But again, perhaps the impact of all these drastic changes merely made the young Chaloner more reticent, more cautious about expressing personal views on such topics. From what we know about the rest of his life, both suggestions seem quite plausible.

We cannot be absolutely sure that Chaloner went to St John's, but there was another student who was definitely there, and who was about the same age as he was. This was William Cecil, whose father, Richard, was a minor employee in Henry VIII's court. Blazer suggests that the fathers were friends, though I have seen no particular evidence of this.[17] It may therefore be that the two sons first got to know each other at university. Miller thinks this is unlikely because when Cecil wrote an elegy for Chaloner, long after the latter's death, he mentions the friendship 'which sprang up between us in the prime of our youth, when the royal court first brought us two young men together'.[18] On the other hand, Cecil in later life was 'notoriously inaccurate in his memory of dates'.[19] It might even be that they did not become close until they were in their late twenties, when they both fought at the Battle of Pinkie Cleugh against the Scots.[20] Whatever the truth of this, the point is that Cecil was a most important contact and friend for Chaloner, especially after 1559 when he became Elizabeth's secretary of state, and therefore Chaloner's superior. Finally, it was Cecil who was to organise Chaloner's funeral and who made sure that the terms of his will were carried out.

In or around 1538 Chaloner quitted Cambridge, his formal education over. Straight away, it seems, he joined the household of Thomas Cromwell, Henry's leading minister. There is a document dated that year and presumably drawn up for Cromwell himself which includes 'Thos. Chaloner' in a list of 'Gentlemen most mete to be daily waiters upon my said lord [Cromwell] and allowed in his home'.[21] Cromwell had a reputation for recruiting promising young men and training them up in his service, which was seen at the time as an important stepping stone to a position within government. Very likely this sought-after post was obtained for Thomas by his father, whom we know had business connections with Cromwell. It is also likely that Roger paid for Thomas's keep while he worked for Cromwell. Later, when Cromwell was defending himself against charges of treason, he denied that he had ever tried to recruit or pay for young men to enter his household in order to create a personal faction:

> He [Cromwell] denies that he ever retained any except his household servants, but it was against his will. Was so besought by persons who said they were his friends that he received their children and friends—not as retainers, for their fathers and parents did find them [i.e. paid for them].[22]

Unfortunately, it is not known how long Chaloner remained part of Cromwell's household, or what tasks he was allotted, but one possibility is that Cromwell sent him off on a mission to Spain, perhaps with a message for the English ambassador there – a message too important or too secret to be dispatched by the usual channels. The ambassador at the court of Charles V at this time was the poet and courtier Sir Thomas Wyatt. It is tempting to visualise the youthful Chaloner remaining at the Barcelona embassy for weeks or even months, becoming a member of the band of highly cultivated young Englishmen who had come to Spain with Wyatt, and who spent some of their leisure hours transcribing the poems of their master, or composing their own. Certainly, this is what Wyatt's most recent biographer, Susan Brigden, suggests, and the fact that Chaloner wrote an elegy for Wyatt on his death a decade later makes the suggestion more plausible. However, all this is somewhat conjectural, and we have no real evidence at all about what Chaloner did until the autumn of 1540, when he set off on the expedition which is the subject of the next chapter.[23]

3

TRAVEL AND DANGER
1540–1541

In 1579, long after Thomas Chaloner's death, his friend William Cecil arranged to have his Latin poetry published for the first time. Cecil chose William Malim, the high master of St Paul's School, to edit Chaloner's manuscript verses and to write, in Latin, a brief account of his life by way of introduction. This included the episode for which Chaloner was perhaps best known by his contemporaries: his shipwreck and near-death off the coast of Algeria when he was just twenty-one. The following translation of Malim's account is by Richard Hakluyt, the Elizabethan chronicler, who inserted the episode into his book about Elizabethan voyages of travel and discovery:

Thomas Chaloner was by birth a Londoner, by study a Cantabrigian,[1] by education a courtier, by religion a devout and true Christian. Therefore after he had confirmed his youth and mind in the studies of good learning, when Sir Henry Knevet was sent ambassador from the mighty Prince Henry the eighth to the Emperor Charles the fifth, he went with him as his familiar friend, or as one of his Council. At which time the said Charles the fifth, passing over from Genoa and Corsica to Alger in Africa in warlike sort, with a mighty army by sea, that honourable Knevet the kings ambassadour, Thomas Chaloner, Henry Knolles, and Henry Isham, right worthy persons, of their own accord accompanied him in that expedition, & served him in that war, wherein Thomas Chaloner escaped most wonderfully with his life. For the galley wherein he was, being either dashed against the rocks or shaken with mighty storms and so cast away, after he had saved himself a long while by swimming, when his strength failed him, his arms & hands being faint and weary, with great difficulty laying hold with his teeth on a cable, which was cast out of the next galley, not without breaking and loss of certain of his teeth, at length [he] recovered himself, and returned home into his country in safety.[2]

Before we get to the shipwreck and the dental resourcefulness described by Malim, we need to look in more detail at the reason Chaloner was sent to meet the Emperor Charles V in the first place. In the autumn of 1540, after much preparation, a splendid delegation crossed the Channel bound for southern Germany. On 16 November the French ambassador wrote home that they intended 'to leave in two days, and their horses are already embarked for Calais. The delay was caused by their preparations, for their company will number 100 horsemen, all in grey velvet, with great gold chains on their necks.'[3] The delegation was led by Sir Henry Knyvet and Stephen Gardiner, Bishop of Winchester, two of the king's most trusted advisers, and Chaloner was a junior member of the party.

The Diet of Ratisbon [today, Regensburg], to which the delegation was headed, was meant to involve all the various princes and dukes of the empire together with other eminent persons, such as representatives from the pope. One of its aims was to try and reach a compromise between Catholics and Protestants, partly so that the empire could present a united front to the growing menace of the Ottoman Turks who were threatening to overrun Hungary. For the English, the point of their mission was to represent their nation at the diet, to impress Europe with Henry VIII's wealth and status, and if possible to establish a closer friendship between Henry and Charles. At this period the dominant factor in European politics and diplomacy was the rivalry between three rulers who were roughly the same age: Charles V, Henry VIII, and Francis I of France. It was vital for each of the three to avoid the other two combining against him. To complicate matters, it was also rumoured that Francis was considering an alliance with the Ottomans against Charles.

This was to be Thomas Chaloner's first mission abroad, and his first introduction to the sophisticated world of international politics (unless we count his conjectural trip to Spain mentioned in the previous chapter). He was only twenty, but viewed as a well-educated and intelligent young man of considerable potential. He could already make himself understood in Italian, the language of diplomacy, which was probably another reason why Knyvet took him on as his secretary.

The English legation pursued a leisurely path, travelling from Calais via Mons to Namur, where they first met the emperor. Charles 'gave audience to the Bishop of Winchester who went to his Majesty with great pomp, being accompanied by some 150 persons on foot, all with gold chains round their necks'. Some two months later they arrived at Ratisbon, having accompanied the emperor on his route by way of Luxembourg, the Rhineland and Nuremberg. The diet went on for several weeks, the main agenda being a series of discussions between Calvinist, Lutheran and Catholic theologians, all of which ended inconclusively. As Miller puts it, 'during the next few months the lords spiritual argued and harangued, the lords temporal drank and feasted, and neither the discussion nor the wine came to any good result'.[4] The English took little part in these theological arguments. They were careful to alienate as few delegates as possible, especially as Henry VIII had already given offence to several German princes by his abrupt rejection of Anne of Cleves earlier the same year.

There was one incident, however, which did affect the English delegation, and in which Thomas Chaloner played a part. To understand the significance of this, one needs to realise that ever since Henry had taken over the headship of the Church of England in 1536, it had been seen as treasonable for any Englishman to appear to favour the pope, to suggest that England should be reconciled with the pope, or even to have any communication at all with the pope. This was perhaps particularly dangerous for someone like Stephen Gardiner, who, although he had helped Henry with his divorce, was known to be strongly conservative rather than reformist in his attitude towards the Church.

The incident started when an Italian merchant named Ludovico happened to meet William Wolfe, one of Knyvet's servants. In the course of conversation Ludovico asked Wolfe 'when my lord ambassador, his master, would make ready his packet for Rome'. It soon became clear that Ludovico did not realise there were actually two ambassadors heading the English delegation: Knyvet and Gardiner. Wolfe reported this conversation to Knyvet, and a plan was arranged to find out more about Ludovico's request by getting him to speak to another member of Knyvet's team, Thomas Chaloner. All this we know because ten years later, long after Henry's death, Gardiner *was* finally charged with treason, and Chaloner, as a witness for the prosecution, gave a long and circumstantial account of what happened, starting as follows:

Sir Henry devised whom he might send, and lastly rested upon me, then being his secretary; for that I could speak a little Italian. And this being passed upon a Saturday, early upon the next Sunday Wolfe called me out of my bed, not telling me one jot of this former matter (for so it was concluded between Sir Henry Knivet and him), to the end I might note what Wolfe afore said, not being afore made privy thereunto. So, therefore, when Wolfe had me called up familiarly, as he was wont to do, having been of long acquaintance with me, he prayed me to walk forth with him to the piazza ... Here, as Wolfe and I walked up and down, that Ludovico (the banker aforesaid) came also into the piazza, and saluted Wolfe.

And they two (I standing by), fell to talk of matters of exchange, which because they touched me not, I smally passed of; till at last (whether it were by Wolfe's motion or the other's I do not well remember), Ludovico said, 'The post departs on the morrow for Rome', and prayed Wolfe to remember our ambassador's secretary ... And, by other talk that he then uttered to Wolfe in my hearing tending to this effect: that the bishop had, at the papal legate's hands, received letters from Rome, and by him was solicited to send other letters for answer.[5]

Chaloner, of course, reported back to Knyvet, and eventually Ludovico got to see the right ambassador, Gardiner, and deliver his message. Gardiner, realising the danger he was in, rushed to the emperor and had Ludovico imprisoned, explaining that he was 'a knave suborned to be his [Gardiner's] destruction'. When Henry VIII was informed by Knyvet of what had occurred, he wrote back putting an end to the affair, saying there should be no further 'outward demonstrations'. There the question of Gardiner's possible treason rested until brought up again in 1551.[6]

In July 1541, after it became clear that the diet had achieved little, Charles V decided to quit Ratisbon and make his way to Spain. However, he then had another idea: he would make a detour on the way and attack the Barbary pirates whose galleys, manned by Christian captives, were a permanent hazard to the ships of all nations attempting to cross the Mediterranean. There were four states used by these pirates as bases: Morocco, Algiers,

Tunis and Tripoli, all of which received support from the Turkish sultan in Constantinople. In 1533 Charles had been hailed as a conquering hero throughout Europe, after mounting a successful attack against Tunis and freeing 20,000 Christian slaves. The main pirate base was now Algiers, which was under the ruthless leadership of a pirate named Hascen-Aga, and from where pirates continuously raided the coasts of Spain and Italy. Charles lacked the power to launch a full-scale attack on the Ottoman Turks in Hungary, and this would also have left the Netherlands and Spain open to possible attack from France. However, to strike the sultan through his Barbary allies seemed to be well within his capabilities. He anticipated a brief campaign, believing that once he had landed his forces the pirates could not put up much resistance. He travelled slowly across northern Italy, building up a considerable army from his noble vassals in Milan, Florence and Lucca, and then set off for Algiers from La Speccia on the Ligurian coast near Genoa. According to Malim, Charles also had with him four Englishmen. They were the ones mentioned by Hakluyt in the quotation at the beginning of this chapter: Henry Knyvet, Thomas Chaloner, Henry Knolles and Henry Isham.

However, things went wrong from the start. The imperial army, consisting of 2,000 cavalry and about 20,000 infantry, managed to land near Algiers unopposed, but on the second day after their landing rain began together with violent wind. The soldiers, who had brought nothing ashore but their weapons, had to spend a sleepless night without tents or cover of any sort. The following day they advanced to within a mile of the town, but came under ceaseless attack from the enemy. Worst of all, the whole army now saw the fleet that had followed their march along the coast, and on which they depended for food and also for a safe withdrawal, completely shattered by a violent storm. In less than an hour, fifteen warships and 140 transports were destroyed with the loss of 8,000 men.

It is not clear whether the four Englishmen were involved in the original landing near Algiers, but it seems certain that Chaloner was by this time on one of the galleys which lost their anchors and were sunk in the storm, either by being blown against the rocks or perhaps by collision with other ships. This is when, according to Malim and Hakluyt, 'Thomas Chaloner escaped most wonderfully with his life' and had to use his teeth to save himself. It was off the coast of a village called Bugia.

Worse was to come. That part of the fleet which had managed to survive the storm was forced to take refuge in a sheltered bay 'beyond the Cape of Metaphuz' and three days' march from the army. Left with so little food that they had to eat their horses, and harassed by Arab horsemen, the soldiers now had to make their way through swampy country along the coast to where the fleet was anchored. Even then fierce storms prevented embarkation for almost three weeks. Back in England, Henry VIII learnt that Knyvet had 'lost 7,000 or 8,000 crowns' worth of money and goods', besides the silver plate with which his ambassadors were usually furnished. No wonder that the king 'expressed wonder that the Emperor made this journey at such a season'.[7]

Finally, a depleted and no doubt demoralised army reached Majorca, from where the emperor sailed on to Spain. Most probably the Englishmen accompanied him, although it is not known how long they remained there. This may or may not have been Chaloner's first visit to Spain, a country in which he later spent several miserable years, and which he was to nickname 'Pain'.[8]

4

LITERATURE AND EMPLOYMENT
1542–1547

The Englishmen must have been astounded by the news that awaited them when they reached Spain. Henry's new wife, Catherine Howard, whom he had married only a few months before they set off to Germany, was now in prison accused of adultery (which amounted to treason if one happened to be married to the king). It seemed she had been extremely foolish. Led by a mixture of vanity, boredom and sexual appetite, she was said to have taken several lovers, both before and during her brief marriage to Henry. Most historians have shared with contemporaries this view of Katherine's behaviour, though some have been more generous, arguing that she might have been blackmailed by former lovers into allowing them sexual favours in return for their silence.[1] In any case, two young courtiers, Thomas Culpepper and Francis Dereham, confessed under torture to having been intimate with her, and both were executed, as was Katherine herself, early in 1542.

Of the four who had fought with Charles in Algiers, it was Henry Knyvet who was most disturbed by the possible effects of this bombshell, because through his mother he was closely associated with the Howard clan, many of whom were now being rounded up and interrogated as possible accessories to Katherine's treason.[2] It was said that the Tower was so full of Howards and their retainers that prison accommodation had to be found elsewhere. Probably, Knyvet deliberately delayed his return to England on the excuse of illness until he was quite sure that he was not in any danger. How long Chaloner remained in Spain – or even whether in fact he ever set foot there at this time – is uncertain. What does seem clear is that he must have been home at least by early 1543, because it was in that year he published the first of his various translations of Latin texts into English.

In fact, it was probably only during the brief time between returning home in about 1542 and obtaining a post as clerk to the Privy Council three years later that Chaloner would have had the time to start his second career as a humanist writer and translator. His first translation from Latin was a short work entitled *Of the Office of Servants*. Miller calls this 'a delightful translation of a delightful book'.[3] The author was a contemporary French humanist named Gilbert Cousin (in Latin, Gilbertus Cognatus). Cousin (1506–72) had been secretary and close friend to Erasmus until the latter's death in 1536. At the time Chaloner made his translation, Cousin was the centre of a circle of scholars which included reformers and Lutherans. Consequently, he was later charged with heresy and spent the final five years of his life in prison.

Chaloner's translation was dedicated to Knyvet, who was clearly still in favour with the king in spite of his Howard connection. He is described by Chaloner in his dedication as his master, and he claims it was Knyvet who advised him to undertake the translation in the first place:

> According sir, as ye bad me have englished this little book, of the
> office of servants ... Trusting your goodness will with as free a

mind receive it as I also went about it, albeit in many places I found the same as a glass to see my own faults in ... I pray God give your mastership long so to serve, as in a lesser degree we your servants ought, and would do. Your humble servant Thomas Chaloner.

The theme of the book is how to select and treat servants, the duties of servants and also of their masters. This was an important topic of the day, especially for those Christian humanists who were seeking a moral reform of society down to its grass roots. In upper-class circles the household was seen as an essential institution in which the (male) householder ruled over a hierarchical structure consisting of many persons, ranging from his own wife and children down through his servants of varying degrees of status, together with their relatives. All of these had their own roles but all were expected to obey the head of the house, and he in turn had obligations and duties towards them. The whole topic might very well seem somewhat irrelevant to us today (though it might be recalled in passing that as recently as 1960 Griffith-Jones, prosecuting counsel at the obscenity trial of *Lady Chatterley's Lover*, asked the jury whether the novel was 'something you would wish your wife or servants to read').

A typical fault of the bad servant, according to Cousin, was to give away to outsiders the secrets of the house which they had overheard. Chaloner explains in typically plain and robust English:

I chiefly wish in them, neither to harken much what is done abroad, nor yet to spread forth things done at home. Which were better untold, namely such as at meals were perhaps spoken under the frankest fashion. For nothing can be more knavish than such, as when so their master having shut the door to him is in secret communication with some friend of his, then holding their breathe, lay ear unto lock hole, or note well if any word, perhaps in drink, escaped him, which straight they report to them about whom the same was spoken, so telling that for earnest, which might be meant but in jest, yea and that with some additions of their own making.

One solution to this is to test a new servant as to his ability to keep to himself whatever he might overhear:

> Then of their blabbing in this wise may ye be instructed, in telling them some trifle upon earnest charge not to disclose the same, and then do suborn some one, who may bait them to utter it, that in case they blab it forth, it skilleth you little, and if they be hushed, ye may well in a greater matter trust them.

Cousin follows this with a story from Plutarch about a wife who couldn't be trusted with the secrets of her husband, a senator. The wife pestered him to tell her what they had been discussing in the senate that day. 'I shall tell thee, said he, provided thou canst hold thy peace. Tush, said she, a stone shall sooner utter it.' The senator then produced an invented tale about an eagle which had been seen flying overhead with a sword in its beak, and he told her that the senate had been discussing whether this portended some great mishap to the city. When he arrived at the marketplace the following morning 'he found all the commons there ready assembled devising of this aforesaid wonder, and thereunto the whole Senate, that marvelled much at the peoples so sudden assembly, did this Senator rehearse this tale upon his wife's goodly silence'.

The book ends with the reflection that 'we all be servants under one master', namely Christ. 'Let a master therefore consider with himself, thus: what ever good turn I do [my servant], I do it as for my brother, he being a member of the selfsame body I am of, and thereby shall I merit of Christ himself.'

In 1544 Chaloner published another translation from the Latin. The previous year Sir John Cheke, a leading English humanist, had translated two homilies by the early church father John Chrysostom (*c.* 347–407) from Greek into Latin, and now Chaloner put Cheke's Latin into English. Chrysostom – the name means 'golden-mouthed' in Greek – was well known for the persuasive power of his rhetoric. Hundreds of his sermons on various passages from the Bible have survived to this day. He himself lived a stormy life, dying in exile because he offended the rich and powerful by suggesting they give up much of their wealth to the poor. What undoubtedly attracted Cheke to these homilies was that they involved practical themes, and were couched in language aimed at the common people. Chaloner's aims were similar. Wherever possible he catered for a wide readership, avoiding long words derived from Latin and opting for a simple English vocabulary. Here are two passages from the book to demonstrate this down-to-earth style. The first is from a sermon by Chrysostom on the Book of Job. The Bible tells us that a messenger comes to Job to tell him that all his children have been killed:

While he was yet speaking, there came also another, and said, Thy sons and thy daughters were eating and drinking wine in their eldest brother's house:

And, behold, there came a great wind from the wilderness, and smote the four corners of the house, and it fell upon the young men, and they are dead; and I only am escaped alone to tell thee. [The Book of Job, I, 18–19]

Chrysostom, in Chaloner's powerful rendering, builds on these verses by imagining a scene tragically familiar in today's world, where a father searches for the bodies of his dead children:

Now put case some one as he dug amongst those ruins, should pluck out now a stone, & then a limb of some one of them, perchance one hand holding the cup, another in the platter, with all the shape of the bodies quashed asunder, the nose frushed down, the head cased, the eyes quisted out, the brain dispercled, and the whole proportion of the body with the diversity of the bruises so disfigured, that the poor father might unnethes [not easily] discern the desired sight of one of his children from another.

In another homily, a public scene is envisaged in which a group of Christian women demonstrate wild grief at the news of some recent death. According to Chrysostom, this proves that these women did not really believe in Heaven or the afterlife:

I am ashamed I promise you, and not meanly I am troubled in my spirit, when I see in the mercate-stede [market place] these flocks of women without shame, plucking their hair, slicing their arms, scratching their cheeks, yes and doing all this afore the Greeks' eyes. What will not they say? What will not they blast of us? These be they that so constantly affirm there shall be a resurrection of the dead: gay words: but their deeds draw not after that line, with their words they maintain the resurrection, but their doings smell of the desperate. If they firmly trusted on the resurrection, they would not do thus; if they were persuaded the dead went to a better state, they would not make this dole.

Chaloner dedicated his translation of Chrysostom to Sir Anthony Denny, a leading privy counsellor and intimate friend of the king, and hence even more important than Knyvet, who in any case was ill, and shortly to die:

TO THE RIGHT WORshipful master Anthony Denny, one of the chief gentlemen of the King majesty's privy chamber.

A SMALL gift agrees with my small ability but not with the greatness of your deserts, which justly to set forth, I leave to such, as may with greater vessels wade more aptly in so large a sea. It may like you therefore of your singular goodness, which so many have proved, if you like not my deed herein, at least to allow my intent, which in great things thought it a second praise to will well. Fare ye no worse than your virtue requireth, the favour of men wisheth, and your own dexterity promiseth.

Your most bounden Tho. Chaloner.

The dedication was clearly a sound move, since the following year Chaloner was promoted to an important office.[4] On 18 December 1545 a grant to 'Thomas Chaloner, the King's servant' of the office of clerk of the Privy Council was signed with a stamp of Henry's signature 'in the presence of Sir Anthony Dennye'.[5] The clerkship was a demanding post since it was, in effect, the Privy Council that ran the country. At the meetings of the council a vast range of matters was considered, ranging from foreign and economic policy to particular cases of civil and criminal law. Unless they were absent on particular missions, which tended to happen quite often, the clerks were expected to attend the council. One of them had to keep detailed minutes, as a memorandum composed by Sir William Paget early in the next reign sets out.

Item: that the clerk having charge of the council book shall daily enter all orders and determinations by the council, all warrants for money, the substance of all letters requiring answer; and the next day following, at the first meeting, presenting the same by the secretary (who shall first consider whether it be made accordingly) to the board, the council shall the first thing they do sign the book of entries, leaving space for the councillors absent to enter their names when they come; and the clerk which keepeth the book shall attend thereunto only, and be burdened with no other charge.[6]

The council was a highly peripatetic body, tending to hold its meetings wherever the king happened to be (though he himself did not attend). During Chaloner's time it met at Westminster, Greenwich, Hampton Court, Windsor Castle, 'the Council Chamber in the Tower' and many other venues. Chaloner obviously had plenty of commuting to do from his house in Hackney. Council meetings were frequent, and lasted for several hours, as Paget's memorandum again explains:

> Item: that the council attendant in the court shall assemble themselves three days in the week at the least for the King's affairs, viz. Tuesday, Thursday, and Saturday, and oftener if the King's affairs so require, and shall meet in the council chamber in the morning at eight of the clock, and sit till dinner, and afternoon at two of the clock, and sit till four, and for private suites they shall assemble upon the Sundays after dinner at two of the clock, and sit till four.

When Chaloner was first appointed there were two clerks – himself and William Honyngs – but in 1547 they were joined by a third, Armagil Waad. To be a clerk to the council was lucrative. Chaloner's salary after 1547 was £40 a year, but this was probably less than he made from occasional fees. For instance, the clerk concerned was entitled to 6s 8d from someone wanting an entry made in the register, 10s from someone appearing before the council, £2 from a new councillor being sworn in.[7] More importantly, this was an office for young, ambitious men, where contacts with powerful councillors could be made easily. If they were seen to be discreet and capable, clerks could soon move upwards in the political hierarchy. Chaloner was efficient, and also trustworthy, unlike his first colleague, Honyngs, who in 1550 was dismissed and imprisoned. He was accused of stealing council papers on behalf of Thomas Wriothesley, a councillor who was under attack for having neglected his duties as Lord Chancellor.[8]

By this time Chaloner had made himself something of a linguist. As mentioned above, this achievement was probably started by tutors hired by his father, but was certainly improved by his time abroad, firstly perhaps with Wyatt in Spain, and secondly when he travelled to Ratisbon, and then accompanied Charles V to Algiers and Spain. Consequently, he was soon being sent by the council on missions that involved meeting foreigners. An early assignment was to deliver £30 to a band of Spanish mercenaries in London who had been instructed to ride northwards to the Scottish border in anticipation of an approaching war against the Scots. Another task concerned the kind of issue he was to become all too familiar with later in his career:

> Upon supplication exhibited by Mr Thorne of Bristol in the behalf of Walter Roberts, captain of a ship of the said town, who being by force of weather driven, with five lawful prizes taken by him of the Frenchmen, to the town of St Sebastian in Spain, was there by them of the Inquisition not only arrested and put in prison with three English merchants more, but also his ship stayed, his chests broken up, and goods set on land and detained, as more at large in the said supplication appeareth, in consideration whereof the council sent Thomas Chaloner to the Emperor's ambassador to declare the aforesaid matter unto him, to the end he thereupon should write unto the Emperor for the speedy redress of the same.[9]

At about the time he was appointed clerk Chaloner was probably completing yet another literary work. This was an original Latin poem extolling the virtues of Henry VIII.[10] It was fairly long – about 1,100 lines in hexameters – and must have taken him many days and nights. Henry, according to Chaloner, was a perfect monarch: 'The beauty of Henry's accomplishments presses upon me; their very number does not allow me to know where to begin.' However, the form of the poem conformed strictly to the traditional principles of *encomia* derived from classical authors, which he would have studied at university as part of his training in rhetoric. Consequently, we should not take his exaggerated praise of Henry too seriously – it was part of the model.

Gabel and Schlam make a persuasive case for the poem having been written sometime during 1545 or early 1546, even though it remained unpublished until 1559. For instance, Chaloner writes of people's displeasure that Henry was demanding new taxes for war, but 'I would like to know what circumstances have ever assailed our state that were more to be feared, in view of the magnitude of the danger'. This was surely written in 1545 when the French were threatening to invade, and landing parties were actually put ashore at Brighton and the Isle of Wight. At this time Henry's response was to impose an extra-parliamentary tax, the 'Benevolence', to pay for coastal defences.

The argument goes that having finished the poem Chaloner decided not to publish, given the uncertainty of what might happen politically after Henry's death. He was probably quite right in his decision, because clearly Mary would not have looked too favourably on the author of a poem that attacked Rome, the Catholic religion and the monasteries. However, on Elizabeth's accession he remembered his poem, added some additional passages in praise of the new queen, had it printed, and sent it to her as a New Year's gift for 1 January 1560. It was published again long after his death as part of his collected Latin verse.[11]

In 1546 Chaloner married a wealthy widow, Joan Leigh. Joan had previously been married to Sir Thomas Leigh, a lawyer employed by Thomas Cromwell to arrange the dissolution of a number of monasteries. Leigh had been one of Cromwell's most active and detested monastic visitors. He was often described by contemporaries in unflattering terms, viz. 'of a very bulky and gross habit of body', 'a doctor of low quality', exhibiting an 'insolent and pompalique behaviour', 'a vicious man'.[12] When it became known, in 1535, that Leigh was marrying the fifteen-year-old Joan, she became an object of sympathy. Her subsequent marriage to the much younger Chaloner was probably seen as a just recompense. Joan Leigh, *née* Cotton, was an heiress in her own right, having inherited property from her father, Sir William Cotton, of Oxenheath, Kent.[13]

Sir Thomas Leigh had died in 1544, leaving not only a widow but a five-year-old daughter, Katherine, who became Chaloner's ward on his marriage to her mother. After Joan's death in 1557, Katherine would marry James, Lord Mountjoy, having inherited from her mother the ex-monastic estate of St Oswalds in south Yorkshire. Katherine also inherited other property, including a large part of a London estate which once belonged to the medieval Hospital of St Giles (today this area is bounded to the north by Charing Cross Road).[14]

5

IN PRAISE OF FOLLY
1547–1550

In 1547, with the death of Henry VIII, the council came to be dominated by Edward Seymour, uncle of the new king, Edward VI, who was aged nine. Seymour became Lord Protector, and awarded himself the title Duke of Somerset. He turned out to be an effective military leader but not a particularly good administrator. Although a somewhat shaky peace had been made the previous year between England and France, England was at this time still at war with France's ally Scotland. Somerset's aim was similar to Henry VIII's towards the end of his reign. He wanted to separate Scotland from France and ultimately to create a union between England and Scotland. This was to be achieved by marrying the young King Edward to the four-year-old Mary Stuart (Mary, Queen of Scots), daughter of James V – a policy colloquially known as the 'rough wooing'. Unfortunately, the powerful pro-French faction in Scotland rejected these suggestions, and the duke decided that the only way he could achieve his goals was by using force. The result was the overwhelming defeat of the Scots at Pinkie Cleugh, alias Musselburgh.

The English campaign was well organised and efficient. An army of 18,000, under Somerset's personal command, advanced along the east coast of Scotland, towards Edinburgh, maintaining contact with an accompanying fleet. The army partly consisted of the usual county levies armed with longbow and bill, but there were also cavalry, and several hundred German and Spanish mercenaries with arquebuses. To stop them advancing on Edinburgh, a larger but less up-to-date Scottish army occupied a strong position on the River Esk. The battle started with a misjudgement by the Scottish commander, the Earl of Arran, who mistakenly thought the English were retreating and gave up his position to launch an attack. During the ensuing battle the English artillery fired from both land and sea while their cavalry and arquebusiers proved too much for the Scottish pikemen. Eventually, the Scots turned tail, defeat turned into rout, and many thousands were slaughtered. It was the most decisive reverse the Scots had suffered since Flodden thirty years earlier, and has been described as the victory of a Renaissance army over a medieval one.

Some of the credit for this successful operation was probably due to Chaloner, who had accompanied Somerset into Scotland and had acted as an accountant to the army, helping to organise and distribute finances. William Patten, an eyewitness who published a detailed report of the battle, wrote that Chaloner was 'as I might call him, Chief Secretary, who with his great pains and expedite diligence in dispatch of things passing from my Lord's Grace and the council there, did make that his merit was not with the meanest'.[1] It is doubtful that he actually wielded a sword against the enemy; Patten mentions him as one of those who were with Somerset on an observation hilltop as the battle started. But regardless of whether he fought or not, this was one of the turning points in his career. Immediately after the victory he was knighted by Somerset on the field of battle. There is also a report (from a book written over a century later) that he was given a jewel by Somerset's wife, Anne.[2]

After Pinkie the newly knighted Sir Thomas Chaloner returned to London. Within a month of the victory he, along with Stephen Vaughan, a business colleague of his father, had been chosen to represent the borough of Lancaster in a new parliament. As far as we know Chaloner had no particular connection with this town. As a Member of Parliament he also had other duties. He served on two commissions for Middlesex, the county where he lived. One was to collect payment of a parliamentary relief, or tax, for that county, and the other to investigate the rapidly mounting cost of living. The commissioners had to 'enquire by any means how the enhancing of prices of corn, victuals and other things therein mentioned grows by the insatiable greediness of divers covetous persons'.[3]

Chaloner now seems to have given up his work as a simple clerk – while retaining the salary – and was seen as a messenger of some status, travelling up and down the land on behalf of the council. First, he had to pay off the Italian arquebusiers under de Gamboa, who had played a significant part at Pinkie. The Privy Council order for this payment gives some indication of the way a mercenary band was organised, not to mention demonstrating the demands this task must have made on Chaloner's mathematical abilities:

Sir Edmund Peckham [Treasurer of the Mints] had warrant to deliver to Sir Thomas Chaloner, to be by him paid over again to Signor de Gamboa and Charles de Guevara, for payment of their two bands of Spaniards, these parcels of money ensuing:-

For ccxxxix soldiers, every at xx s. the month, accounting xxx days to the same, beginning tomorrow, the first day of February, and ending the second of March following inclusive, ccxxxix li.[£]. For ii captains, every at xii li. x s.; for ii alpheres, every at vii li. x s.; for ii sergeants, every at iiii li.; for x capos de squadra, every at xl s.; for iiii drummers and two fifes, every at xl s.; and for two banderades, ii chaplains, two harbingers and two surgeons, every at xx li. the piece, appertaining to the said two bands by the said space, amounting to lxxxix li.x s. ... [plus various back payments owing]

All which sums amount to mlxxxx li. xviii s. viii d.; whereof, deducting cl li. already to them impressed, and the price of cc arquebuses at x s. delivered to them out of his Majesty's store, must remain to them in full satisfaction until the said ii of March, dcccxl li. xviii s. viii d.[4]

In spite of their crushing defeat at Pinkie, the Scots refused to go along with Somerset's policy. He set up a network of garrisons stretching as far as Dundee, but found that his finances did not allow these to be maintained for long. Meanwhile, Mary Stuart was smuggled off to France, where she was betrothed to the dauphin, Henry II's son Francis. Somerset's aggressive and expensive policy towards Scotland was now seen to have failed completely. Even more alarming to the other members of the council was the failure of his domestic policies. At this time enclosing landlords were threatening the livelihood of peasants, and there was growing unrest culminating in two serious rebellions: in Norfolk, and in Devon and Cornwall. These summer uprisings of 1549 were the most serious threat to the government during the whole century, with the possible exception of the Pilgrimage of Grace in 1536.

Somerset, it is true, had been responsible for a series of commissions and proclamations about the dangers of enclosure, but the main result of these was to convince many of the rebels that they were acting in his name. By now Somerset was showing himself to be proud, stubborn and aloof from his colleagues. The most experienced and long-serving member of the council, Sir William Paget, a close friend of Somerset, was not afraid to warn him: 'How it cometh to pass I cannot tell, but of late your Grace is grown into great choleric fashions whensoever you are contraried in that which you have conceived in your head.'[5] A majority of the council saw the rebellions, and the uncertain way Somerset dealt with them, as a colossal failure of government, and they decided he had to go. On 11 October 1549 he was arrested and sent to the Tower. At the same time, great efforts were made to explain to the nation why the ex-leader, still a popular hero to many, was in fact a villain.

Chaloner was involved in these efforts. This is one of the times in his career when one has to admire his sense of political timing, while perhaps wondering about his loyalty to former patrons. His career had made excellent progress under Somerset, culminating in the important role he was given in the Pinkie campaign, and then his reward – a knighthood. Now, two days before Somerset's arrest, we find Chaloner riding round the city on instructions from the council, and reading aloud to Londoners a proclamation declaring the Lord Protector a traitor. It purported to explain 'the very truth of the Duke of Somerset's evil government, false and detestable proceedings'. As a diarist recorded:

> The proclamation of 8 October was read out at several places in London just after four in the afternoon by the Sheriff of London and Sir Thomas Chaloner, a clerk of the privy council; they were preceded by two trumpets, four heralds, two kings of arms, with the sergeant of the trumpeters and the common crier riding with their maces before them.[6]

With Somerset's fall, John Dudley, Earl of Warwick, and later Duke of Northumberland, became the dominant member of the council. Northumberland was a more cautious and less arrogant politician than Somerset. For instance, he willingly accepted advice from other councillors, and he never employed the royal 'we' in documents and letters as Somerset had done. However, he did continue the religious reformation that Somerset had started, and to do this he made sure that any conservative opposition was reduced. Two leading churchmen who were dismissed and imprisoned not long after Somerset were Edward Bonner, Bishop of London, and Stephen Gardiner, Bishop of Winchester. Both were conservatives in religion and therefore out of place during Edward VI's reign, a time of rapid religious reformation. Gardiner was the more significant of the two. During the 1530s he had been Thomas Cromwell's chief rival, and he had continued in high favour with Henry until the king's death.

Chaloner played a small part in the fall of each of them. Bonner, an effective administrator in the previous reign, found himself denied power and influence under both Somerset and Northumberland. Consequently, he had become deviously obstructive towards the new reformist policies. One issue which got him into trouble was his refusal to allow copies of Erasmus' *Paraphrases* to be sent to churches in his diocese. He was given a last chance by the council, and ordered to preach a sermon at St Paul's Cross in which he was to show his allegiance to the regime and his agreement with its policies. The sermon failed to satisfy the council, and a commission of enquiry deprived him of his bishopric and sent him to prison. Chaloner was one of those testifying that he had attended the sermon, and that Bonner had breached the council's orders. Gardiner was then treated in a similar manner, but he was more difficult to pin down because he knew the law so well. Eventually, towards the end of 1550, he was brought to trial, found guilty and imprisoned in the Tower, where he spent the rest of the reign. Chaloner gave evidence at his trial that he had disobeyed Henry VIII back in 1540 by secretly communicating with the pope during the Diet of Ratisbon.[7] Both Bonner and Gardiner were lucky to escape with their lives, and both were to rise to power again in the reign of Mary I.

Both before and after the fall of Somerset, the council entrusted Chaloner with various highly sensitive missions, as befitted his new status as a knight. One of them concerned the arrest of Thomas Seymour, Somerset's younger brother and uncle of Edward VI. Seymour was ambitious and reckless, and said to be attractive to women. He was described by one contemporary as 'fierce in courage, courtly in fashion, in personage stately, in voice magnificent, but somewhat empty of matter'. After Henry VIII's death he married the king's widow, Catherine Parr, but when she died after giving birth, Seymour turned his attentions to the fifteen-year-old Princess Elizabeth, whom he hoped to marry. He also had plans to gain control of the person of the young king, and perhaps make himself Lord Protector instead of his brother. He was arrested, accused of treason and executed. The day after his arrest, Chaloner was sent down to Wiltshire to search his house at Bromham for evidence of treason. Subsequently, he was ordered to ride to Sudeley Castle in Gloucestershire, another of Seymour's possessions, to take an inventory of its contents and report back to the council.[8]

Another delicate matter involved the Archbishop of York Robert Holgate, who, at the age of sixty-eight, had caused some scandal by marrying a Yorkshire woman, Barbara Wentworth,[9] who was over forty years younger than him. A certain Anthony Norman claimed that, because he and Barbara had been betrothed when they were children, Holgate's marriage was invalid. Chaloner, along with Sir Thomas Gargrave and Dr John Rokeby, an ecclesiastical lawyer, was appointed by the council to investigate the affair.[10] It seems they found in Holgate's favour, and decided that the marriage was perfectly valid. However, a few years later when Mary came to the throne, Holgate's position worsened dramatically. All priests, and especially bishops, were now expected to be celibate, and Holgate found himself imprisoned in the Tower. While there, he wrote his *Apology*, in which he claimed that he had only married because the Duke of Northumberland had insisted he do so. He was later released from prison but never recovered his see.

In spite of all his work and travelling, Chaloner somehow had time to produce another book. This was his best-known translation, and it was from another Latin work, *The Praise of Folly*, by Desiderius Erasmus.[11] This had first been published in 1511, and was allegedly written over one week when Erasmus was staying with his close friend Thomas More. It was a hugely popular work which had gone through several editions before Chaloner worked on it, and had already been published in French, German and Czech as well as Latin. By 1549, when the English edition came out, Erasmus had been dead for over a decade, yet his influence was still high, especially in Protestant countries, even though he himself had been an orthodox member of the Catholic Church all his life. In England his name was associated with the Reformation. A royal injunction two years earlier had ordered that a copy of his *Paraphrases of the Gospels*, rendered into English with the support of Henry VIII's widow, Catherine Parr, be placed in every church in the land.

In the introduction to his translation, Chaloner made crystal clear his views concerning the inevitability of a rigid system of social class. He wrote, 'The high god, who made us all of one earth, hath nevertheless chosen some to rule, and more to serve.' The general population must never aspire 'to things above their reach'. Nor would they, if only they understood the stresses and problems affecting the rich and powerful: 'For surely, if a man of the poorer sort, whose eye is dazzled in beholding the fair gloss of wealth and felicity which the state of a great lord or councillor in a commonwealth doth outwardly represent, and did inwardly mark the travails, cares and anxieties which such a one is driven to sustain in serving his master and country, now I believe he would not much envy his state, nor chose to change conditions of life with him.'

The Praise of Folly was ostensibly a light, humorous work. Folly was said to be a goddess whose mother was a nymph and her father, Plutus, the god of wealth, the implication being that much of the world's folly is caused by human greed for riches. As Chaloner writes in his introduction, 'Folly in all points is not so strange unto us … she will be sure to bear a stroke in most of our doings.' Through the mouth of Folly, Erasmus castigates many aspects of society, especially with regard to religion. Folly has a lot to say about superstition, and also about monks, bishops, cardinals and even popes – although Leo X, the pope of the day, is said to have found the book highly amusing.

Erasmus's book was couched in Renaissance humanist style, with classical references and quotes in other languages on practically every page. As Miller says, it is a very learned book, aimed at an educated elite, and even those who could read the Latin could not always cope with the Greek or Hebrew phrases. Chaloner wanted to make his translation accessible to a much wider readership. He apparently saw no contradiction between this ambition, which we might see as laudably democratic, and his deeply held views about class and hierarchy. In his introduction he wrote, 'For which purpose I also soonest moved to English it, to the end that mean men of baser wits and condition, might have a manner comfort and satisfaction in themselves.' To achieve this aim he used, whenever possible, simple vernacular terms rather than words derived from Latin.[12] Often, too, he tried to find appropriate expressions and proverbs in English that every reader would recognize, instead of Erasmus's references. He wrote,

> Likewise in all my translation I have not pained my self to render word for word, nor proverb for proverb, whereof many be Greek, such as have no grace in our tongue: but rather marking the sense, I applied it to the phrase of our English. And where the proverbs would take no English, I adventured to put English proverbs of like weight in their place.

Some examples of where he does this are, 'they know well enough on which side their bread is buttered'; 'as far wide, as from hence to the man in the moon'; and, with regard to Erasmus's unflattering verdict on educated women, 'so that if any woman studieth to be counted wise, she doeth naught else but labour to be twice foolish, as if ye would force a cow against her nature to leap through a hoop'.

Very occasionally Chaloner alters, or even omits entirely, passages from Erasmus, either because he does not agree with them, or because such passages would not go down well with the English authorities – or both. For example, when Erasmus, who inclined towards pacifism, writes about war, he somewhat sarcastically describes the kind of people he thinks make the best soldiers. They are 'parasites, pimps, robbers, assassins, farmers, dolts, bankrupts, and suchlike scum of mankind'. Chaloner's list is much more polite: 'good bloods, venturers, companions, swashes, dispatchers, bankrupts, with such like'. And when it comes to kings there is a paragraph in Erasmus which Chaloner felt he must completely omit from his English version. In a later translation the passage reads as follows:

[Kings] grant no hearing to anyone unless he knows how to speak pleasant things, because solicitude must not get a foothold in their minds. They believe they have played the part of a sovereign to the hilt if they diligently go hunting, feed some fine horses, sell dignities and offices at a profit to themselves, and daily devise new measures by which to drain away the wealth of citizens and sweep it into their own exchequer. All this, of course, is done in due form, under new-found names, so that even when most unjust it shall carry some appearance of equity; and they take care to add a little sweetening so that in any event they may secure for themselves the hearts of the people.[13]

Miller sums up the virtues of Chaloner's translation as 'vividness and vigor, deft additions and adaptations, and faithfulness to the original'. It was, he says, the most accurate English version of *The Praise of Folly* for almost the next 400 years.[14]

In 1550, Roger Chaloner died. He had lived to see his eldest son obtain his knighthood, and rise steadily in the ranks of government. It is obvious from his will that, although he still owned Abbott's Inn – his 'greate mansion', which was left to Isobel – he and his wife were actually then living at another house he owned, in Tower Street. The will assumes that Isobel would continue to live there with her two unmarried stepdaughters, Ellen and Elizabeth, daughters of Roger's first wife, Margaret. The two younger sons, John, aged twenty-nine, and Francis, twenty-five, clearly by now had their own establishments.[15]

6

SCOTLAND
1551–1552

In spite of his victory at Pinkie in 1547, the policies of Edward Seymour, Duke of Somerset, regarding Scotland and France, proved to be totally unsuccessful. After this battle the French had sent powerful forces to Scotland, and Mary Stuart, now in France, had been betrothed to the dauphin rather than to Edward VI as both Somerset and Henry VIII had hoped. The 'rough wooing' now had to be abandoned. Somerset's Scottish policy had been expensive, and money was short. And England's ally, the Emperor Charles V, had failed to help them against France when help was most needed. Consequently, Somerset had been forced to make a humiliating treaty whereby the recently acquired port of Boulogne would be returned to France.

Scotland, now under the control of Mary of Guise, mother of Mary Stuart, was a party to the treaty of Boulogne, which ended all hostilities between England, Scotland and France, but it was also felt necessary to make a separate treaty between England and Scotland, because there were a number of issues to sort out. These included terms for the release of hostages taken at Pinkie and earlier, rules concerning trade between the two countries, and discussions about the precise location of the English-Scottish border in certain disputed areas. In April 1551 the Privy Council chose four commissioners to meet with the Scots at Norham Castle and negotiate the treaty. They were Richard Sampson, Bishop of Lichfield and Coventry, Sir Robert Bowes, Sir Leonard Beckwith and Sir Thomas Chaloner.[1] The instructions given to the commissioners give some idea of the complexity of the issues involved:

Memorial by the King's highness to the Bishop of [blank], Sir Robert Bowes, Sir Leonard Beckwith, and Sir Thomas Chaloner knights, his commissioners, &c.

Taking with them copies of (1) the last treaty with France, (2) the treaty between the late Kings of England and Scotland of 11 May 1534, and (3) between Edward IV. and James III. of 1 June 1467, also of Sir John Mason's letters to the French King touching Edrington *alias* Cawmills, the Debatable ground, and the Tweed fishings, and informing themselves by good evidence of the true ancient bounds of the three marches, they shall meet the Scottish commissioners at some neutral place near the frontiers:—saying generally,

First: that though England by conquest, &c. might justly claim enlargement of its old limits, yet the King agrees to a friendly and indifferent view of the old true bounds, and that the same shall be as before the late wars, and plainly set out. Is also content to give up Roxburgh and Eyemouth, Edrington *alias* Cawmills, and the fishings known to be within Scotland. The Debatable land in the West Marches shall remain neutral as before. These matters being so compounded, the King agrees that the hostages yet lying for the prisoners taken at Solom mosse [i.e. the battle of Solway Moss, 1542], shall be enlarged free of ransom or any other demand.[2]

In May, Chaloner travelled up to Norham. There is a slight problem here about dating. In the calendar of state papers for

Scotland, a letter from Chaloner to William Cecil dated 14 May shows that he had arrived at Norham for the negotiations with the Scots. However, another letter from Brussels in the calendar of state papers, foreign, seems to prove that he was in Brussels on 20 May. This letter, from Nicholas Wotton, says, 'Next morning Sir Thomas Chaloner and I sent notice of our arrival [in Brussels].' Miller suggested that Chaloner might have made a rapid trip from Norham to Brussels and then returned, but this seems scarcely credible considering the nature of sixteenth-century travel. However, a glance at the actual manuscript of Wotton's letter as opposed to the summary in the state papers shows that he wrote, 'Sir Thomas Chamberlain and I,' rather than, 'Sir Thomas Chaloner,' and thus the mystery is solved.[3]

Norham Castle – which still stands today, though a ruin – was a suitable place for the meeting. A few miles from Berwick, it commanded a ford across the Tweed and was said to have been the stronghold most often attacked in the long history of Anglo-Scottish wars. Yet apparently Chaloner did not particularly enjoy his visit. In the letter to Cecil mentioned above, he reported progress in the negotiations, complained about the weather and also complained that he had heard nothing from the council, whereas the Scots commissioners were kept well informed of current events:

My long letter to my lords suffers no longer letter to you than may contain salutations, wishing our matters here were done, and we on return. I little like this country, and me thinks October is fairer here then May! I dare not ask letters of you, knowing how smally ye can spare time, yet if you said how my lords take our doings, it would much satisfy me. We marvel that in 11 days we have no answer from court to our letters – we need have speedier word, or it will hinder us. Their Governor lieth hard at their noses, and so may they nightly send unto him. I chiefly desire we may hear well of all things there, and, trusting our affair shall go on a good foot.[4]

The Treaty of Norham was concluded in June. It was long and detailed. Fugitives who had crossed the border during the wars were to have the same rights as natives, and all prisoners were to be returned. Piracy was to be dealt with harshly. One article noted that large bands from both sides of the border were in the habit of crossing over even in broad daylight to cut down and steal trees for building, and that both governments had a duty to put a stop to this. Having helped to write out the treaty in Latin, Chaloner returned to London to report to the council.

Between September of this year and the following March, we know from his accounts that Chaloner was mainly living at home in Hoggesden, Middlesex. We also know that he attended the court at Greenwich for seven weeks during the Christmas and New Year period:

> Laid out for boat hire and board wages for my men attending on me at the court during vii weeks per estimaton   iiii l.

> Laid out for certain extraordinaries touching my self and for rewards given to sundry persons during this while   xl s.

> Out of my purse upon Saint Stephens day [Boxing Day] at my going to Greenwich   *xxx s*

What was he doing at court during this extended period? The answer is that he was participating in the annual court revels, which that Christmas were particularly prolonged and expensive. This was perhaps because the council felt it necessary to distract attention from the plight of the Duke of Somerset, who was imprisoned in the Tower awaiting execution, and whom many felt had always been a champion of the people. This, at any rate, was the view of the chronicler Richard Grafton:

> The people murmured against the Duke of Northumberland, and against some other of the Lords for the condemnation of the said Duke [of Somerset], and also as the common fame went, the King's majesty took it not in good part: wherefore as well to remove fond talk out of men's mouths, as also to recreate and refresh the troubled spirits of the young King, it was devised that the feast of Christ's Nativity commonly called Christmas then at hand, should be solemnly kept at Greenwich with open household, and frank resort to the court.[5]

These celebrations took place mainly at Greenwich Palace, and lasted until Twelfth Night [6 January]. We know a little about them due to recorded disputes between the two main organisers. One was Sir Thomas Cawardine, who was Master of the Revels, which meant he was in charge of all dramatic performances at court, and also of the finances and administration of these elaborate and sumptuous end-of-year presentations. He had held this office for several years and disliked being interfered with. But for 1551/2 the ancient role of Lord of Misrule was revived and allotted to George Ferrers, a lawyer and poet. Both he and Chaloner had been servants of Thomas Cromwell in their youth, and both had served in the campaign leading to Pinkie Cleugh. It was now Ferrers' task to actually present the various plays, masques and processions required, although he found it very difficult to get Cawardine to spend the money needed to provide the expensive costumes and props thought necessary, and he frequently had to appeal to the council over the head of the Master of the Revels.

According to *Grafton's Chronicle*, the choice of Ferrers as Lord of Misrule was a great success:

There is one appointed to make sport in the court, called commonly Lord of Misrule ... There was therefore by order of the council a gentleman both wise and learned, whose name was George Ferrers, appointed to that office for this year ... Which Gentleman so well supplied his office, both in show of sundry sights and devises of rare invention, and in act of divers interludes and matters of pastime, played by persons as not only satisfied the common sort but also were very well liked and allowed by the council and others of skill in the like pastimes. But best of all by the young King himself, as appeared by his princely liberality in rewarding that service.[6]

One of the highlights of the revels took place on Twelfth Night, and the likelihood is that it was written and produced by Chaloner. The previous day the council had sent an order to Cawardine: 'We shall require you to put order and prepare the apparel of two personages which tomorrow at night shall play a dialogue before the King's majesty. This bearer Sr Thomas Chaloner shall declare unto you the rest of the matter, how they are to be trimmed, whom we pray you credit.' The following evening the dialogue was performed. All we have is the following anonymous account:

The same night was first a play, after [i.e. afterwards] some talk between one that was called Riches, and the other Youth, whither of them was better. After some pretty reasoning there came in six champions of either side ... All these fought two to two at barriers in the hall. Then came in two apparelled like almains [Germans], the Earl of Ormond and Jaques Granado, and two came in like friars, but the almains would not suffer them to pass until they had fought. The friars were Mr. Drury and Thomas Cobham. After this followed two masques, one of men another of women. Then a banquet of 120 dishes. This was the end of Christmas.[7]

The significance of these revels for Chaloner was that it was probably here that he first got to know a group who were to be his lifelong friends. His participation in these festivities showed that he now moved in the same literary circles as George Ferrers, Walter Haddon and William Baldwin, all of whom were also involved. Chaloner, Ferrers, Baldwin and others would come together again in the following reign over a joint publication, *The Mirror for Magistrates*.

The next year, 1552, between March and October, Chaloner was once more employed in an important capacity to do with Scotland. This, along with his role in the Christmas revels, was significant because it meant that he was still in favour after the fall and subsequent execution of Somerset, who had knighted him and been his patron. He was now appointed member of another commission – this time to fill in a particular gap left by the Treaty of Norham. Their task was to meet with a Scottish delegation in order to divide up the so-called Debatable Lands between England and Scotland. This area was a rectangle about ten miles long and four miles wide on the border near Gretna Green and north of Carlisle. The Debatable Lands extended from the Solway Firth near Carlisle to Langholm in Dumfries and Galloway. Over the centuries the area had become totally ungoverned and ungovernable, under the grip of various warlike local clans such as the Armstrongs, Nixons and Grahams. These border clans had their own fortified towers, and they could use the Debatable Lands as a base for raids on neighbouring areas. They profited when there was hostility between England and Scotland, but now that there was peace it was hoped something could be done about them, and the first step was to fix a precise border.

Some discussion took place between the two governments as to where and when to proceed, and how many ought to attend on each side. At first the Scots wanted to send ten commissioners, but the English said that this was far too many and would be too expensive. Also, the point was to confer in privacy, and not alert those with a vested interest in keeping the Debatable Lands lawless. It was finally agreed that the meetings should take place in Carlisle, and also that the French ambassador to Scotland, a Monsieur Doysell, should attend as a referee:

> The number of the Commissioners named by the Scots be too many, and shall not without much charge and trouble be answered from hence, the place being hence so far distant.
>
> Wherefore if a plat [i.e. map] were truly made by the consent of some men to be appointed on both parts, it is thought that there might be some reasonable and equal division made by men which should have indifferent respect to the quiet and concord of both the realms, and not to be led with any private affection to the people dwelling on either parts of the said Debatable.
>
> And, in deed, the less privy the Borderers be made to the division hereof, the more likely it is the thing shall take place.
>
> And for that the city of Carlisle is nigh thereto, and no place else either of the English or the Scots fit for this assembly, it is thought best that the meeting be there.
>
> If Monsieur Doysell shall require to know the names of such as shall be appointed in Commission, it shall be showed that it shall be the Earl of Westmorland, the Lord Wharton, Sir Thomas Chaloner and Sir Thomas Palmer, knights, and to be there upon the Borders within the month of March.[8]

The Scots agreed that discussions should be at Carlisle, and this certainly would have suited Chaloner because he could fairly easily reach that city from St Oswalds, his wife's estate near Pontefract. In fact, it is unlikely that he himself ever found it necessary to visit the Debatable Lands. We know from his accounts that he spent several weeks during April and May of 1552, and again in

July, in Carlisle. The only evidence in the accounts about what he was doing there are two consecutive entries concerning hospitality shown to the Scottish commissioners:

> delivered the second of May to John Stather [Chaloner's agent] upon account for board, wages etc. iii l. and towards the provision of his dinner for the Scotts iii l.   vi l.

> delivered to Stather the viith of May upon account for the banquet to the Scottish   xl s.

In early August we find Chaloner 'riding in company of the D. of N. [Duke of Norfolk] to the court at Salisbury'. This was to report on the result of the negotiations to the council, and probably to deliver them a copy of the map showing the newly agreed boundary between England and Scotland. The large and attractive map which was produced can be seen today in the National Archives.[9] The boundary cut the Debatable Lands diagonally in half, giving the south-western section to England and the north-eastern part to Scotland. It was agreed that a ditch should be dug along this new border with a stone pyramid at each end. Chaloner and his fellow commissioners had completed their task. Unfortunately, the lawlessness and border raids continued unabated, but Chaloner's role was over. Apart from a brief mission towards the end of Mary's reign, he would have no further dealings with the Scots.

7

ACCOUNTS
1551–1554

When I came across these accounts in the British Library I was surprised to discover that no one had seriously attempted to transcribe them before.[1] The accounts are from Michaelmas (29 September) 1551 until Michaelmas 1554, with one additional page in a different hand, dated February 1556/7. Out of over a hundred foolscap pages, twenty concern receipts, mainly from rents; the rest deal with expenditures. However, there is a gap in the accounts because the months Sir Thomas spent on official business in France during 1553 are not covered. He may possibly also have visited the Scottish borders in the summer of 1552 in order to view the Debatable Lands, but this too goes unmentioned.[2] Nevertheless, from these pages, plus other sources, it is possible to deduce much information about his interests and activities during these three years.

Transcribing these pages has been an enjoyable though sometimes frustrating business. They are in Chaloner's handwriting, but were obviously written rapidly and spontaneously. The task of decipherment is complicated by the fact that most of the items listed are not dated, and often his location when he made a particular payment or received a rent payment is not given. I have quoted directly from the accounts without altering grammar or punctuation. All items are stated in Roman numerals and in pounds, shillings and pence (abbreviated in the accounts as l., s. and d.) for instance, xxxi l. vi s. viii d. is thirty-one pounds, six shillings and eight pence.

On the death of his father in 1550, Thomas Chaloner became the head of his family. He was now a man of some status, comfortably off and with excellent prospects of moving still further up the diplomatic ladder. However, his family was large, and tended to look to him for support. He had a wife, Joan, together with Katherine, a young daughter from her previous marriage, and two unmarried sisters, as well as two younger brothers, neither of them, one assumes, particularly well off. Then there was his stepmother Isobel, and also his elderly mother-in-law, Margaret, as well as various other more distant relations.

At the time these accounts were composed, Chaloner and Joan owned, or leased, three large estates in different parts of the country, together with smaller properties in London and elsewhere. The estates were St Bees on the Cumberland coast, Guisborough in north-east Yorkshire and St Oswalds, near Pontefract, south Yorkshire.[3] Guisborough and St Bees had come to Chaloner by dint of his status and hard work on behalf of the Privy Council, but St Oswalds belonged, in fact, to his wife and her daughter. During this period he made repeated visits to the north of England, partly to administer his lands and partly on official business. As mentioned, it was fortunate that this business, which consisted of discussions with Scottish commissioners about the Debatable Lands on the Scottish border, took place mainly, or entirely, in Carlisle. This town was conveniently placed roughly in the centre of the triangle formed by his three northern country estates.

Income and Residence

Chaloner's properties provided a substantial income, although in the cases of Guisborough and St Bees he merely owned the leasehold at this time, and had to pay annual sums to the Crown as the freeholder. He also owned or leased bits of property in other parts of the country. For instance, we hear of two chantries in Berkshire which he owned. Chantries consisted of small chapels intended for a priest to say regular prayers for the soul of a wealthy individual in perpetuity, but, like the monasteries, they had been taken over by the king and had then passed into private hands.

[1554]
> Rec. of a man of Hungerford in county Berks who bought of me the lease of two chantries besides iiii l. that he paid me two years past   vi l.

He also leased 'Leeds parsonage' from an Oxford college and then rented it out:

[1552]
> paid to Mr Doctor Cope Dean of Christ's College xvii June by the hands of Leonard Bristow parcell of the last Lady Day rent for Leeds parsonage   xxiiii l.

At this time Chaloner was still receiving his two official salaries as clerk of the Privy Council and teller in the Exchequer, according to an entry in the autumn of 1551:

> rec. for my fees of clerkship of the council and mine office of the Exchequer both due at Michelmas last past   xxviii l. vi s. viii d.

This sum was presumably half a year's payment, in which case his annual salary for his clerkship was £40, and as an Exchequer official, £16 13s 4d.[4]

In addition to his regular salaries he was also paid separately for each day he was sent up north on official business. Between

May and the end of August 1552 he received a pound a day, as these two entries show:

> rec. at London of Sir John Williams [Treasurer of Augmentations] xv June 1552 by the council warrant parcel of my diets until the x of June at xx s. per diem   xxxi l. vi s. viii d.

> rec. at London ultimo augusti upon a warrant of my dues from the xth of June last past forwards at St John Williams hands   c l.

After their marriage, Chaloner and Joan lived with Katherine in Hoggesden (referred to here as Hogden) in Shoreditch, now part of London's East End, in a house Chaloner's father-in-law had left to Joan during her lifetime, and then to her daughter.[5] This house was probably on or near the site of the present-day Geffrye Museum.[6] Another member of the household was Chaloner's sister Ellen, who was to marry Thomas Farnham in March 1551/2. A younger sister, Elizabeth, most likely lived with his stepmother Isobel, who seems to have moved back to Abbot's Inn, the house in which she and her husband, Roger Chaloner, had once lived. However, as the accounts make clear, Chaloner himself was often away from home, and Joan spent much of her time at St Oswalds, where her elderly mother was probably still living.

One measure of Chaloner's status at this time can be gauged from a licence exempting his household from the Lenten dietary restrictions imposed by an act passed in the second year of Edward's reign and recorded in the Patent Rolls for 1 June 1550. The prohibition against eating flesh during Lent and other fast days, although seen by many as a popish survival, had been retained by the Protestant reformers in the interest of the fishing industry, on which depended recruitment for the royal navy. Exemptions from these dietary rules represented a kind of status symbol. Chaloner's licence was restricted to himself and family, 'not exceeding ten in number'. But people of the highest status, such as the Archbishop of Canterbury and the nobility, had licences which were unlimited as to numbers of people, whereas the licence for one Thomas Powle, for instance, covered 'one or two guests at the most'. Powle was controller of the Hanaper (part of the Exchequer). Chaloner came in between him and the nobility.[7]

Travel and Servants

Chaloner spent many hours and days in the saddle, travelling on behalf of the council, or up and down to his various properties. In this extract he refers to riding with his servants from St Oswalds to Hogden and back again.

[1554]

spent as well for my riding down to London with vi of my servants and vi horses as for the charges of their remaining there viz. For board wages and horsemeat and boat hire and for the charges of my return to Saint Oswald in all by the space of xxxix days viz. xvi die aprilis usque [until] xxvth die May in toto   xix l. iiii s. ii d.

'Boat hire' meant the cost of hiring a boat from Stepney, probably to Greenwich where the court and council were often based. As befitted his status, Chaloner always travelled with a number of servants. The following extracts show how much these servants were paid for food and accommodation when they were on the road (in addition to their normal wages).

[1553]

The charges and expenses of my riding down from Saint Oswalds to London the xviii of August with my charges and expenses at London and of my return back again to Saint Oswalds upon Thursday the xiiith of September 1554

> paid by estimation for the board wages of viii of my servants from Friday the xxiith of August that I came to London until Sunday the ix of September. viz. For Wright Brakenbury[8] Bennett Johnes Alisander Ketrich Tedde and Small by the space of xviii days at viii d. per day each of them being v s. iiii d. per diem   v l. ii s.

From these two extracts one can also calculate how long it took the group to ride from St Oswalds in south Yorkshire to London, the answer being four days. However a previous trip had lasted six days.

[1551]

> spent for all my charges by the way from London to St Oswalds by the space of vi days with viii horses and viii men   v l. x s.

Another extract makes clear that the route from London to St Oswalds lay via Royston and Grantham.

It is also likely that occasionally, when on official business, Chaloner made use of post horses rather than using his own. We know that early in the century three lines of post stations emanating from London, each station about twenty miles from the next, had been set up. One of these routes ran from London to Berwick.[9] Some extracts make it likely that post horses were being hired, although the majority of Chaloner's journeys were certainly made on his own horses.

[1551]

> delivered to Stather at Wetherby upon account for charges of my posting xl s. and at Rychemont xxvi March upon like account xl s   iiii l.

[1551]

> delivered to Robert Grindall at Raby Castle upon account and at Penrith upon like account for post horse and other charges as from Raby to Carlisle xxvi s.   l s.

[1552]

Memorandum defrayed by the way from Carlisle to Saint Oswalds where I arrived xxix September as well for post horses as otherwise   iii l. x s. iiii d.

When goods such as furniture needed to be transported from St Oswalds to London, the best method was by sea.

[1552]

paid to my wife the xixth of December for the carriage and freight of my stuff from Saint Oswalds to Hull and from there to London   v l.

delivered Henry Ketrich to pay for the going to Gravesend and taking up of part of my stuff   x s. in prest

Chaloner, of course, had more servants than the eight referred to above. In the book which he had earlier translated from Latin, *Of the Office of Servants*, there is a passage which accuses English gentlemen of possessing an unnecessary number of servants for reasons of status, and this criticism perhaps applies to him. For instance, in 1554 he seems to have kept at least twenty servants or retainers at St Oswalds without counting those waiting for him back at Hogden. In October they received their wages for the last quarter:

paid to my servants ensuing for Michelmas quarter their wages as followeth 1554 viz

To John Johnes whom I put to my Lord of Cumberland for his quarters wages and in reward   xx s.

To Brakenbury   xiii s. iiii d.
To Butler   xiii s. iiii d.
To Tho. Wright   xiii s. iiii d.

To John Stable	x s.
To Charles the coke	xx s.
To Alixander in reward	vi s. viii d.
To Tempest in reward	vi s. viii d.
To Avison	i s. viii d.
To Raphe	vi s. viii d.
To Cliff	vi s. viii d.
To Shepherd	x s.
To Pypott	xiii s. iiii d.
To Robinson	x s.
To Garlike	x s.
To Hoyle	vi s. viii d.
To Besse Young	vi s. viii d.
To Margery Shepherd	v s.
To Courtany	vi s. viii d.
To the boy of the buttery [crossed out]	
sum of wages of this parcel	ix l. vi s. viii

This list does not include Henry Ketrich, Chaloner's invaluable clerk, always on hand to carry out varying tasks:

[1551]

paid xiii March to Henry Ketrich for the charges of the house since my wife's going [to St Oswalds] all paid till this instant day

xl s. ii d. ob [½d.]

paid to him also that he dispursed for two males [mails, i.e. travelling bags] for me a little and a greater and a yard of cotton to trussle [?] in

xi s.

delivered to Henry Ketrich to pay to the smith upon his taile [tally] at my wife's going and all paid

v s. iiii d.

paid to H Ketrich to be by him paid over to the goldsmith that
set my diamond for the gold being iiii French crowns and for the
fashioning   xl s.

All these retainers no doubt wore their master's livery, but
precisely what colour this was remains uncertain. Chaloner
was not very good at describing colours. One item does refer to
livery:

[1551]
    paid to Snokeld a drapers servant for a pece of sheep colored cloth
    at xxiiii s. the yard to make my men's liveries   ix l. iiii s.

Another item may or may not refer to livery:

[1552]
    for xiii yards of horseflesh coloured damask   v l. iiii s.

And a third item, definitely for himself, again relies on animal
comparisons:

[1552]
    paid to H. Ketrich ultimo augusti for iii yards rat coloured cloth for
    a cloak   xxxiii s.

With all this travelling it is no surprise that many items are
about shoeing horses, mending saddles or buying new ones. For
instance, in the autumn of 1554 there was much preparation in
the neighbourhood of St Oswalds for the long journey south:

    the charges of my saddles newly bought and repaired etc circa iiii
    October 1554

paid to a saddler of Wakefield for two new saddles and for mending of certain of mine old saddles and bridles with stirrups

xxi s. iiii d.

paid to a saddler of Pontefract for iiii new saddles with all kinds of harness to the same and for two days' work at Saint Oswalds to mend mine old saddles and to stuff them as by the bills appeareth

xl s. ii d.

paid the viith of October to a man of Pontefract for two Spanish skins for the covering of my saddles

xiiii s.

Very occasionally, Joan rode with her husband, either to or from her home in St Oswalds.

[1554]

paid the smith of Wakefield's bill for new horse shoes and removes as well of old debt v s. as for shoeing at my riding to Skipton and to London with my wife xii October

xix s. iii d.

At this time, too, a new pillion was bought, presumably for Joan. According to the *OED*, one meaning of the word 'pillion' is 'a woman's light saddle'.

Item for a yard of fustian of Naples and for making of a new pillion and for his iiii days labour vi s.

Household

Under Chaloner's overall supervision, he and Joan shared the running of the two households: Hogden and St Oswalds. Some items seem to indicate that he kept a fairly close check on what money he gave Joan to spend on herself. For example,

[1551]
    Given to my wife upon Christmas day to play at cards   x s.

and about the same time,

> Given to my wife xviii Decembris towards the russet damask for
> her night gown   xl s.

This last may have been a New Year's Day present. These, rather than Christmas presents, tend to feature in the accounts.

Joan was in charge of *acates*, meaning purchases of items, such as food, which the households could not produce from their own resources. Consequently, there are numerous references such as

> delivered to my wife for acates Saturday xix Febr 1551   iiii l.

but few references as to what kind of food was actually acquired. Very occasionally, Chaloner himself did the shopping, or at least got involved:

[1552]
    delivered to a woman of the country for a quarter of pork ii s. iiii d. / for a quarter of veal ii s. ii d. / for two hens ii s. ii d. / the woman's name was Goodwife Larkin / pd. as to the steward

                                        vi s. viiii d.

[1554]
    bought then at York for my wife groundseed aniseed also ii lb. of sugar and quarter ounce of mace   iiii s. vi d.

This was especially true if the order concerned something unusual:

[1552]

Paid upon Candelmas day [2 Feb.] by the hands of Farnham to Mr Tonson Treasurer of the ships for an old debt of a chest of sugar which my wife had being prize ware and answerable to the king   xii l.

There are many references to the buying and selling of silver and gold items. Usually the weight of each item is specified.

[1552]

paid to a goldsmith in Lombard Street upon a bargain of exchange of iii goblets and a cover with one covered pot of silver weighing in all xciii ounces et di [a half]/ for two wine pots of silver parcel gilt and iii small bowls parcel gylt weighing in the whole lxxxvii ounces di/ the pots at vi s. the ounce/ So for the superplusage of the new plates exchanged for the old paid him in money by Letham   liiii s. iiii d.

In December 1551 Joan asked Chaloner to buy her a gold chain, perhaps to go round her waist. However, it seems she did not fancy the one he bought, so he had to return it to the goldsmith at a loss of £1.

rec. of my wife for a chain of gold weighing xiiii ounces   xl l.

Received of my brother Farnham for the price of a chain weighing xiiii ounces Crown gold sold to a goldsmith by mine order   xxxix l.

As a representative of the court, Chaloner gave considerable time and thought to his own clothes, and there is much mention of silks, satins and furs.

[1552]

paid to an old man a skin for furring of my gown of caffa[10] and for two marten skins   xxxvii s.

In an age of conspicuous display and magnificence, what the various professions and classes of society wore was highly significant. According to Ian Mortimer, the sumptuary regulations of 1553 specified that only lords, knights, or those with annual incomes of over £200 were permitted to wear velvet gowns or velvet coats.[11] The following examples involving the creation of a new velvet outfit by Sir Thomas, who himself probably qualified in two of these categories, are all from the summer of 1554:

paid for a rapier dagger and sword girdle per manus Ketrich   xxxiii s. iiii d.

paid for a doublet of Spanish taffeta the outside   xiii s.
the lining buttons and making   xx s. iiii d.

paid for a new velvet cap   xii s.

paid for a pair of velvet shoes   v s. iiii d.

paid for points[12] and socks   ii s.

paid for a yard and a quarter of velvet for a pair of hose xxi s./
paid to the hosier for the lining of secemett [?] iii s./ for the woollen lining iii s./ for two pair of socks x s./ for the making and silk v s.   xliii s.

paid for a quarter of velvet for the cape of my gown embroidered   iiii s. vi d.

paid for xii new coney [rabbit] skins and the laying of the fur in my damask gown guards with velvet   x s.

Leisure

Many items in the accounts give some indication of Chaloner's leisure interests. He was always buying books, though unfortunately their titles are seldom mentioned.

[Nov. 1554]
  bought ii books in Fleet Street   v s.

Other items relate to his interest in foreign languages:

[May 1554]

    for certain Spanish books bought then at London   x s.

[1551]

    given to a Frenchman that presented me a book of verses   x s.

The following item indicates fluency in Latin and an awareness of both classical and Renaissance authors:

[Oct. 1554]

    paid to a bookbinder of Pawles [St Pauls] for binding of divers Latin books and for certain new books bought of him viz. Plinius Livius Suetonius etc./ Celius Rodiginus and Alexander ab Alexandro et Macrobius[13]   iii l. x s.

And at the same time,

    paid for a Greek lexicon[14]   xx s.

Chaloner was clearly fond of music. He owned viols,[15] virginals and several lutes. Probably on occasion he hired professional musicians to play for himself and his family, but also he presumably played himself, or he would hardly have needed his own scores.

[1551]

    Paid to Pointes for the mending and tuning of my virginals   xiii s. iiii d.

[1551]

    Laid out at an other time for lute strings and given in reward to Herome [?] the lute player   x s.

[1552]
    paid for v set of books of Italian music   xvii s.

There are several references to a John Rose, who supplied and
mended Chaloner's vials, and also to the purchase of a surprising
number and puzzling variety of lute strings:

[1552]
    datum to John Rose for an other vial to be made xxix October of
    the finest sort   xl s.

[1554]
    bought v dozen of minor key lute strings at ii s. viii d. the dozen
    and one dozen cat lines   xiiii s. iiii d.

When he was away from home and in suitable company, there
was always card playing and other pursuits to account for:

[1552]
    lost at tables bowls etc and given to the poor   x s.

[1552]
    lost at cards during the said time as partner to Sir Thomas Palmer

                                                               xx s.

[1552]
    lost sundry times at tables   iii s.

[1551]
    paid ibidem die to Sir Thomas Palmer lost overnight to my Lord
    Wharton at Irish[16]   x s.

Wagers between gentlemen were also in fashion:

[1554]

    given to Thomas Wright to buy iii yards black satin for Sir Thomas
    Holcroft that I lost to him upon a wager   xxx s.

Transactions involving money were complicated by the fact that
there were so many different coins available. Chaloner mentions
marks [not a coin, but a unit of account, i.e. two-thirds of a
pound], groats [a silver coin worth four pence or more], testoons
[low-quality silver shillings], angels [gold, worth ten shillings],
nobles [gold, worth perhaps one mark at this time], half-
sovereigns [gold coins worth about fifteen shillings], and double
ducats [gold coins, perhaps minted in the Netherlands]. It was
clearly important whether a transaction was to be in gold or
silver. Here are a few examples to illustrate the complexities of
coinage.

[1551]

    delivered to my wife upon Sunday morning vith March to be
    converted into gold to carry with her into the country twenty
    pounds   xx l.

[1552]

    delivered to Henry Ketrich the last of August parcel of my warrant
    money to pay over to Quarles the draper upon my bill of xl mar
          xx l. sic debeo [thus I owe] xx nobles

[1553]

    rec. of my wife xxix October 1553 angels at x s. and French
    crowns at vi s. iiii d. parcel of the gold she had in a bag at my
    coming home [i.e. from France]

          lix l.

[1553]

    Memorandum Sir John Mason upon Wednesday before Michelmas
1553 for five c crowns of the sum which I delivered unto him by
John Taylor/ his servant repaid me in new coined groats

                                                 clviii l. vi s. viii d.

[1556]

    pd. to a goldsmith for exchanging of v l. of white money into
pistlates[17]   iiii s.

    given to my brother Francis xxvii May 1554 as angells   xxx s.

Relations

On his marriage Chaloner had become the guardian of Katherine,
the daughter of Joan and Sir Thomas Leigh, who was then about
thirteen. The accounts show some of the efforts he made towards
her education:

[1553]

    bought of James Wonesh [?] a vocabulary in Latin which I gave to
my daughter   iii s. iiii d.

And at the same time:

    given to a Flemming maistair [master] who teacheth my daughter
for ii books Italian in a pair   x s.

His brother Francis had married Agnes, the illegitimate daughter
of Sir William Bowyer, who had been mayor of London from
1543 to 1544. At this time the couple probably lived in Hoxton,
which was part of Shoreditch and not far from Sir Thomas's

house in Hogden.[18] The accounts show that Francis frequently received gifts or loans from Sir Thomas:

[1551]
    given to my brother Francis xiiii March left with Farnham to give
    him   xl s.

[1553]
    delivered eodem tempore to my brother Francis for the hire of a
    horse for his maid   vi s. viii d.

    delivered iii November to my brother Francis by way of loan to
    pay his daughters nurse   xiii s. iiii d.

Francis's brother-in-law, John Bowyer, was also helped:

[October 1553]
    lent to my brother Francis to bestow upon John Bowyer   x s.

Chaloner's other brother, John, is mentioned less frequently. He was probably spending much of his time in Ireland during the period of the accounts. He was engaged in various petitions to authority in order to secure the right to mine for minerals in the island of Lambay, off the coast near Dublin.[19] However, there is one interesting reference to him:

[1553]
    given to the mariners of my brothers ship in reward when I supped
    there   v s.

This would have been the ship *Eugenius*, bought by John and about to set sail for Ireland carrying a cargo of materials for his mining operations in Lambay. Unfortunately, this ship was captured by pirates and it took nearly three years for John Chaloner to get his equipment back.[20]

Chaloner's sister Ellen married Thomas Farnham in March 1551/2. Farnham seems to have acted as Chaloner's agent, trusted with large sums and frequently buying goods for him or lending him money.

> Received xii March 1551 by the hands of my brother Farnham for the price of a silver basin and an ewer and of three bowls with a cover weighing in all clvii ounces di/ viz the basin and ewer lxxvi ounces and the bowls with the cover lxxx ounces at v s. the ounce/ sold to a goldsmith   xxxix l. vii s. vi d.

[1551]

> paid to Farnham for so much lent by him aforehand to my wife at her going this last summer to St Oswalds which sums he took up of my fees in the Exchequer due at mich. last   xxxv l. xvii s.

Clearly, Chaloner had paid a dowry to Farnham on behalf of his sister:

> Memorandum also paid to my brother Farnham mense [month] December 1553 parcel of my sister Ellen's marriage money   xiii l.

Ellen's wedding was celebrated at length at Hogden, as Chaloner records, possibly somewhat resentfully as to the expense:

[March 1551/52]

> memorandum/ the charges of meat and drink with the play and other things at Shrovetide for my sister's marriage with her apparel cost me above xx l.
> for iii days meat and drink x l. and iii l. sithyns [since]

An interesting item connected with the wedding festivities was the performance of a play in Chaloner's house by masked players, with whom he later socialised, perhaps unwisely taking them on at a game of dice:

> given on Shrove Monday to the Kings Players who played the play of Self Love etc.[21]   xx s.

> played amongst the maskers at dice   x s.

At different times Ellen's younger sister, Elizabeth, received what were probably New Year's gifts:

[1553/4]
> bought at London certain Florence taffeta [and] white damask for a kirtle and sleeves/ certain wrought velvet for guarding and other trifles for my sister Elizabeth   v l. vi s.

The following entries seem to imply that Elizabeth was living at this time with Thomas's stepmother at Abbot's Inn.

[March 1551]
> given to my mother Chaloner ix March for black cloth to upp ... [?] a frock for my sister Elizabeth   viii s.

> given upon Thursday morning x March to my mother Chaloner to bestow smock linen gre [?] and a gown of frieze for my sister Elizabeth   liiii s.

Chaloner gave his stepmother Isobel an annuity:

[1553]
> paid to my mother Chaloner the ixth of October in full payment of the bill of annuity that I made her of xvi l. per annum   viii l./ and
>   viii l. was paid by my wife afore

He also converted her lease of Abbot's Inn – the rent of which he was already paying – from a leasehold tenancy to freehold. Presumably this property had been sold to new owners at some point between 1535 and 1552 (see chapter 1, note 6).

[1552]
  paid to Randall Haward and the Lady Powes his wife for redemption of the lease of the Abbots Inn circa x February 1552

  cc marks

8

QUEEN MARY AND *THE MIRROR FOR MAGISTRATES*
1553–1558

In April 1553 Chaloner was appointed ambassador in France in the place of Sir William Pickering. At the same time Chaloner, Pickering and Dr Nicholas Wotton, Dean of Canterbury, were instructed to meet the French king, Henry II, and offer England's services to mediate a peace between him and Emperor Charles V.[1] The three of them travelled to Poissy, had an audience with the king, visited the queen, Catherine de Medici, and sent a nineteen-page report back to the Privy Council, of which the following is an extract:

> Dr. Wotton, Sir William Pickering, and Sir Thomas Chaloner, to the council, May 1st 1553.
>
> The Dean of Canterbury and Sir Thomas Chaloner arrived at Poissy on Friday the 21st ult., Sir William Pickering having met them at Pontoise on the preceding day.
>
> As his Majesty was going to ride on hunting next morning, audience to the three joint commissioners was deferred till Tuesday, St Mark's day, on the eve of which the Constable[2] sent to the Dean of Canterbury part of the venison killed by the King, and forgot

not the next day, before the Dean had leisure to return thanks, to put him straight in remembrance thereof. Audience had, the King gave them most gentle entertainment, and after due attention to their credentials, referred them for consideration of the objects of their mission to the Constable and the other ministers. After the interview the Constable presented them to the Dauphin,[3] who for his years is of handsome stature, and better liking, than his late sickness doth well suffer him to be.

They were then brought to the Queen's bed-chamber, who within these fourteen days looketh to be delivered of child, to whom, and the rest of the young Princesses, they did the salutations appertaining. After leaving, they were in daily expectation of being sent for by the Constable, but did not hear from him till Friday, when M. Villandry informed him that next day was appointed for the meeting. At this were present only the Constable, the Cardinal of Lorraine, and M. Bertrandy, the Garde des Sceaux [keeper of the royal seals], when the grievances, complaints, and demands preferred by the French against the Emperor were rehearsed at great length, and are by the said commissioners fully set forth. These demands of the French, according to the instructions received, they have sent in cipher to the Bishop of Norwich and his colleagues.[4]

At this time the duties of a fully fledged ambassador were rather new to Chaloner. He wrote apologetically to Cecil:

I cannot tell, nor am not yet well acquainted with, the usages of this court, but by report of others my predecessors. I am not yet in room to have recourse unto me of such as know the estate of things here; which after Mr. Pickering's departure hence, I shall have more occasion to confer withal, and then will travail to attain to the perfect understanding of things which as yet I have none entry unto.[5]

At the end of May he was instructed by the council to explain to the French king that Edward VI was in excellent health. In fact, the reverse was true. The fifteen-year-old Edward was dying, and the Duke of Northumberland was waiting for his death, ready to put Lady Jane Grey on the throne. For those in the know, a major crisis was fast approaching. According to the will of Henry VIII, the heir to the throne after Edward should have been Henry's elder daughter, Mary. However, many saw major drawbacks to this. Mary was Catholic, and would inevitably try to undo all the Protestant legislation of Edward's reign. Also, she would probably want to restore the wealth of the Church which had been taken away in the 1530s, and which of course included the monastic houses whose lands and possessions had long since been parcelled out to nobles and gentry. It was probable that Mary would get married, most likely to a Catholic prince such as Philip, the son of the emperor, and this would totally alter the course of England's foreign policy.

A plan was therefore devised whereby the Duke of Northumberland, who had dominated the council since the fall of Somerset, would be able to retain power when Edward died. He had married one of his sons, Guildford Dudley, to Jane Grey, who had a claim to the throne since she was the granddaughter of Mary, sister of Henry VIII. On Edward's death Northumberland planned to proclaim Jane queen. The young king had given his approval of the plan, and may in fact have originally suggested it. The advantages of Lady Jane Grey over Mary were that she was a committed Protestant and already had a Protestant husband. Also, the couple were young, and therefore presumably amenable to guidance.

Very quickly, however, the entire scheme unravelled. It had involved gaining control of Mary's person so that she could not raise an opposition or flee abroad, but she showed initiative by moving from London to Norfolk the moment she heard of Edward's death and before she could be detained. Northumberland had assumed that Lady Jane would be the natural choice of the majority, but there he was wrong. Over the course of the next few days Mary attracted more and more support, while in London Northumberland and the council dithered. When he tried to lead an army to recapture her, he found his forces evaporating and going over to her side. Mary was proclaimed the successor, and Jane, queen for just nine days, was imprisoned in the Tower. There is a strong possibility that if Mary had not taken the initiative, the plan to alter the succession might have succeeded. Jane remained a prisoner until the rebellion of Sir Thomas Wyatt the following year. After this she was regarded too much of a risk as a figurehead for opposition to Mary, and she and her husband were executed.

What did Sir Thomas Chaloner make of Mary's accession? He had been appointed ambassador by the previous regime, and he was now recalled by Mary in favour of Wotton. However, there is no evidence that she disapproved of him or of his work at the French court, nor that he supported Northumberland's scheme in any way, especially as he was out of the country when the plot was being hatched. Although he returned to the status of a private citizen within a few weeks of Mary's accession, he was recalled to service in February 1556, and again given an important mission. He was therefore certainly not out of favour during the whole of Mary's reign, as were many others, one of them being his friend William Cecil. The eighteenth-century historian Andrew Kippis wrote about Chaloner, 'Under the reign of Queen Mary he passed his time, tho' safely, yet very unpleasantly, for being a zealous Protestant, he could not practise any part of that compliance which procured some of his friends an easier life.'[6] However, there is also no evidence that he had an 'unpleasant' time under Mary's rule, and in fact there is some to the contrary. It was during this reign that Chaloner acquired, or started to acquire, two valuable properties: Steeple Claydon in 1557, and the manor of Guisborough in 1558.[7] On the other hand, we do know that Chaloner greatly admired Lady Jane Grey and berated Mary for executing her. This is very clear from a Latin poem he wrote extravagantly praising Jane. When this poem was composed is unknown, but it seems unlikely that it was during Mary's reign. In any case, it was not published until after his own death.[8] To sum up, perhaps all we can say is what he himself wrote years later in a letter to a friend, 'I could conform myself to all tolerable things, reserving my opinion to myself.'[9] Possibly, too, if Mary had never come to the throne and re-established the old religion, his career might have moved forward a little faster than it did at this juncture.

Among those granted a general pardon by Mary for failing to oppose Lady Jane Grey as queen[10] we find listed 'Thomas Chaloner of Hoggesden, co. Middlesex, knight' opposite the date 9 October 1553. This Pardon Roll, very useful to economic historians, is a long list of what appears to be a cross-section of affluent English society. In total about 1,600 names appear, along with each person's occupation and where they lived. Clearly, all those who could afford the twenty-two-shilling fee and thought it worthwhile to avoid possible accusations of disloyalty in the future applied to go on the list and be granted a pardon. There are members of the nobility and privy councillors mixed in with every kind of tradesman and professional, from tinkers, watermen and shoemakers, to schoolmasters and 'barbosurgions'. Next to Chaloner is a fishmonger from Southwark.

In Chaloner's own accounts there is a neat confirmation of his application:

[Oct. 1553]

paid to Mr Cotton clerk of the Hamper xii October for my pardon
xxii s.[11]

On 16 January 1554 it was announced in Parliament that Mary was to marry Philip II of Spain. Within a few days news reached the council of a rising in Devonshire for the 'resisting of the king of Spain's coming'. The discovery of the conspiracy before the rebels had coordinated their plans caused their activities in Devon and other counties to be quickly subdued, but by the end of the month a large force of Kentish men under the leadership of Sir Thomas Wyatt[12] was advancing on the city of London. There was consternation within the city and the court, and it is the general consensus among historians that 'had London been less loyal, Wyatt more swift, or the Queen less resolute, Mary might have lost her throne'.[13] As it was, she stood firm, refused to flee the city, and rallied the Londoners to her defence. The gates were closed against Wyatt, and the help he had expected from within the city never came.

Many friends and colleagues of Chaloner were involved in the revolt, or at least accused of involvement. Some fled to the continent, including Sir William Pickering, who had been a commissioner in France with him the year before. There were also Henry Killigrew and his brother Peter, who escaped to France and turned to piracy; Lord Cobham and three of his sons; William Thomas, once a clerk to the council with Chaloner; and Sir Nicholas Throckmorton, who defended himself successfully at his subsequent trial for treason. We have no direct knowledge of what Chaloner did or thought during the revolt, though, in view of what he wrote about Mary in his poem about Lady Jane Grey, he may well have sympathised with the rebels. On the other hand, he may, for all we know, have taken some part in opposing Wyatt, as did his friend George Ferrers, who actually fought the rebels at the city gate.

One of Chaloner's activities during the time he was free of diplomatic commitments was to return to poetry. He was one of a group of seven literary friends who met together to compose

a joint work entitled *The Mirror for Magistrates*.[14] The leader
of the group was William Baldwin, and among the others were
George Ferrers, Thomas Phaer and also, better known today, the
authors Thomas Sackville and Thomas Churchyard. It is striking
that Baldwin and Ferrers in particular, like Chaloner, already had
literary reputations, but all of them were also skilful political
operators in dangerous times. As the literary historian Lily
Campbell explained:

> If we are to see the *Mirror* in true perspective, it is necessary
> to understand that it was written, not by literary hacks nor by
> minor writers of the day, but by learned men who were accepted
> as important figures in their own time ... First, they were
> adroit enough not to suffer from a change of rulers. So far as
> we know their history, most of them might have written their
> autobiographies as favourites under four reigns. Second, they were
> accepted as distinguished men of letters. Third, they had ample
> opportunity to know the affairs of the court and the nation. In
> other words, they had the necessary qualifications for writing
> a political *Mirror* which should take its place in literature: they
> kept their heads on their shoulders, which required a good deal of
> political wisdom; they had more skill in their craft of writing than
> did any other group to be listed during the reign of Mary.[15]

The *Mirror* was the successor of a very popular work from a
century earlier, John Lydgate's *The Fall of Princes*. As such, it
was an attempt to satisfy the contemporary demand for works of
history and politics that painted a moral which the readers could
understand and perhaps profit from. The format of this collective
work was as follows: members of the group were each asked to
research the lives of selected leading figures from history, and
compose poems explaining about their lives, and especially how
they had all eventually come to grief, punished by God for their

misdeeds. Each poem would be as if spoken by the character's ghost, warning others not to commit the same mistakes and sins as he or she had. All these ghosts were to address their remarks to William Baldwin, who was also the editor of the entire series of poems. In between each poem was a linking passage in prose, explaining why the different characters had been chosen.

Chaloner picked Richard II, the king who was overthrown in 1399 by Henry Bolingbroke, the future Henry IV, and then murdered when a prisoner. In his introduction Chaloner wrote, 'To further your enterprise, I will in the king's behalf recount such part of [Richard's] story as I think most necessary. And therefore imagine *Baldwin* that you see him all to be mangled, with blue wounds, lying pale and wan all naked upon the cold stones in Paul's church, the people standing round about him, and making his moan in this sort'.

There followed a poem of some 120 lines, in ten-line stanzas, titled, 'How king Richard the second was for his evil government deposed from his seat, and miserably murdered in prison.'

One can learn something of Chaloner's philosophy of life from his participation in this project. The book was called *The Mirror for Magistrates* because its message was that all those in authority, from kings to magistrates, had a duty as God's representatives to rule wisely and not selfishly. For instance, Chaloner's contribution starts:

Happy is the prince that hath in wealth the grace to follow virtue,
keeping vices under,
But woe to him whose will hath wisdom's place:

All the contributors subscribed to the following doctrine: if a king is virtuous then the people will be happy, but if he is greedy and immoral, all will suffer. However, this by no means implies that subjects may rebel against an unjust monarch. Their duty is, under all circumstances, simply to obey, leaving it to God to punish, if necessary, his unworthy lieutenant. In other words, this group of poets, like practically all their class, firmly believed in the Tudor and early Stuart doctrine of the divine right of kings. Shortly before they set to work, court and country had been rocked by Sir Thomas Wyatt's rebellion against Mary, yet in his final speech on the scaffold Wyatt himself uttered sentiments that could have come straight out of Chaloner's contribution to the *Mirror*:

I must confess myself guilty, as in the end the truth of my case must enforce me ... For peruse the chronicles through, and you shall see that never rebellion attempted by subjects against their prince and country from the beginning did ever prosper or had better success, except the case of King Henry the fourth, who although he became a prince: yet in his act was but a rebel, for so I must call him. And though he prevailed for a time, yet it was not long, but that his heirs were deprived and those that had right again restored to the kingdom and Crown, and the usurpation so sharply revenged in his blood, as it well appeared that the long delay of Gods vengeance was supplied with more grievous plague in the third and fourth generation. For the love of God all you gentlemen that be here present, remember and be taught as well by examples past as also by this my present infelicity and most wretched case.[16]

The *Mirror* was finished sometime in 1555, but it was not printed. This was owing to a royal proclamation of June that year which prohibited books thought to be heretical or otherwise disliked by Mary's government. Among these was Edward Hall's history of the Wars of the Roses, known as *Hall's Chronicle*, which had been the chief source used by the authors of the *Mirror*. Hall's history, published in 1542, had celebrated the reign of Henry VIII, including his attack on the pope and the monasteries. John

Wayland, the group's printer, clearly thought this was not the moment for a new publication based on Hall. In fact it was not until 1559 that the *Mirror* first appeared in print, but after that it quickly became a bestseller, going through several enlarged editions during Elizabeth's reign.

It is possible that the *Mirror* was not merely a series of innocent tales following on from Hall and Lydgate. In the characters of Humphrey, Duke of Gloucester, and Cardinal Beaufort there may have been a disguised eulogy to the executed Duke of Somerset, and an attack on his old enemy Stephen Gardiner, Bishop of Winchester.[17] Chaloner, and others in the group, had once been close to Somerset. He had been knighted by the duke, and later had been used in such confidential business as procuring evidence against Thomas Seymour, the protector's brother and rival. Chaloner had also been a witness against Gardiner at his trial for treason. If this theory is true it may have been Gardiner, then Mary's Lord Chancellor, who was responsible for the suppression of the book.

The potential printer of the *Mirror* was probably wise to avoid publication during Mary's reign, but there is no evidence that its authors got into any kind of trouble. As already mentioned, Chaloner was soon to be given another diplomatic assignment by the queen. Baldwin, Ferrers and Phaer also all continued to prosper. The sole casualty was Chaloner's name as one of the original contributors, which was left out of subsequent editions. The only reason we know at all that he wrote the poem about Richard II is the chance survival of a single leaf from the suppressed 1555 edition, which starts, 'When master Chaloner had ended this so eloquent tragedy.'

Chaloner's wife Joan died on 5 January 1557. One wonders whether her death was brought on by the effects of the long winter journey she had just made from St Oswalds to Hogden. She may, however, merely have been a victim of the influenza epidemic of the winter of 1556/7. The following two items occur close together on the final page of the accounts, which is written in a different hand – perhaps that of Chaloner's clerk, Henry Ketrich:

[1556]

to Joyce for moneys lent to my Lady viz money laid out for her
charges from St Oswald to London   *ix s.*

to Willm Parlar for blacks bought at my Lady's burial   xx l.

A contemporary diarist gives this account of Joan Chaloner's funeral:

The xj day of January was buried my lady Challenger the wife of Sir Thomas Challenger, and was the wife of Sir Thomas Lee of Hogston, and buried at Shoredich church, with ii white branches, and ij dozen staff torches and iiii great tapers, and a herald of arms, and iiii banners of images and viii dozen of escutcheons of arms, and the street hanged with black, both the street and the church and arms.[18]

This was clearly a very costly and elaborate funeral, and perhaps an unusual one for a Protestant lady, particularly with regard to the 'iiii banners of images'. It may be that Chaloner organised it with one eye to the likely approval of the Catholic queen.

A few months after Joan's death Chaloner's stepdaughter, Katherine, married James Blount, 6th Baron Mountjoy. In the accounts there is a brief reference to Mountjoy, presumably already a suitor for Katherine's hand:

[Feb. 1556/7]

to my Lord Mountjoy's man that brought venison pasties   ii s.

Unfortunately, Katherine's husband rapidly proceeded to get into debt, and he soon started to dissipate his wife's fortune and mortgage her estates. St Oswalds, heavily mortgaged, was finally sold to Sir Thomas Gargrave in 1568 for £3,560. Throughout his life Mountjoy was obsessed with the search for rare minerals, in particular alum and 'copperas',[19] and he was also something of an alchemist, believing that he could find a way of transmuting iron into copper, a more valuable mineral. He was far from being alone in these obsessions; many prominent figures, even including William Cecil, were fascinated with mining and the transmutation of metals. Mountjoy was always begging Queen Elizabeth I to grant him a monopoly on the mining of alum, and he brought over specialist Italian workmen to set up mines on his estates in Dorset – all ultimately to no avail. Katherine died in 1577 and her husband four years later, deeply in debt. Appropriately, one of his sons became a close friend of the Elizabethan magus John Dee.[20]

At the beginning of 1556, Chaloner was given a delicate mission which embroiled him in the complicated relations between Ireland and Scotland. He was to travel to Edinburgh to meet the regent, Mary of Guise, mother of the young Mary Stuart, and protest about the actions of Scottish settlers in Ulster. These, under the leadership of the O'Donnell clan, were making themselves a nuisance and attacking various castles garrisoned by the English. They had formed an alliance with the powerful Earl of Argyll in Scotland, who had even given his daughter in marriage to the chief of the O'Donnells. After his meeting with Mary of Guise, Chaloner had to report back to Thomas, Lord Wharton, who was warden of the East and Middle Marches. The two knew each other well, since they had both been commissioners for the Debatable Lands in 1552. According to his accounts, Chaloner had played card games with him and once borrowed a horse from his stable:

[Sept. 1552]

given also at that time in reward to my lord Wharton's horse keeper
that provided me with a gelding one di [a half] sovereign   x s.

Chaloner's instructions from the Privy Council give some idea of the complexities of the Irish situation:

Instructions for Sir Thomas Chaloner sent to the Dowager of Scotland [Mary of Guise] in February 1555 [i.e. 1556].

First.—To declare the Queen's [Mary I's] forbearance of the disorders committed by Scots in her realm of Ireland, as she considered they were done without her good sister's [Mary of Guise's] knowledge, and her hope that she will redress them in time.

Item.—That of late Callough O'Donnell, a subject of England, has rebelled, and meaning unnaturally to depose his father O'Donnell from his estate, and usurp it, has married the Earl of Argyll's daughter, which earl has sent his own son with many of his men, and money to help him, while James McConnell and his brethren with a strong force of men, vessels, and brass ordnance, are in the north of Ireland. These rebels and Scots have not only sieged and taken our castles of Lough Foile, Lyffer, Fynne Doungall &c., but have burned and spoiled 60 miles compass, and slain many loving subjects, taking besides others the said Callough's father, whose unnatural son keeps him prisoner, the Scots keeping the others and the castles.

The said Sir Thomas, on receiving answer, shall return to Lord Wharton, advertise him thereof, and report to us his whole proceedings. While in Scotland, he shall make diligent inquiry in all ways at his discretion, as to their feelings towards peace, practices with France, and especially in Ireland, what their meaning is, who are the principal doers, &c., and advising thereon with Lord Wharton, whose experience, we know, shall much further his charge, report to us.[21]

We have no idea how this assignment worked out, nor how long Chaloner remained in Scotland. A year later we do know he was with English forces in France fighting against the French and on the side of Mary Tudor's husband, Philip. A large Spanish army under Philibert, Duke of Savoy, who was Philip's ally, was advancing towards Paris from the east, and had besieged the town of St Quentin in Picardy. A smaller French army which was trying to reach the town was caught in an unfavourable position and routed by Philibert with great loss of life. The English forces arrived somewhat later, as Froude explains: 'The English did not share in the glory of the battle, for they were not present; but they arrived two days after to take part in the storming of St Quentin, and to share, to their shame, in the sack and spoiling of the town. They gained no honour, but they were on the winning side.'

It is likely that Chaloner took part in the storming and the sacking because, six months later, the Privy Council ordered the Lord Mayor of London to deliver to him 'a Frenchman, presently remaining in the Counter [a prison] in London, who was taken prisoner by the said Sir Thomas at the beginning of the wars'.[22] Presumably, Chaloner was entitled to receive the ransom paid for the release of this French soldier. Early the following year the tide turned in the war, and the French besieged and captured Calais. Dunkirk, along the coast, was still in English hands, however, and Chaloner was appointed to take charge of providing carriages for the troops stationed there.

January 10 1558, The Queen to Sir Thomas Chaloner

We send at present a power to Dunkirk to be thence employed as the Earl of Pembroke (whom we have appointed lieutenant-general) and others of our council with him think best. We have, in respect of your experience of those countries appointed you to have chief charge of provision of carriages for our army; forthwith put yourself in order with such able men as you have about you, to attend our lieutenant [i.e. after he has arrived at Dunkirk].[23]

9

ELIZABETH – THE MARRIAGE QUESTION
1558–1559

In November 1558 Mary died, and the cautiously Protestant Elizabeth succeeded her devoutly Catholic sister. At the same time there were other major changes in the political and diplomatic map of Europe. Earlier that year Emperor Charles V retired, handing over his German lands and the imperial title to his brother, Ferdinand, and to his son Philip not only Spain, but also Flanders, parts of Italy, and the wealth of the New World. The following year Henry II of France died, leaving his widow, Catherine de Medici, regent for his three young sons, who succeeded to the throne in turn.

One of the first things Elizabeth did was to appoint William Cecil as her permanent secretary (he had previously held this post during the second half of Edward VI's reign). When Cecil took his oath as secretary Elizabeth is reported to have told him, 'This judgement I have of you, that you will not be corrupted with any manner of gifts, and that you will be faithful to the state; and that without respect of my private will you will give me that counsel that you think best.' The two of them made an effective team, and proceeded to run the country together for most of her reign.

As far as Chaloner was concerned, his closeness to Cecil meant that from now on he was seldom without employment.

Elizabeth and her Privy Council faced many problems both at home and abroad. In a highly pessimistic memorandum, Armagil Waad set out the situation as he saw it. Waad had been a clerk to the council along with Chaloner, and their careers ran closely parallel. His memorandum was addressed to William Cecil.

> The Queen poor, the realm exhausted, the nobility poor and decayed. Want of good captains and soldiers. The people out of order. Justice not executed. All things dear. Excess in meat, drink and apparel. Divisions amongst ourselves. Wars with France and Scotland. The French king bestriding the realm, having one foot in Calais and the other in Scotland. Steadfast enmity but no steadfast friendship abroad.[1]

The threats from abroad were the most pressing. It is true that the long struggle between Hapsburg and Valois came to a temporary conclusion with the Treaty of Cateau Cambrésis, signed in April 1559, but this left England in a dangerous situation. The treaty confirmed the loss of Calais, England's last Continental possession. Scotland was occupied by French troops under the rule of Mary of Guise who was acting as regent for her seventeen-year-old daughter, Mary Stuart. And most worrying for Elizabeth was that this daughter, known to history as Mary, Queen of Scots, also had a strong claim to the English throne, a claim that was supported by the French. She was the grand–daughter of Henry VIII's elder sister, and was seen by many, even in England, as the rightful heir to the throne rather than Elizabeth. England during the early years of Elizabeth's reign was militarily weak and vulnerable to attack from either France or Scotland, or both. Moreover, if England was attacked, Philip of Spain was unlikely to help. He would have been reluctant to antagonise the

French, with whom he had just made peace, by coming to the aid of Elizabeth, who was in his eyes an illegitimate and heretical monarch.

Elizabeth, however, did hold a crucial asset: her possible marriage. As Chaloner was to express in a letter to Cecil, 'The queen's hand is the card of our negotiations.' She was far and away the best match to be had anywhere, and was hardly on the throne before she was besieged by the messengers of potential suitors from all over Europe. No one thought for a moment that she would stay single; she clearly needed a husband to guide her in a man's world and relieve her of weighty decisions. Even Cecil believed this at first. At about this time he is said to have told an envoy from abroad that he ought not to have discussed a certain issue with the queen, since it was 'a matter of weight, being too much for a woman's knowledge'.

The earliest and perhaps the most obvious husband for Elizabeth was Philip himself, the widower of Mary Tudor. In spite of Elizabeth's obvious drawbacks, his advisers were all for the match, including the Spanish ambassador in London. This was the Count de Feria, a Spanish grandee who was to become a good friend of Chaloner's. Feria had been ambassador at Mary's court and a crucial link in helping to arrange Mary's marriage to Philip. Although a Catholic himself, he was not unsympathetic to England, having just married an Englishwoman, Jane Dormer, who had been one of Mary's ladies-in-waiting and was from a well-connected Catholic family. Within a few months of Elizabeth's accession, Feria resigned as ambassador, and he and Jane left the country. They stayed briefly in Flanders, where Jane gave birth to her first child, and then went on to Spain. Feria's estate was at Zafra, near the Portuguese border. He was one of Philip's most influential and trusted councillors, and he and his wife were useful contacts for Chaloner when he became ambassador in Madrid.

Both Philip and Feria felt sure Elizabeth could not possibly refuse an offer of marriage. Philip wrote a letter to Feria in which he weighed up the pros and cons from the Spanish point of view, ending by instructing that his offer be put to the queen. He was, he thought, granting the queen the most splendid alliance in the world, and an end to all England's worries about France. He explained to Feria the conditions on which he would be prepared to marry her, though he instructed him not to inform the world about these conditions straight away. His letter reveals his patriarchal assumptions and his overconfidence that Elizabeth would see things the way he did:

> I have decided to sacrifice my private inclination in the service of our Lord, and to marry the Queen of England.
>
> Provided only and always that these conditions be observed: first, and chiefly, you will exact an assurance from her that she will profess the same religion which I profess, that she will persevere in it and maintain it, and keep her subjects true to it.
>
> Secondly, she must apply in secret to the Pope for absolution for her past sins, and for the dispensation which will be required for the marriage; and she must engage to accept both these in such a manner that when I make her my wife she will be a true Catholic, which hitherto she has not been.
>
> You will understand from this the service which I render to our Lord. Through my means her allegiance will be recovered to the Church.[2]

In announcing his resolution to make this cruel sacrifice, Philip added that though he was ready to marry her she must not expect him to remain long with her. He was absolutely needed in Spain, and to Spain he must go whether he left her pregnant or not.

Unfortunately, Feria made the mistake of showing Philip's letter to certain of Elizabeth's ladies-in-waiting, who told the queen what they had seen, with the obvious result. Philip was not refused directly, but nevertheless the wedding was off. This was not to the liking of Feria, who clearly thought his royal master the obvious choice of husband for the new queen. However, even without the conditions Philip wanted to attach to his proposal, the marriage was never a realistic possibility. His previous marriage to Mary Tudor had been highly unpopular in England, and there would have been large-scale opposition to another Spanish match. Nor was Philip himself particularly enthusiastic about marrying someone he saw as an illegitimate heretic, even though Feria thought he should make such a sacrifice in the interests of his country and his faith.

Another early suitor was Eric, King of Sweden. His brother John, Duke of Finland, arrived in London at the head of a large delegation to plead Eric's case. John's retainers wore, pinned to their red velvet coats, hearts pierced by javelins, symbolising their king's love for Elizabeth. John spent money like water on gifts to courtiers, as well as to the poor of Southwark, where he was allocated a palace during his stay. Londoners got the impression that Sweden was easily the wealthiest nation in Europe. A courtier reported that John – and presumably therefore also his brother – 'was a very proper man, well learned, well nurtured and had the commendation of all men', while Cecil noted that he was well spoken in Latin. Above all, of course, the King of Sweden's main attraction was that he was a Protestant. His suit continued intermittently until 1561, when he received a final rejection.[3]

During this time Thomas Chaloner found himself fully involved in the issue of a possible royal match. He was first dispatched to Germany to meet with Ferdinand I, who had now formally succeeded his brother, Charles V, as Holy Roman Emperor. Feria gives us a rare glimpse of Chaloner at this time, as seen by a foreign diplomat: 'He is a gentleman who in the time of King Edward was one of the three secretaries of the Council, and when troops were being raised a year since to succour Calais he went as commissary to Dover, where I saw him. He is a man of a little over 40, and speaks Latin, Italian, and French well.'4

Chaloner set out from England in the first week of December 1558. His journey was dangerous due to the ending of the late war between Spain and France. He reported that the roads were 'difficile through the extreme frost, and dangerous from the men of war who on either side have been dismissed'. On Christmas Eve he reached Augsburg, where an interview with the emperor was arranged. Chaloner's instructions specified that he was to conclude the interview with an apparently vague statement that 'if any other thing should occur to further the amity between England and the emperor's patrimonial dominions, [Elizabeth] would be glad to give ear thereto'. Both sides knew what this meant. The implication was that Elizabeth might possibly be interested in a suggestion of marriage between herself and one or other of the emperor's two available sons.

Actually, Ferdinand had no less than fifteen children – ten daughters and five sons – but it was generally understood that the eldest son, Maximilian, was one day to succeed his father as emperor. It was the next two sons who were apparently on offer. They were Archduke Ferdinand, then aged thirty, and his younger brother Archduke Charles, about ten years younger. In fact, although this was not generally known until some months after Chaloner's visit, Ferdinand was not available because two years earlier he had secretly married a German lady who was not of royal blood. This was Philippine Welser, from a wealthy family of bankers. Philippine was a beautiful and gifted lady about whom much has been written (in German), both in fiction and fact.5

Back in England, Chaloner soon received confirmation that his hints had been understood and reciprocated. The emperor dispatched to England an envoy, Count von Helfenstein, who arrived at Chaloner's house, was introduced by him to the court, and an audience with the queen was arranged. Feria's successor as Spanish ambassador, Alvaro de Quadra, wrote to Philip, 'Count Helfenstein is in good spirits about the prospect of his affair, and is all for the archduke coming over. Once here, he thinks the archduke will find so many friends that she will be obliged to consent, whether she likes it or not. Nothing can be worse than to let her go on as she is going.'[6] On meeting Helfenstein, Elizabeth said little, and for several weeks she prevaricated while still giving the impression that she favoured the match. Feria, still in England, reported back to Philip:

> When the Emperor's ambassador arrived here I understand he had no instructions to treat of the matter [i.e. the marriage of Elizabeth and the Archduke Ferdinand], but so many loose and flighty fancies are about, some of these people who went to and fro with him to the palace must have broached the subject to him. One in particular I know of was Chaloner, who went to visit the Emperor on the Queen's behalf when she succeeded to the throne. He is a great talker, but a person of no authority.[7]

By 'no authority' he perhaps only meant that when in Germany Chaloner did not have official permission to discuss the marriage proposal openly. Feria himself, like others who were in the know, thought the marriage to Ferdinand quite likely to take place. He probably also felt that if Elizabeth would not have Philip, then another Hapsburg union in the shape of Philip's cousin would be the next best thing. Chaloner himself was rather more enthusiastic. A few months later he wrote to Cecil from Brussels concerning the Archduke Charles: 'He is not a Philip but better for us than a Philip.'

During the spring and early summer the court was agog with rumours about the impending Austrian marriage. No one seemed certain which of the two archdukes were in the lead, which presumably means that Ferdinand's earlier marriage was still a secret. In May, a gossipy letter to Philip from Quadra contained this excerpt:

> The council tell me they will not have the Archduke Ferdinand. They hear he is a bigot and a persecutor. They think best of Charles, only Cecil says he is not wise, and that he has as big a head as the Earl of Bedford.[8]
>
> The Emperor's ambassador has had an interview. The Queen told him jokingly her fool had said that he was one of the archdukes in disguise, who had come over to see her. She spoke warmly of the Emperor, calling him a good and upright man; and Maximilian, she said, was a friend of the true religion. She ridiculed Ferdinand; she was told, she said, that he was a fine Catholic, and knew how to tell his beads and pray for the souls in purgatory. Of Charles she seemed to know nothing; but she declared she would never have a husband who would sit all day by the fireside. When she married it should be a man who could ride and hunt and fight.[9]

In the same month Helfenstein organised an agent from Germany to arrive in London bearing a letter from the emperor, as well as a portrait of the Archduke Ferdinand, which he was to deliver to the queen.[10] Helfenstein himself wrote to Chaloner, '[He is] a most comely person, but his mind and inward abilities exceed his person.' The canvas was damaged during its journey to England, however, and Helfenstein promised to send Chaloner another 'of the Duke's whole body, and of his brother also', so that he could compare the two. However, when she got to see it, Elizabeth was apparently not impressed with the portrait of Ferdinand. Perhaps she recalled the time her father had been attracted by a portrait of Anne of Cleves, only to reject the lady herself. In any case, she insisted that the archduke appear in person before she could make any decision. 'You ask me to be frank with you,' she said to Quadra in September, 'If the Emperor would have me as a daughter-in-law, let him send over his son to see me. I am a queen and a lady. I cannot ask a man to come to England and marry me. I would die a thousand deaths first. Others marry for interest; I if possible would marry for affection.'[11] Sometime after this it is likely that news of Ferdinand's secret marriage became public, because he never did come to England, and one does not see his name again as a possible suitor. Instead, his younger brother Charles took up the running, although he too was finally rejected several years later.

For all these foreign candidates for Elizabeth's hand, there was a sinister cloud threatening their various plans. It was public knowledge that the queen had long been attracted to a certain Englishman, Robert Dudley, and rumours of a sexual affair, a secret marriage, and even of the murder of his existing wife, Amy Robsart, were rife, not only throughout England, but also in foreign courts. Dudley became thoroughly unpopular. Quadra wrote home that 'Lord Robert is the worst young fellow I ever encountered. He is heartless, spiritless, treacherous, and false. There is not a man in England who does not cry out upon him as the queen's ruin.'[12] William Cecil now saw Dudley as a real threat to his own plans, and even to his position in the court and council. A few years later, when Archduke Charles was still the leading foreign suitor and Dudley, now Earl of Leicester, his only serious rival, Cecil set down a table comparing the two candidates – perhaps somewhat sarcastically:[13]

CONVENIENT PERSON	CHARLES	LEICESTER
In birth.	Nephew and brother of an Emperor.	Born son of a knight, his grandfather but a squire.

In degree. In age.	An archduke born. Of __ and never married.	An earl made. Meet.
In beauty and constitution.	To be judged of.	Meet.
In wealth.	By report 3,000 ducats by the year.	All of the Queen, and in debt.
In friendship.	The Emperor, the King of Spain, the Dukes of Saxony, Bavaria, Cleves, Florence, Ferrara, and Mantua.	None but such as shall have of the Queen.
In education.	Amongst princes always.	In England.
In knowledge.	All qualities belonging to a prince – languages, wars, hunting, and riding.	Meet for a courtier.
In likelihood to bear children.	His father, Ferdinando, hath therein been blessed with multitude of children. His brother, Maximilian, hath	*Nuptiae steriles.*[14] No brother had children, and yet their wives have. Himself married, and no children.

	plenty. His sisters of Bavaria, Cleves, Mantua, and Poland have already many children.	
In likelihood to love his wife.	His father Ferdinando, *ut supra* [as above].	*Nuptiae carnales a laetitia incipiunt et in luctu terminantur.*[15]
In reputation	Honoured of all men.	Hated of many. His wife's death.

FLANDERS
1559–1560

Chaloner was allowed less than four months in England to settle his affairs before being sent off on another mission. This time he was to go as English ambassador to the court of Philip II, which at this moment was based in Ghent. His instructions were that if Philip decided to return to Spain he was either to accompany him or to remain where he was, as ambassador to Margaret of Parma, Philip's regent in the Netherlands. The choice was to depend on Philip himself. So Chaloner was now seen as a fully fledged ambassador to a foreign ruler, and not merely as an envoy with a specific and temporary mission.

During Chaloner's seven months in Flanders, important changes took place on the international scene. One was that Philip, having been rebuffed by Elizabeth, married Elizabeth Valois, daughter of the French king Henry II, thus consolidating peaceful relations between the two leading powers in Europe. However, from the English point of view, worse was to follow. Froude takes up the story:

In honour of the marriage of his daughter with Philip of Spain, Henry II held a gorgeous tournament. The King himself took his place in the lists. On the last day of the festivities he was running a course with the Count Montgomery de Lorge, captain of the Scotch Guard, when de Lorge's lance striking full upon Henry's casque, tore it away from the helmet; the point broke short off, and the ragged staff pierced the king's forehead above the eyes, bearing him senseless to the ground. The surgeons at first believed that there was no danger; but a splinter had reached the brain. He lingered ten days, and died; and Francis and Mary Stuart were King and Queen of France.[1]

Henry's death turned out to be a severe blow for England, because it meant that the ultra-Catholic Guise faction now came to dominate France. Mary Stuart was an ambitious and energetic nineteen-year-old whose husband was a sickly child some four years her junior. She was now Queen of France and Scotland as well, where her mother, Mary of Guise, was still ruling as regent in her name. But she also had a strong claim to the throne of England, since her paternal grandmother was the sister of Henry VIII. She took this claim seriously, added the arms of England to her escutcheon, and in all her public acts styled herself Queen of England. Her claim was fully supported by her five uncles, the brothers of Mary of Guise, of whom Francis, Duke of Guise, nicknamed Balafré [the scarred], was the warrior brother.

Chaloner's task was to attend Philip's court, to interview the king as soon as possible, and to send back to England as much as he could discover about the attitudes and plans of the Spanish rulers of Flanders. During his time as ambassador he wrote and received a stream of letters and dispatches, both official and personal. Normally he sent frequent, sometimes weekly, reports to Elizabeth, often accompanied by less formal covering notes to Cecil, whom he regarded as a friend as well as his superior. On delicate matters, especially to Cecil, Chaloner often wrote in a rather allusive style, using references and Latin phrases understandable to an educated elite but not to others who might intercept and open his letters. Sometimes, too, the names of important people were put into a simple cipher, substituting numbers for names. The following example from a letter to Cecil expresses Chaloner's pressing hope that the queen would marry for the security of the country, especially after Philip's recent marriage to Elizabeth Valois. The Spanish, he claims, believed that the English were provoking the French to declare war by their policy in Scotland:

This strait amity between the two mighty neighbours proceeds to the knot by consummation of the marriage. God knows what they will brew against us! Were it not good to have an Oliver for a Rowland?[2] I assure you they count our force nothing, the Scotch much less; they suppose division at home will be both our ruins; and that the French wiliness and tolerance will at length weary them. They judge here again that we have been the covert setters on. Wherefore, whether our parts be in it or not, it is good to look unto it, seeing, as well without cause as with, they impute it to England. If 13 [the Earl of Arran, England's ally] could bring his feat about, *nihil prius* [nothing more], but if always *mora trahit periculum* [delay involves danger], then what doth it impart in such kind of enterprises, which stand altogether upon celerity? If we, as spectators of their doing, should lose the occasion elsewhere of concluding honourable *partito* [wager] for our stay and reputation in the world, I wot not what to say or think in it. I hope the Queen will lose no more time, for *non nobis nati sumus sed patriæ* [we are not born for ourselves but for our country]. Antwerp, 10 Nov. 1559.[3]

To fully grasp what Chaloner is saying here, one needs to take account of an event that had occurred shortly before his arrival in Ghent. In Scotland the rule of Mary of Guise, the French-backed regent, had come under threat from a revolt by the Scottish Protestants. This provided an opportunity, but also a danger, for

Elizabeth. Should she send them help, either financial or military? If she did, and if they were successful, their gratitude to England might lead ultimately to a union between the two nations, a policy which both Henry VIII and Somerset had attempted and failed to successfully implement. However, intervention could also lead to retaliation by France, now under the leadership of the Duke of Guise, and the French were quite capable of defeating the combined forces of England and Scotland. Nor would Philip, now the husband of a French princess, be inclined to help. Typically, Elizabeth's response to this problem was to procrastinate and compromise. She sent money to the Scottish rebels, and she also helped the Earl of Arran, a rival Protestant claimant to the Scottish throne, to return to Scotland from his exile abroad.

Chaloner arrived in Ghent on Friday 28 July 1559, but was kept waiting for a week before he could meet Philip, 'not having been visited by any of the court since my coming, nor bidden welcome from the king'. This was partly due to the rituals of the Order of the Golden Fleece, the most prestigious order in Europe, which were being held this year in Ghent with great pomp and ceremony. Although he suspected that he was also deliberately being kept waiting for his royal audience, Chaloner watched the procession incognito, and wrote home to Cecil admiringly:

The ceremonies of the Order were as follows. The King and the Knights of the Order passed to the great Church yesternight to evensong. I did behold, disguised, in a house, the solemn pomp thereof; where first, the procession, with xxi mitred bishops and abbots *in pontificalibus*, and amongst them the Bishop of Arras, went before. Then the officers of arms and trumpets followed, next whom those of the Order, of the number of a xxiiii, and amongst them the Duke of Savoy, two and two together, and next them the King, all clad in robes of the Order, with their chaperons [hoods] upon their heads, very rich and fair to behold. And last, a great number of his other Lords and gentlemen of his court, closing up the pomp at the King's back. Ambassadors saw I none there. They say the King, with those of the Order, this Sunday, the Mass ended, dineth at the Town House at the cost of the Lords of Gand [Ghent].

These ceremonies have been celebrated here in very solemn sort with great concourse of beholders, and continued three days, from Saturday last at evensong till Tuesday following; each day with a peculiar change of robes and chaperons, viz. crimson, black, and white. Every of these three days the King with the Knights of the Order were sumptuously feasted at the Town House at the several charge of the three estates of the said town.[4]

While he was waiting to meet Philip, Chaloner took the opportunity to discover what leading Spanish officials, including Feria, thought about England. Feria was now in Flanders waiting for his wife to recover from a troublesome childbirth before the two set off for Spain. He told Chaloner that he and his colleagues did not rate England's military might very highly, and also that they were aware of the latest gossip in Elizabeth's court (i.e. her alleged affair with Robert Dudley). Chaloner's advice to Elizabeth was to strengthen the armed forces:

These men have learned the first school point of deep dissimulation, yet a mind alienated cannot so be covered, but that on some side it will show itself. Omitting the vulgar sort, the greatest of them at their houses and tables speak unseemly of your affairs, and procure your evil subjects both here and at home to forget their liege duty. If occasion served, they would produce their evil meaning to effect.

All this contempt arises because they repute us unarmed. One of the Count de Feria's terms was, 'that we had matter, but we wanted form.' I hope that the next to God you will put your surest trust in the right hand; for I never heard but an armed prince had ever the quietest friendship of his neighbours. 200 gentlemen pensioners at 100 marks apiece, everyone with four horses, swartrutters [horsemen who wore black and blackened their faces, the crack mercenaries of the time], in the whole but 1,000 horsemen, were but 20,000 marks by the year, besides the furniture of Your Grace's Court, with servants and gentlemen, the service and surety were great. A prince so banded may the bolder command.[5]

Finally, Chaloner did get to meet Philip, presenting him with letters from the queen. According to his report, Philip could not have been more charming to him:

Coming to the Palace I was brought to the King's privy and bed chamber, where at the first were only Don Antonio de Tolledo and Don Juan Menriquez, with whom I passed reciproque salutations. Soon after the King himself came forth of an inner garderobe, clad in a plain black cloak with cloth cap (for he mourneth) very plainly. I did my due reverence, even to the kissing of his hand, which offer the King would not permit, but made me straight be covered. I then presented the Queen's letters, which gently he received, read distinctly, and paused to hear my credence, which I uttered in Italian, as by a note enclosed appears. The King showed his good acceptance thereof by his countenance while I was speaking, and at last made answer in Spanish, declaratory of his amity and of his intention to observe the leagues and treaties which had passed heretofore, concluding with many good words, in such gentle fashion and such smiling countenance as one might not well desire more at so great a Prince's hands.[6]

In spite of finding Philip so gracious, Chaloner still found it difficult in Ghent, and in Flanders generally, to acquire the kind of information he was expected to come up with. In one letter to the Queen he suggested he should be allowed more money with which to pay spies: 'To repair to the court were over suspicious; to come to their churches were for me dangerous; so these two conferences being taken from me, what resteth but a good table and liberal rewards to espies? Without tools no work is done.'[7]

Philip told Chaloner he was about to leave the Netherlands for Spain, and the issue then was whether Chaloner should accompany him. The queen and Cecil now wanted him to stay where he was, partly because he would be on the spot to deal with the important issues concerning trade, which constantly cropped up between England and the Netherlands. Chaloner agreed. Even at this date he seems to have developed a strong antipathy towards Spain, that 'land of heat and Inquisition' as he called it. He already suspected that the role of English ambassador would be difficult in such a Catholic nation: 'The favour that any of our nation should find in Spain, when travelling from place to place, should be very meagre, and great circumspection would be necessary'.[8] Eventually, much to his relief, it was agreed by all concerned that he could remain in Flanders as ambassador to Margaret of Parma, the half-sister whom Philip left to rule the Netherlands when he was not there.

Chaloner thought that the primary reason Philip was anxious to leave the Netherlands for Spain was that he was worried about the spread of heresy, even in this most Catholic of nations. He heard reports about the Spanish Inquisition, which, now that the king was at home, seemed to be increasing its power and activities. With each successive report reaching Antwerp the stories grew more horrendous, and Chaloner duly passed on what he was told to Elizabeth:

I have heard also more particularly of the terrible or tyrannous severity of the Inquisition in Spain. Men there be called on to account for words of two years past. A great number of the best sort are touched therewith, some executed, others committed to perpetual prison, their goods and livings confiscated to the king, the value whereof, as I am informed, ariseth to an incredible sum. So zeal is somewhat kindled with the thirst of gold.[8]

In one report he went on to relate a particularly horrific incident – one has to remember, of course, that these stories were passed on to him by his Flemish contacts, most of whom were likely to be Protestants:

There chanced, amongst sundry there executed, that a priest, not bound with chains but ropes only to the stake, half scorched and broyled, through struggling, when his hands were burst asunder, broke from the stake and ran amongst the press, every man giving way to the poor and miserable spectacle of the carbonade; but, being taken again by the ministers of the justice and demanded whether he would deny his opinions, he answered constantly no, and so was eftsoons committed to the fire.[9]

In his reports home Chaloner could wax satirical about the activities of the Inquisition. When he heard a report that the corpse of a certain Spanish nobleman accused of past heresies had been dug up after seven years in his grave, he commented, 'If he be convicted, woe be to those bones.'[10]

After Philip left for Spain in September Chaloner found that he had less official business and was able to enjoy the autumn of 1559, which he spent mostly in Antwerp, a prosperous and lively port which thronged with merchants and entrepreneurs of every nationality. As he reported to Cecil, he had 'leisure now after the king's departure to take a breath and look about him at things not costly but rare and delectable, either maps, books, or other like trinkets he may chance to light upon here'. He continued to send

Cecil all the news he could find, although there was little enough without the presence of Philip and his court:

> Since my letters from Flushing of the 23rd inst. to the Queen little has occurred, save that on Friday last the King embarked with his whole fleet towards Spain. The foolish Nostradamus, with his threats of tempests and shipwrecks this month, did put these sailors in a great fear. The Count de Feria tarries behind until the countess be delivered of child. Much honour is done here unto her; the King sent Don Antonio de Tolledo in his name with xl gentlemen in post to visit her.[11]

Cecil requested that Chaloner send him detailed information about all the knights of the Golden Fleece. Another task was to interview various inventors and speculators who were hoping he would tell Elizabeth about their schemes. For instance, he met a German miner who was sure he could discover new sources of minerals, especially alum, in England and Ireland. Chaloner was sceptical, but more enthusiastic about an Italian engineer who wanted the queen to be informed about various 'machines' he had invented and which, according to Chaloner, were 'very rare and strange':

> By his talk it seems he is a practiser in alchemy. He can speak a little broken English, and was among the merchants at Antwerp then suspected to be a spy. This perchance is untrue; but sure his inventions are strange and worth a reward, if he can perform his word, as he demands no trifling sums. His hand mill, made in form of a mace for a man of arms, is a right pretty invention. The engine, all of steel, is no bigger than a man's fist, that in one quarter of an hour, with one maiden's work, will grind bread-meal to serve six men by the day. By chance I saw the inward privity of the instrument, and with help of a workman could make such another with a noble's cost [i.e. ten shillings].[12]

Chaloner was also asked to arrange for various purchases of military materials, such as gunpowder, from Antwerp merchants. However, while trying to obey his instructions, he also strenuously recommended a policy of self-sufficiency for England, rather than reliance on foreigners: 'As touching powder, where may it better cheap be made than in England? Englishmen should be set at work for so much as may serve the realm; also for armour, for surely such necessary instruments of defence ought never *precario* [by request] to be sued for at our fickle neighbour's hands, but be had within our own power.'[13]

One issue that caused considerable trouble was when the queen asked Chaloner to arrange for delivery to England of four horses for her own stables. These had already been bought from an Italian merchant and paid for, but the Netherlands government refused to grant a licence for their export. The regent argued that all horses were needed to supply her own garrisons, although Chaloner knew that other foreigners had been allowed to take horses out of the country. Elizabeth was forced to make a personal appeal to Margaret of Parma, and it was not until Chaloner himself sailed for England in January 1560 that permission was granted, and the four horses sailed with him.

From Brussels Chaloner wrote to Cecil that he still hoped the match between Elizabeth and the emperor's son the Archduke Ferdinand, first mooted the previous year, might take place. In this letter he returned to the awkward topic of Elizabeth's feelings for Dudley, whom she had appointed her Master of the Horse. Chaloner again reported that foreigners were gossiping about this relationship, which was damaging for the queen's reputation and therefore for the nation. I give a passage in this letter in its original form as an example of Chaloner's style and spelling:

I assure you Sir thies folks ar brod mothued, when I spake of oon to muche in Favour as they esteem, I thinks ye gesse whom they named, if ye do not I will upon my next letters write furder. To tell you what I conceyve, as I count the slawnder most false, so a yong Princesse canne not be to ware what countenance or familiar Demonstration she maketh more to oon than another. I judge no oon mannes service in the Realme woorth the Entertagnment with such a Tayle of Obloquie or Occasion of Speeche to such men as of evil will are ready to find faults. The delayne of rype tyme for maryage, beside the lossse of this Realme (for without posterite of her Highness what hope is lefte unto us) Mynistreth matter to theyre lewde Towngs to descant upon and breedeth Contempt. I would I had but oon Hourse talkes with you. Thinke if I trusted not your good nature I would not write thus muche, which nevertheless I humbly praye you to reserve as written to yourself. Consider how ye deale now on the emperors matter, much dependeth on it. In myne opinion (be it said to you onlie) the Affinite is great and honourable. The Amitie necessary to stoppe and coole many Enterprises. Ye neede not feare his greitness should overrule you. He is not a Philippe, but better for us than a Philippe.[14]

In this letter Chaloner phrased his advice to the queen concerning her relationship with Robert Dudley very carefully, but it was still clearly a lecture to 'a yong Princesse' from an older man. It seems that he worried that he had perhaps gone too far, because in his next report he wrote, 'On my knees I beseech you to interpret what I have written touching your royal affairs as being according to the bare and very truth of matters, as represented unto me by those with whom I have had to treat.'[15]

Meanwhile, Elizabeth's relations with France and Scotland were coming to a head. The Scottish Protestants, led by the so-called Lords of the Congregation, had succeeded in defeating Mary of Guise's small French garrison so that the French were now holed up in the walled fortress of Leith, the port of Edinburgh on the Firth of Forth. However it was rumoured that a powerful French army under the command of Marquis d'Elbeuf, brother of the Duke of Guise, had set off for Scotland. If they succeeded in landing at Leith it would be the end of Protestant rule in Scotland. As usual, Elizabeth hesitated. Leith was well defended and the Scots by themselves were incapable of capturing the port. Should she send English forces to help them before the relieving French fleet arrived? This would be highly expensive; it would provoke open war with the French and at the same time alienate Spain. Typically, Elizabeth produced a risky compromise. She sent Sir William Winter, a young and aggressive naval captain, with fourteen ships to patrol the Firth of Forth and, if possible, stop Elbeuf landing. But Winter was to do this 'as of your own courage', and deny that he was under the queen's orders. Luckily, as with the Spanish Armada many years later, nature stepped in at this point to help Elizabeth. In January 1560, Chaloner reported home the good news:

> Yesterday in post came hither a gentleman out of Holland to the Prince of Orange, governor of that country, with advertisement, that the Marquis d'Elbœuf, M. d'Andelot and other French lords, who lately took shipping at Calais towards Scotland with seventeen ships fraught with men and horses, had suffered great shipwreck by reason of a late sore storm upon the coast of Holland, where four of their fleet, with men and horses drowned, were cast on land.
>
> P. S.—Even now I have learned that of the seventeen ships charged with men, horses, and munition, four wrecked about Egmond, four leagues on this side of Amsterdam. One great ship of 500 tons (*ut dicunt*) lost eighty horses, others swam to land; divers men saved, 800 by count drowned cast on land, an evident argument that more are lost not yet extant.[16]

Events in Scotland then continued to favour the English. The French decided not to risk any more fleets at this time of year.

English forces from Berwick were sent against Leith, which surrendered after a long siege. Mary of Guise died, and finally the French signed the Treaty of Edinburgh with England, whereby they promised to allow the Scots to worship as they wished, and not to send any more French soldiers to Scotland. Elizabeth, by a combination of luck and caution, had secured what she wanted: a peaceful and friendly Scotland.

For several weeks before this Chaloner had been pleading to be allowed home. His diets were always months overdue and money was becoming a real problem. Several times he complained to Cecil about the cost of living in Flanders. He said that he used 'all convenient means' to save, but still ran into debt due to the high price of everything. At one point he wondered whether the queen might possibly grant him a commercial licence to export beer from England to sell in Flanders:

Antwerp, 16 Nov. 1559

Not without great cause do I make motion to have the warrant of my diets renewed; for being with much ado now paid for September, I have not yet received it over by exchange, and am now unpaid for two months more, expiring the 20th inst. You are not ignorant how costly a country Flanders is, well nigh the double of France, though I use all convenient means to husband all things; but everything here is so extremely dear, wood, wine, bread, extraordinaries and house room, which alone, with my host's plate of meat, stands me in 10s. a day. I beg the Queen that in lieu of the two months diet already due and unpaid, and of other two months now next to be due as by way of advancement before hand, she will grant me a licence for so many tons of beer free of impost, as the said four months shall amount to after the rate of 13s. 4d. custom and impost to the Queen upon every ton; and so the Queen, saving the sum of four months diet, without any charge to herself will do me a great benefit to have ready payment, with some gain in the exchange.[17]

Soon after this his mission in Flanders was ended, therefore presumably he never received his beer export licence. All things considered, he was no doubt pleased to return home, but his pleasure was spoiled by the knowledge of what the future had in store for him. During his final months in Antwerp there had been some discussion between him and Cecil about whether now was the time to send a permanent resident ambassador to the court of Philip at Madrid. Chaloner had advised Cecil 'to send none to King Philip but those perfect in the language', and 'who can as perfectly understand the king whose soft speech is hard of a young beginner in Spanish to be well at the first comprehended'. He suggested that either Sir Henry Sydney or Sir William Pickering might be suitable – or possibly Mr Henry Knollys, an excellent linguist – 'but as yet Cecil has not given him reputation. King Philip in so great a matter will look for a great person.'[18] However, in January 1560, when he received his recall from the Netherlands, Chaloner was dismayed to learn that he himself was the one who had been picked to go to Spain.

11

ALVARO DE QUADRA
1559–1564

Between 1559 and 1564 Alvaro de Quadra, Bishop of Aquila, was Spanish ambassador at Elizabeth's court. Quadra was an exceptionally able diplomat who created and maintained a network of correspondents throughout England. He was skilled at obtaining the latest information from courtiers and noblemen, and he had a close relationship with both the queen and Cecil. His long dispatches to Spain have been a boon to historians of this complex period. As Froude says, 'The state of parties in England, the court intrigues, the political aspects of the situation will be seen most clearly in the correspondence between the Spanish ambassador in London, Philip II, and other Spanish noblemen.'

Quadra had some similarities with Chaloner, who for part of the time was his opposite number in Madrid. Both ambassadors were continually short of funds, since their respective governments invariably delayed paying them their salaries. Chaloner was always wanting to leave Spain as soon as possible; Quadra, after his first year or two, shared this longing for home. In early 1562 he wrote to Cardinal Granvelle, Margaret of Parma's chief minister in Flanders, that he asked 'only for payment of what is owing to me so as to be able to serve my king in this prison where I have been four years'. His letter continued, 'I beseech your Eminence to aid me to get out of this place without offence, even though it be without reward. This will content me as I am not ambitious and care little about being rich.'[1] Quadra, being a priest, had no family or heirs to worry about, unlike Chaloner. He also, of course, received a second income as a bishop.

Yet the differences in the positions of Quadra and Chaloner as well as their respective characters were enormous. Quadra's instructions were firstly to support Elizabeth, especially when threatened by France, and secondly to work for the restoration of the true religion in England and to support and reassure the English Catholic community. These two aims were fundamentally incompatible, which is why Quadra ultimately failed in spite of all his talents. As regards English Catholics, the Spanish ambassador was their link to the outside world and in the course of his duties he met and listened to their projects and their grievances. Unlike Chaloner, he was not a stranger in a strange land, bereft of partisans. The trouble was that these contacts gave Quadra a distorted view of the facts. According to him the government was full of opportunists and heretics, the persecution of devout Catholics was bad and getting worse, the virgin queen's private life was an abomination, and the whole realm was becoming disaffected.

Bishop Quadra put religion at the top of his priorities. He had a Manichaean view of the world: in his opinion people were either Catholics or heretics. He was convinced that the vast majority of the English still remained true to the old faith, and consequently with skill and good judgement the nation could be steered away from the pit of heresy and back to the true Church. The concept of toleration totally eluded him. He once wrote to Philip, 'The Swedish ambassador here says that his king will meddle with no man's religion; as far as he is concerned every man may believe what he pleases. I am not so much appalled at the expression of such monstrous views as the fact that a man could be found to hold them.'

When Elizabeth came to the throne the Spanish had high hopes she would continue the good work of her sister and support the true religion. Quadra thought that as the queen was so young perhaps he himself could educate her, teach her to see the necessity of an alliance with Spain and of retaining the religion of her sister. However, he was soon disillusioned. He was horrified by the Elizabethan religious settlement and by Elizabeth's support for Protestant rebels abroad, first in Scotland and then in France. In his dispatches home he did not modify his language: 'This woman is possessed with 100,000 devils; and yet she pretends to me that she would like to be a nun, and live in a cell, and tell her beads from morning to night', and again, 'I have lost all hope in the affairs of this woman. She is convinced of the soundness of her unstable power, and will only see her error when she is irretrievably lost ... her language is so shifty that it is the most difficult thing in the world to negotiate with her. With her all is falsehood and vanity.'[2] Yet, in spite of what he wrote home, Quadra personally could be quite charming and he seems to have got on well with Elizabeth, who allowed him to visit her frequently and seems to have tolerated his fatherly lectures.

In his letters to Spain, Quadra was also scathing about leading English ministers. Cecil was 'a great heretic', and Dudley, 'treacherous, and false'. Nevertheless, when the occasion arose he was quite prepared to work with either of them. For instance, in September 1560, Cecil was on the verge of resigning his post as he felt that nothing could stop the marriage of Elizabeth and Dudley, which would be disastrous for himself and also the country. According to Quadra, Cecil came to see him:

I met the secretary Cecil whom I knew to be in disgrace. Lord Robert, I was aware, was endeavouring to deprive him of his place. With little difficulty I led him to the subject, and after many protestations and entreaties that I would keep secret what he was about to tell me, he said that the Queen was going on so strangely that he was about to withdraw from her service. He could perceive the most manifest ruin impending through her intimacy with Lord Robert. The Lord Robert had made himself master of the business of the state and of the person of the Queen, to the extreme injury of the realm, with the intention of marrying her. He was therefore determined to retire into the country although he supposed they would send him to the Tower before they would let him go. He implored me for the love of God to remonstrate with the Queen, to persuade her not utterly to throw herself away as she was doing, and to remember what she owed to herself and her subjects.[3]

But Cecil was not out of favour for long, and the marriage he was afraid of did not take place. However, another extraordinary project involving Quadra was suggested by Dudley himself a few months later. He approached the ambassador with a suggestion which Quadra was invited to put to his master: if Philip would support the marriage of Elizabeth and Dudley, then they in turn would do their best to bring England back to the Catholic faith. It is not clear whether either the queen or Dudley were serious about this offer or whether it was merely a ruse to gain Spanish support when England was threatened by the French. In any case, this plan too was soon rejected.

Meanwhile, ever since he had been appointed ambassador, Quadra was establishing links with the English Catholic community, much to Cecil's disapproval and suspicion. Quadra had his agents and correspondents in every part of England and even in the royal household, and through him all his co-religionists received comforting messages from Philip sympathising with their situation under a hostile government and urging them to be patient. However, Quadra saw things in a more urgent light. He constantly urged Philip to prepare the English Catholics for the inevitable war that he was sure was round the corner, and even to be prepared to send a Spanish army to England if and when Elizabeth's 'disastrous' policies led to a French invasion, possibly through Scotland. Philip, on the other hand, was far more cautious. He personally found war uncongenial and hoped the Treaty of Cateau Cambrésis meant an era of peace. He instructed his ambassador to be as polite to Elizabeth as possible, and in particular to try and dissuade her from ever giving the French 'an excuse for putting their foot in England'.

The first time Quadra's machinations got him into trouble was actually due to Chaloner, who in the summer of 1559 received news that he passed on to Cecil. The news concerned Katherine Grey, who was the sister of the executed Lady Jane Grey. Katherine, like her sister, had a claim to the English throne through her grandmother, Henry VIII's younger sister. But Katherine had made the mistake of marrying without Elizabeth's consent. News of the marriage leaked out when she became pregnant, and she was consequently locked up in the Tower and her name no more to be mentioned by members of the court. It now seems that Chaloner was approached by one Robert Hogyns, an Englishman living in the Netherlands, who told him that certain Spaniards in the Netherlands were involved in a plot concerning Katherine:

These men, fearing the French King's pretended titles for the Scottish Queen, sought means to solicit and get into their hands my Lady Katherine Gray, whom further, as events should out, they might either marry to the Prince of Spain, or with some other person of less degree. By this tale they take her to be of a discontented mind, as not regarded or esteemed by the Queen or of her friends.[4]

Hogyns also informed Chaloner that Quadra was involved in the plot. However, on this occasion Cecil did not act, having apparently decided that these rumours were not worth the awkward business of insulting Philip by making charges against his ambassador.

But two years later Cecil, who constantly kept a close eye on what Quadra was up to, had a stroke of luck. One day Quadra sent his private secretary, an Italian named Borghese, to see Cecil on a matter of business. It was Borghese whose role involved putting Quadra's letters into cipher and filing his correspondence. When he met Cecil he offered to tell him all he knew about Quadra's scheming. Quadra soon found out about Borghese's betrayal and tried to persuade him to go abroad, perhaps to a place where he could be conveniently assassinated. As he wrote to a colleague, he knew that to kill was against his priestly vocation, but in this case it was justified: 'I have done my best to repair this disaster, but I have failed. The devil that has entered into my servant will not be exorcised. I have tried to induce him to leave the realm, I have entreated, bribed, threatened, promised, all to no purpose; and to put him to death as he deserved would have been awkward. I would have consented to it myself, and for the nonce would have broken the rule of my habit; but I should only have irritated them the more and increased their suspicions.'[5]

Cecil shielded Borghese from Quadra's revenge, and he warned Chaloner that the Spanish authorities might take counter measures against him, as Quadra's opposite number in Madrid. Quadra was closely examined by Cecil's lawyers about the various schemes he and leading Catholics had been up to, but no positive action was taken against him, partly because Elizabeth did not want to make public her and Dudley's scheme to persuade Philip to support their marriage by promising to make England Catholic again. Quadra's influence at court was much reduced by the Borghese affair, though he continued to nurture his network of disaffected sympathisers, and Cecil continued to monitor his activities closely.

A few months later Cecil had another chance to curtail Quadra's activities. Durham Place on the Strand, which was Quadra's headquarters as ambassador, had access to the Thames via a water gate in the back garden. This allowed those who did not want to be seen visiting the embassy to arrive and leave by barge. Some Catholics came to discuss plots against the government, others merely to celebrate Mass, which was forbidden elsewhere in England. One day there was a street brawl outside the main entrance after an attempt to murder an Italian officer. The subsequent report stated, 'The pellet lighted betwixt his left arm and his body, and pierced the side of his coat, and clean through his Spanish cloak, and glanced over the street into a shop, where it also missed very narrowly the killing of an honest Englishman, grazing the top of his shoulder.' The would-be assassin fled the crowd by taking refuge in the embassy, where he was protected by Quadra's servants and finally escaped via the river. Cecil investigated, and discovered that the gunman often visited the house and had been interviewed by Quadra after the incident. He was able to use this information as an excuse to change the locks on the water gate and later to insist that Quadra move to a less prestigious embassy with no access to the river.

All this was duly related to Chaloner in Spain, but he replied that he thought Quadra could have been treated more politely: 'It had been better, without setting any lock on the water gate, to have appointed to him a fitter house, telling him that the queen would otherwise employ the other. Hereafter, using him ceremoniously for the while, ye may both take a guard to his trades, and find the means to shift him off without demonstration or giving matter of pique, which needeth not'.[6] By 'matter of pique' Chaloner meant that the Spanish authorities might avenge the treatment of Quadra by reprisals against himself.

By 1564 Quadra was thoroughly disillusioned with his role as ambassador and with the impossibility of modifying, as he saw it, England's descent into heresy and chaos. Worn out by years of stress, he died still in harness, his last words being, 'I can do no more.' He was so heavily in debt to local tradesmen that they seized his body and it was not buried for over a year. Chaloner believed that his influence had reduced England's reputation abroad. He wrote, 'I beshrew that bishop that set in his foot so much to our loss and shame.' He, Chaloner, 'very well knew that much of the ill treatment this ecclesiastic suffered was revenged upon him'. Yet Quadra had merely been doing his job as he saw it. He was charming, clever and adroit, and had, one might say, given up his life for his faith and his king.

12

JOURNEY TO MADRID
1561–1562

Between February 1560 and November 1561 Chaloner was in England, but there is little evidence about this period in his life. We do know he bought land and built himself a large house in St John's precinct, Clerkenwell. According to the *Survey of London* this house is not to be confused with Chaloner House nearby, which was built later and belonged to his son, another Sir Thomas.[1] He himself could not have spent many months in his new house, but it was where some of his family, including his brother Francis and his newly widowed sister, Ellen, lived for some of the time he was absent in Spain. It was also the house to which he returned from Spain to die. His former home in Hoxton was probably sold – there is a letter in the archives from the Earl of Westmorland asking if he could buy it.[2]

Very likely Chaloner spent time visiting his properties at Guisborough, St Bees and also Steeple Claydon, Buckinghamshire, the new estate he had been granted by Queen Mary. It was first here, and later at Guisborough, that future generations of Chaloners were to reside. Being a gregarious soul and an eligible bachelor, he no doubt also enjoyed a full social life. He certainly got to know at least two ladies well enough to entertain hopes of marriage to one or other of them. One was Elizabeth Sands from Kent, a gentlewoman of the queen, to whom he was later on the point of proposing when she decided to marry someone else. The other was Audrey Frodsham, who was to visit him in Spain and whom he eventually did marry.[3]

This time of comparative leisure was a rare interval in Chaloner's crowded career of government service. It was overshadowed, however, by the knowledge that sooner or later he expected to be dispatched to Spain, to attend once again the court of Philip II. To us it might seem odd that Chaloner was far from welcoming the prospect of a trip to Madrid, there to take up a high-status post on a comfortable salary. But he was already familiar with the stresses of life as an ambassador, not to mention the physical demands of sixteenth-century foreign travel. Also, it seems that since his time in Flanders he had developed a thoroughly negative image of Spain. When the call came he put off his journey for as long as possible and was reprimanded for doing so. When he finally did embark from Dover in early November 1560, he took with him just three servants, the rest, together with his possessions, being sent to Spain by sea from Plymouth. He also took Henry Cobham, a young nobleman who was seeking an introduction to the diplomatic service, much as Chaloner himself had accompanied Gardiner and Knyvett to the court of Charles V in 1540. Cobham was the younger brother of Elizabeth Parr, Marchioness of Northampton, whom Chaloner counted as one of his intimate friends.[4]

On 18 November Cobham and Chaloner arrived in Paris to be met by Sir Nicholas Throckmorton, the English ambassador to France.[5] Within a few months of their visit, war was to break out in France between the French Protestants, known as Huguenots, and the Catholic majority. It was then that Throckmorton, who advised the queen to intervene on the side of the Huguenots, and Chaloner himself was to be imprisoned for several months by the French authorities. Throckmorton arranged for Chaloner and Cobham to have an audience with Catherine de Medici, Regent of France and widow of King Henry II, who had been killed in a jousting tournament and had left her with three young sons. At this time the French king was the nine-year-old Charles IX, in whose name Catherine attempted to run the country, but she had to contend with powerful and independent nobles, in particular, Francis, Duke of Guise, and his brothers. She tried – but ultimately failed – to steer a middle course between the Catholic Guises and the Huguenots. It seems that nothing came of this audience save the usual diplomatic courtesies and assurances of continued friendship, but Throckmorton also secured for Chaloner interviews with the Huguenot leader Antoine de Bourbon, King of Navarre, and with his queen, Jeanne. According to Throckmorton, Jeanne was especially taken with Chaloner, holding him by the hand and making him sit by her. She told him that the young Charles IX did not really believe in the Catholic Mass in spite of what his mother and his schoolmaster had tried to instil into him. In other words, when he grew up he might well support the Huguenot cause. Unfortunately, she said, he was not very robust, and was perhaps 'too good to tarry long amongst them' – just like Edward VI of England.[6]

By the end of November, having completed their interviews, Cobham and Chaloner and their three servants set off from Paris to ride the overland journey to Madrid. Meanwhile, their baggage, consisting of a number of 'males', or chests, had been dispatched from Plymouth, and most of Chaloner's servants, together with their horses, had left London on 1 November. A week later the servants split into two groups: five men with their horses crossed the Channel from Rye to Dieppe, while two others, plus more horses, waited for another ship bringing the luggage from Plymouth. The first group made their way gradually to the south of France, crossing the Spanish border near San Sebastian, and then on to Vitoria where they finally met up with their master on 19 December. We know quite a lot about their forty-day journey because accounts were kept by one of them, Henry King, who meticulously recorded everything that was spent en route. King's accounts are all the more impressive since he had to cope successively with the currencies of England, France and Spain.[7]

Chaloner himself arrived in Bilbao in early February to learn that his chests from Plymouth had only just arrived, having been delayed by bad weather. His servants, led by Henry King, were on their way and would meet him at Vitoria. But what would annoy Chaloner the most when he found out was that both his servants and his luggage were to attract the attentions of the Spanish Inquisition. The Inquisition was a powerful force in Spain, and even the nobility and the king himself hesitated to challenge its decisions. Its officials saw it as part of their duties to search the baggage of travellers crossing into Spain, and they would also go on board any merchant ships arriving at Spanish ports and seize 'heretical books'. What kind of book was meant is shown from another incident which occurred shortly afterwards at Bilbao, when a calendar was confiscated and those in charge arrested merely because the names of the pope and St Thomas à Becket had been scored out by its owner.[8] In Chaloner's case a chest of books had been taken away to be searched and not yet returned. Worse still, after the second group of servants arrived by sea all of Chaloner's chests and coffers were broken into because the keys had not been handed over. When presented with a demand for diplomatic immunity, the officials replied that if they refrained from searching they themselves would be excommunicated, which threatened them with eternal damnation. Chaloner was aware that such high-handed actions were commonplace in Spain, but this did not stop him protesting vigorously to Philip as soon as he could:

Being informed that certain chests containing books, clothes, and other necessaries belonging to myself and my servants, which had come from London to Bilbao by sea, had been broken open by the ministers of the Inquisition, under the pretext of searching for prohibited books; I sent thither one of my people to enquire into the matter. The messenger not only found that it was so, but was told by the said ministers that they would do the same to any other chests coming from abroad. Relying on my privileges as an ambassador, I desire that not merely should I and my household be in security from violence, but also that the King will send his letters to the ministers of the Inquisition and command them for the future not to meddle with anything belonging to myself, on oath being made by my servants that it is my property. It is not proper that under colour of searching for prohibited goods, matters of state should be revealed to persons whom they do not concern. It is all the harder to bear, because the ambassadors of all other princes and states receive their chests intact and unsearched.[9]

Chaloner spent a few days in Bilbao in the house of John Cuerton, a friendly and genial English merchant who had been settled there for several years. Cuerton was to be his most important agent in Spain, supplying him with information as well as fulfilling orders for clothing and food from abroad for the Chaloner household in Madrid. It was also useful that he stood in good favour with the Spanish authorities, being in fact himself a junior member of the bureaucracy of the Inquisition. Cuerton took Chaloner and Cobham hunting for wild boar, and later sent them presents.

He seems to have taken a particular fancy to Cobham. A few months later he ended one letter with 'I would I had Master Cobham here for 8 days to go a hunting'. When Cuerton's wife Joan gave birth to a girl Chaloner sent him congratulations, but added 'next time take better footing for a boy'.

Having met up with his servants, Chaloner finally arrived in Madrid to discover that not only had his possessions still not arrived, but also that no house was available for him until the previous ambassador was ready to quit. It had been, Chaloner told Cecil, the most painful journey he had ever made

> both for ill stony ways of the mountains and miry ways of the plain country, and also for the worse fare and lodging, such as in eight weeks journey, for want of my own things I came not three times in naked bed, almost famished for want of bread to my taste, until I came to Madrid, where, until Chamberlain left, I could only get but one sorry chamber for my lodging. The servants which came with myself in post are at a village three leagues distant, and to this misery is to be added the want of my stuff, which I sent from London to Plymouth three weeks before my departure, esteeming well (though I was chidden for tarrying) that I would come hither to find neither men, apparel, plate, linen, or other stuff to serve my turn at need.

In the same letter Chaloner told Cecil about the search of his possessions and requested his opinion: 'I beseech you Sir let me have your advice concerning this troubling matter of these inquisitive inquisitors. I did always write to you out of Flanders what I should find here. I send you a copy of the petition which I exhibited to the king in that behalf.'

He was also horrified to learn that the diets of his predecessor, Sir Thomas Chamberlain, who had not yet left, were over six months in arrears, especially when he came to realise the exorbitant cost of living in Spain:

> My diets will not bear at the prices here, for all kinds of victuals are double, treble, or quadruple the price they are in England. If I keep but a dozen servants, their wages, liveries, and clothing will cost myself above 600 ducats per annum, besides lodging and bedding, which amounteth to thirty-eight ducats a month. The dearth of things here is such that I know not how to deal, and that my predecessor has felt, being at his departure unpaid of his diets since last June, and was fain to borrow upon Mr. Gresham's credit at a large interest.[10]

Chaloner's steward, Henry King, continued to keep the accounts of the ambassador's household after they all arrived in Madrid. The historian Gary Bell, who has worked over King's accounts, thinks that Chaloner's statement about prices in Spain as compared to England was reasonably accurate.[11] At this time the Spanish were suffering consistently high inflation, well above the rest of western Europe. Bell has compared the costs of some basic commodities in the two countries and finds them twice as high in Spain:

> Chaloner's steward paid, for instance, 6½d per pound for the same tallow candles in Madrid that had cost him approximately 2d per pound in London. Paper, an important purchase for a constantly corresponding diplomat, was something more than fifty per cent higher, while Spanish butter was two and a half times again as much as the English product. Mutton was about three times in Spain what it cost in England, though eggs were only 2d per dozen more (8d compared with 6d). From the data available, where comparable items with convertible measures permit comparisons, it

seems that Sir Thomas was warranted in expressing shock at price differentials, and that he paid, on an average, about twice in Spain what the same goods would have cost him at home.[12]

However, even if prices were high, it seems Chaloner was not the man to stint when it came to food. Unfortunately, Lent started shortly after he arrived, and meat could not be obtained in Madrid, at least certainly not without someone reporting him to the Inquisition. Nevertheless, Henry King's accounts reveal that during Lent Chaloner and his ten servants still enjoyed a varied and healthy Mediterranean diet. I quote the household expenses for one particular day.[13]

At Madrid. Monday the xvi[th] of February 1561 [i.e. 1562]

Item. Paid for xvi loaves of bread for my Lord at iiii m. the piece	i R. xxx m.[14]
Item. Paid for viii loaves of bread for the household at x m. the loaf	iii R. xii m.
Item. Paid for xii herrings at viii the piece	iii R.
Item. Paid for iii lbs. of salmon	iii R.
Item. Paid for xi lbs. of salt fish for my Lord at xvii m. the lb.	v R. xvii m.
Item. Paid for ix lbs. of salt fish for the household at viii m. the lb.	ii R. iiii m.
Item. Paid for leaks and parsley	xiiii m.
Item. Paid for endives & lettuce	xiii m.
Item. Paid for ii lbs, of peas	xii m.
Item. Paid for a cheese weighing v lbs. x ounces at xliii m. the lb.	vii R. xvi m.
Item. For ii lbs. of apples	xxviii m.
Item. For iiii lbs. of sardines at xliii m. the lb.	ii R. xx m.
Item. For iii lbs. of butter at xlviii in the lb.	iiii R. vi m.
Item. For a lb. of sugar	ii R. xii m.

Item. Paid for iii dozen of egges at xxxviii m. the dozen	iii R. xii m.
Item. Paid for a load of water	vi m.
Item. Paid for a dozen of oranges	xxiiii m.
Item. Paid for capers	xii m.
Item. Paid for watercress for salads	xviii m.
Item. Paid for iii roves xxi lbs. of coal at li m. in the rove	v R. xxvi m.
Item. For the bringing of them home	xv m.
Item. Paid for ii loads of wood	vi R.
Item. Paid for a lb. of soap	i R. vi m.
	xviii R. xvii m.

Things improved slightly when all Chaloner's goods and his other servants finally arrived in mid-March. By then Chamberlain had left for England, leaving free the spacious residence allotted to the ambassador in Porte del Sol, not far from the Alcazar palace where king and court were in residence.[15] However, Chamberlain's departure produced another headache. He wrote from London requesting that 'his plate and other such things as he had left' for Chaloner's convenience be shipped to England 'well packed so that the same will not be bruised by the way, and also my Guaderezelles'.[16] Getting his predecessor's baggage back home caused Chaloner a great deal of annoying correspondence involving export licences. The guadamazilles were a particular problem. When they finally got through the Spanish bureaucracy and survived the voyage to England, they inexplicably went missing. After investigation, Chaloner's brother Francis accused Mrs Percival, a former servant of Chaloner's who was looking after his house in Clerkenwell, of having stolen and pawned them, but the matter was never satisfactorily resolved.

It goes without saying that Chaloner hated Madrid. As well as the Inquisition and the cost of living, there was the climate. As he wrote to one correspondent in June, 'Here is now so ill-favoured, raw, and cold weather as if it were Christmastide in England. This air of Madrid is subject to sudden heats (as all March past it was like our English May) and straight again to sudden cold, as a man shall not know how to govern himself.'[17] The following months and years only served to give him more reasons to want to leave his post and go home.

13

MARY STUART AND WAR IN FRANCE
1562–1563

With the Treaty of Edinburgh, Elizabeth had achieved her first major success in foreign policy. The French had agreed to withdraw their forces from Scotland and not to come back. But there was another issue which could not easily be solved, and which was to dominate most of the reign. This was the question of who was to succeed Elizabeth. She was the last of the Tudors and it looked increasingly possible that she might never marry. If she died childless there was no generally accepted successor, and this could plunge the nation into civil war and anarchy. In October 1562 she did in fact nearly die, having caught smallpox, and the council found itself completely divided as to whom to declare her successor.

At the time Chaloner arrived in Spain there were two likely candidates. Some still supported Katherine Grey, who had been named in Henry VIII's will and also had the advantage of being a Protestant. However, she was still completely out of favour and locked in the Tower, as was Edward Seymour, Earl of Hertford, the man she had secretly married. Everything therefore hinged on Mary Stuart, the other candidate with a good claim to the succession. Mary's first husband, Francis II of France, had died in December 1560, so Mary, aged nineteen, then ceased to be Queen of France. She was still Queen of Scotland, however, and now she decided to go there and take up her role. She was a talented and ambitious woman, determined to make the most of her claim to be recognised as Elizabeth's successor. In fact, in the eyes of many Catholics she had a better claim to the English throne than Elizabeth herself, since they held that Elizabeth was the illegitimate daughter of Anne Boleyn, Henry's unlawful second wife. In support of this claim, and with the backing of her uncles, the powerful Guise brothers, Mary had actually quartered the arms of England on her own shield. Now she was in Scotland, but she had never endorsed the Treaty of Edinburgh; this meant that conceivably she might one day invite the French back there.

Should Elizabeth recognise Mary as her heir? On the one hand, the recognition might be traded for Mary's acknowledgement of the Treaty of Edinburgh. Also, it would please Mary's subjects, the Scots, and it might mean that one day the union of Scotland and England, which Henry VIII and Somerset had wanted, would become a reality. On the other hand, Elizabeth, although she did not dislike Mary, was reluctant to name a successor. She knew that if she did she would become a focus for plots against her life. She once famously said, 'She was not so foolish as to hang a winding-sheet before her eyes or make a funeral feast while she was alive.'

Another question which troubled Elizabeth and her council was, what if Mary were to marry someone threatening, such as a Hapsburg or Valois prince? Philip II had a son, Don Carlos, and if she married him this would unite the thrones of Scotland and Spain. From Philip's point of view the Catholic Mary would be a most suitable bride for his son and heir. Having recently managed to eject the French from Scotland, the last thing

Elizabeth wanted was to see the Spanish take their place. She would have much preferred to see Mary married to an English or Scottish nobleman.[1] Luckily for everyone concerned except Mary, Don Carlos ceased to be marriageable material after the summer of 1562.[2]

The obvious way to try and get a solution to these various problems was for Elizabeth and Mary to meet and reach an agreement. In May the two queens agreed to meet later that summer. As Sir John Mason explained to Chaloner, not all the council were in favour of the meeting:

Sir John Mason to Chaloner, 3 July 1562.

At present they are all preparing northward to see the Scottish Queen, who has made such request to have a meeting that the Queen has yielded thereunto, without any great number giving her counsel so to do. The meeting will be at Southwell, and from thence they will repair to Nottingham and remain there seven or eight days. They will set forward about the eighth or ninth of August. It will be a costly journey. You know what the opinion of Philip de Comines is concerning the interview of Princes.[3]

However, events in France meant the meeting had to be postponed – or cancelled. Elizabeth and Mary never did meet each other. As Cecil explained in a letter to Chaloner, such a meeting would have appeared to be giving support to Mary's relations, the Guises, just when they were attacking Elizabeth's Protestant co-religionists.

By the time the long set of wars between Hapsburg Spain and Valois France had come to an end with the Treaty of Cateau Cambrésis (1559), a new process was beginning in western Europe, something much more significant than particular changes of monarch. If the first half of the century had been the era of dynastic conflict, especially the rivalry between Charles V,

Francis I and Henry VIII, the second half would add a new dimension: religious conflict. From Calvin's Geneva a particularly divisive form of Protestantism was starting to spread, especially in neighbouring France where the Calvinists were known as Huguenots. When it came to fighting for their faith Huguenot forces were committed and disciplined. In some ways they were like Oliver Cromwell's Puritan forces in the English Civil War, a century later. A contemporary French writer – admittedly a Protestant himself – gives this description of a Huguenot encampment: 'Their modesty of demeanour was beyond example. Each company in this army had its minister; and daily prayer was said throughout the camp. Their songs were psalms. When they played they played for sport, and blasphemy was never heard among them. No *filles de joie* [prostitutes], as among the Catholics, loitered among their tents. If a soldier was found with a woman he was forced to marry her.'[4]

By now heresy, in the eyes of contemporary rulers and many of their subjects, was increasingly equated with treason. Calvinists were seen as a political as well as a religious threat because of the intensity of their convictions, as well as their internationalist outlook. These dedicated revolutionaries did not believe in kings any more than in bishops or priests. Most ordinary Catholics were starting to think that until Calvinism was exterminated there could be no real peace and security in France. Huguenots, on the other hand, believed that their security required the complete destruction of the evil Church of Rome.

The Huguenots were commanded by a section of the French nobility including Louis de Bourbon, Prince of Condé, who soon became their leader instead of his vacillating elder brother Antoine, who changed sides when the real fighting began. The brothers were directly descended from an earlier monarch, Louis IX, which meant they were 'princes of the blood'. Condé's main opponents were the ultra-Catholic Guise family, led by the Duke of Guise, commander of the royal forces. By the spring of 1562 it was obvious to all that war was imminent and merely needed a spark to set it off. Nicholas Throckmorton sent a report to Cecil about Paris, a predominantly Catholic city which, he said, 'now more resembles a frontier town, or a place besieged, than a court, a merchant city or university'.

Throckmorton to the Queen, March 20 1562.

Since my last letter the Duke of Guise, accompanied by his brothers, has come to Paris accompanied by the Constable, his sons, the four Marshals of France, and twenty-one knights of the Order, which train amounted to 3,000 horse. Numbers rejoiced at his coming, as though he was their protector. Having arrived at his house, the Provost of the merchants of Paris, accompanied by many of the principal merchants here, made an oration testifying their joyful welcome, with an offer of two millions of gold to serve him in defence of the Catholic religion and quietness of Paris, where they desired him to reside. The Duke thanked them, and said they need not be so suspicious of their state, for the Queen Mother and the King of Navarre would (with the advice of the King's council,) give such order that all troubles should be appeased.

On the same day the Prince of Condé, returned from the court to Paris, being resolved to depart for Picardy to his house, changed his purpose, and at the same hour the Duke entered, the Prince, accompanied with seven or eight hundred horsemen, went from his lodging to the place where ordinarily the Protestant ministers preach, and heard a sermon, whereat there were twelve or fourteen thousand people.

Condé suspecting the intention of the Duke of Guise and the Constable to persecute the Protestants, remained in the town as long as the Duke did, and for better safety he caused many of those affected to his religion to repair here, whereupon great numbers come daily from all parts, so now the Protestants think themselves strong enough to resist their adversaries. When the Duke of Guise and the Constable saw the Protestants so little abashed, and perceiving the numbers increase daily, they sent to increase theirs also. There must be in Paris, on both sides, about nine or ten thousand horse, whom it will be difficult to keep from disorders.[5]

The spark was finally struck at the end of March 1562 when the Duke of Guise and his train visited the village of Vassy in north-east France. They were attending Mass at the village church when the service was interrupted by noisy singing from the Calvinist meeting house nearby. There were scuffles, the duke was hit by a stone, and his men then attacked the Protestant congregation, killing about sixty of them. This was the 'Massacre of Vassy', and it started the first of some eight rounds of religious war during the next fifty years. Fighting followed throughout France with terrible atrocities committed by both sides. The Huguenots initially held a number of cities, but the professional royal armies soon turned the tide. It was now that Condé, on the brink of defeat, made his appeal to Elizabeth. He asked for money to buy arms, and he wanted English forces to fight beside his own. In return he made a seemingly attractive offer. He said that as the Huguenots still controlled Normandy he would allow the English to occupy Le Havre and Dieppe, and then when peace came they could exchange these towns for Calais. Elizabeth disliked having to spend money on armies, disliked Calvinism, and disliked helping rebels against their own government, but the recovery of Calais, lost in Mary's reign after having been held by England for centuries, was one of her dearest ambitions. Calais trumped the other drawbacks, and after negotiations a treaty was signed with the Huguenots.

The situation in France demanded all Chaloner's tact and diplomatic skills. In Madrid his main duty as ambassador was to keep Elizabeth and her council informed of events in Spain, especially about Philip II's intentions regarding France. Might he intervene on the side of the Catholics, and what would be his response if England helped the Huguenots? The problem was that the Spanish court was secretive, and even an audience with Philip often did not produce much of substance. Also, there was the lack of fresh news from England about which Chaloner often complained. Regarding the agreement with Condé, Cecil and the queen wanted to keep the news secret for as long as possible. There was a fear that Philip II would feel himself bound to send Spanish forces to help the Guises if he heard about England's intervention. Consequently, in early June Cecil told Chaloner to deny rumours that any such agreement was in the offing, which he did for nearly two months. Cecil wrote to Chaloner, 'As to the affairs of France, that which is rumoured of the queen aiding the Prince of Condé with money is false, and you may put it out of doubt in the [Spanish] court as you see cause.'[6]

However, in August Chaloner was seriously embarrassed to learn that not only was there such an agreement, but an English army was on its way to garrison and fortify Le Havre, the key port handed to them by Condé. This was one of several occasions when Chaloner complained vigorously about being kept short of news from England, feeling that he was being used as a pawn.

Chaloner to Cecil, 21 August 1562.
Three days ago a Flemish courier arrived here with letters and reports, not only of the Queen having sent divers armed ships to sea, but also that she has a hold in Normandy that is taken by her folks, to the number of 10,000, landed there to aid the Prince of

Condé. Yesterday the French ambassador was with me, to feel of me what he could. I knew not what to say or think, as your letter of the 8th of June affirmed nothing.[7]

Meanwhile a strong English garrison commanded by the Earl of Warwick, Robert Dudley's elder brother, had occupied and fortified Le Havre. But Condé, trying to link up with Warwick, was attacked by the Duke of Guise. The Battle of Dreux, which followed, was a draw, except that Condé himself was captured, thus tilting the balance towards the Catholic side. He finally accepted terms which included limited toleration for Huguenots throughout France, and he wrote to Elizabeth explaining that, as this had been his object in the first place, the war was now over and the English should quit Le Havre. The queen was furious, since there was no mention of Calais in his letter. She instructed Warwick to hold on at all costs until better terms were offered, and this at first seemed the logical thing to do, as the town's defences were considered impregnable by land, while reinforcements and supplies could be brought in by sea. The English felt confident even when they were put under siege by the Duke of Guise.

Disaster, however, lay ahead. Early in June Warwick reported that 'a strange disease' had appeared in the garrison, of which nine men had suddenly died. Froude recounts what happened next:

This strange disease was the plague; and in the close and narrow streets where seven thousand men were packed together amidst foul air and filth and summer heat, it settled down to its feast of death. On the seventh of June it was first noticed; on the 27th the men were dying at the rate of sixty a day; those who fell ill rarely recovered; the fresh water was cut off, and the tanks had failed from drought. There was nothing to drink but wine and cider;

there was no fresh meat, and there were no fresh vegetables. The windmills were outside the walls and in the hands of the enemy; and though there was corn in plenty the garrison could not grind it. By the 29th of June the deaths had been five hundred. The corpses lay unburied or floated rotting in the harbour. The officers had chiefly escaped; the common men, worse fed and worse lodged, fell in swathes like grass under the scythe, and the physicians died at their side.[8]

Reinforcements were sent over from England but they too became rapidly infected, until the garrison was down to a few hundred men and the position was untenable. Warwick finally surrendered and the shattered remnants of the garrison were allowed by the French to leave for England. Even worse, the returning soldiers brought the epidemic back with them as they returned to their various homes. Before the plague struck Le Havre, Chaloner had been given new orders by Cecil. He was instructed to request another audience with Philip, and to put forward Elizabeth's justifications for the campaign to the king, which he duly did. He was told to make it clear that Elizabeth's motive for intervening in France had been purely to get back Calais, and was nothing to do with religion, and all this Philip appeared to accept. Chaloner also was instructed to ask Philip if he personally would now agree to broker a settlement between France and England along these lines. But again, Chaloner was unfortunately overtaken by events and caught out by the lack of up-to-date information from England. News arrived that Condé had made peace and that Le Havre had surrendered, and now there was no question of Philip or anyone else brokering a treaty with France which involved Calais.

Elizabeth's intervention in the French religious war had turned out to be a fiasco and a major waste of resources. She had not helped the Huguenots and she had not regained Calais. Also, once again Chaloner felt humiliated by his inability to play a useful role due, as he repeatedly wrote home, to never being put fully in the picture. However, to look on the plus side, the attempt to retain either Le Havre or Calais would have led to many years of hostility and probably war between England and France. Furthermore, the queen had learnt a valuable lesson. She would not dispatch English forces to the Continent again – not, at least, until 1585 when she sent a small contingent to the Netherlands to support the Dutch Revolt against Spain.

1. A woodcut of Chaloner's head taken from the frontispiece of his book of Latin poetry published after his death. (Courtesy of the British Library's English Short Title Catalogue)

2. Portrait of Chaloner, aged 28. (Private collection, courtesy of Lord Gisborough; photograph by Peter Morgan)

3. *Left*: Library of St John's college, Cambridge. (Courtesy Flickr user bengallagher)

4. *Bottom*: Norham Castle today. Chaloner was one of the commissioners chosen to negotiate the treaty of Norham with the Scots here in 1551. (Courtesy Flickr user europealacarte)

5. *Above*: A seventeenth-century view of the old Palace of Madrid. (Courtesy of Rijksmuseum)

6. *Below*: A sixteenth-century *auto da fé* organised by the Spanish Inquisition. (Courtesy of Rijksmuseum)

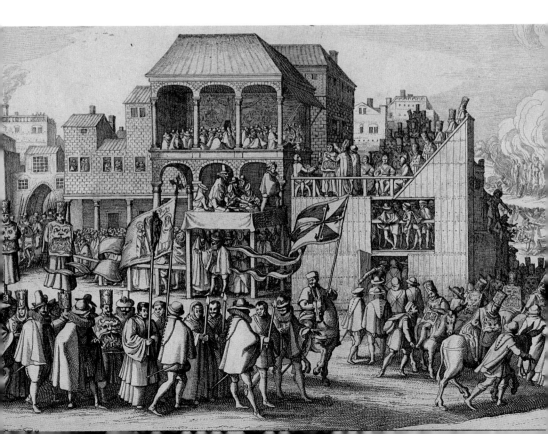

7. An anonymous portrait of Queen Elizabeth painted in about 1559. (Courtesy of Rijksmuseum)

8. Philip II, King of Spain. (Courtesy of Rijksmuseum)

9. Thomas Cromwell, whom
Chaloner served after university.
(Courtesy of Rijksmuseum)

10. William Cecil, lifelong
friend of Chaloner. (Courtesy of
Rijksmuseum)

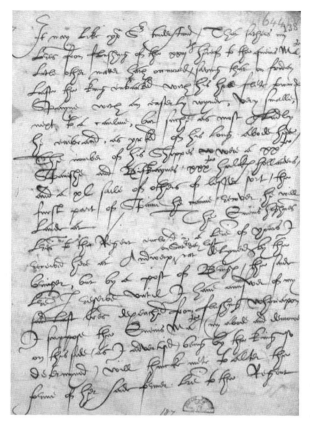

11. An example of Chaloner's rather ornate handwriting. Part of a letter written to Cecil in August 1559; see transcript below. (Courtesy of National Archives)

It may like you Sir t'understand, that sithens my
letters from flushing of the xxiij[th] hereof to the quenis Ma[jeste],
litle other matter hath occurred, saving that on friday
Laste the king embarked with his hole flete towards
Spayne with an easterly wynde, Very smalle,
next to a caulme, but suche as most gladly
he embraced, as yrkd of his long abode here.
The nomber of his shippes were a xx
Spanishe and Biskaynes, xxxx hulks hollanders,
and a xl saile of others of lesse sort, the
furst part of Spaine he canne recover, he will
Land at. The Quens highnes
L[ett]res to the Regent enclosed in a L[ett]re of yours I
received here at Antwerp, on Sat'day last, not delyvered by the
bringer, but by a post of Bruges, the said
L[ett]re I reserve until I have aunswer of my
said last l[ett]res depeached from flushing whereapon
I suppose the Quenis Ma[jes]te (my abode and demoure
on this side, as I advertised, being by the king so
determyned) will thincke mete to alter the
forme of her sayde former l[ett]re to the Regent

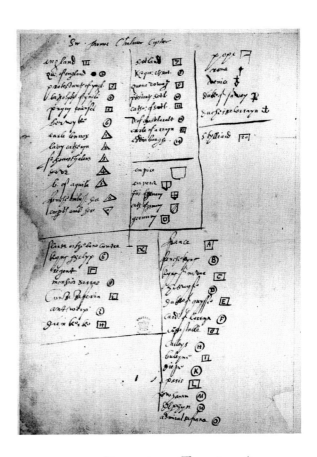

12. Chaloner's cipher in 1559. (Courtesy of British Library, Cotton MS Vespasian C VII f. 99b)

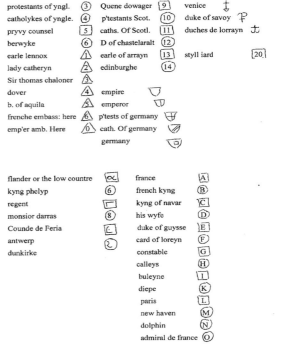

protestants of yngl.	③	Quene dowager	9	venice	‡
catholykes of yngle.	④	p'testants Scot.	10	duke of savoy	℗
pryvy counsel	5	caths. Of Scotl.	11	duches de lorrayn	±
berwyke	⑥	D of chastelaralt	12		
earle lennox	△1	earle of arrayn	13	styll iard	20
lady catheryn	△2	edinburghe	⑭		
Sir thomas chaloner	△3				
dover	△4	empire	⊍		
b. of aquila	△5	emperor	⊎		
frenche embass: here	△6	p'tests of germany	⊞		
emp'er amb. Here	△0	cath. Of germany	⊘		
		germany	⊍		

flander or the low countre	⊠α	france	Ⓐ
kyng phelyp	⑥	french kyng	Ⓑ
regent	⊓	kyng of navar	Ⓒ
monsior darras	⑧	his wyfe	Ⓓ
Counde de Feria	⌐	duke of guysse	Ⓔ
antwerp	⊋	card of loreyn	Ⓕ
dunkirke		constable	Ⓖ
		calleys	Ⓗ
		buleyne	Ⓘ
		diepe	Ⓚ
		paris	Ⓛ
		new haven	Ⓜ
		dolphin	Ⓝ
		admiral de france	Ⓞ

13. Author's transcription of Chaloner's cipher.

14. The ruins of Guisborough Priory today. The priory estate was acquired by Chaloner in 1550. (Courtesy Flickr user glenbowman)

15. Portrait of Sir Thomas Chaloner, aged 38. (Private collection, courtesy of Lord Gisborough; photograph by Peter Morgan)

14

SIR NICHOLAS THROCKMORTON
1515–1571

It might be useful at this point to compare Elizabeth's resident ambassadors in Paris and Madrid. Throckmorton's personality, and therefore his behaviour as an ambassador, could hardly have been more different to Chaloner's. Throckmorton was ideologically committed and keen to help the Protestant cause throughout Europe, whereas Chaloner kept his personal views about religion separate from his public duties. Throckmorton was not afraid to make enemies when he felt it was necessary, while Chaloner avoided conflict whenever possible. Hence, it is not surprising to learn that during his career Throckmorton was imprisoned no less than four times, either by the French or the English authorities.

The Throckmortons were an old, established English gentry family with useful connections to important people. Nicholas was the cousin of Catherine Parr, Henry VIII's last wife, and his career started as a member of her household. Like Chaloner and William Cecil, he fought under Somerset at the Battle of Pinkie Cleugh against the Scots, and was subsequently knighted by Edward VI. There is a contemporary poem about Throckmorton's life which describes how close he was to the ten-year-old king and tells a little story about how he came to be knighted, much to the resentment of other courtiers:

> The King me fancied daily more and more,
> For as his years so did my favour grow ...
>
> And on a time when knighted I should be
> The King said, 'Kneel'. Yet then I went my way.
> But straight forth himself ran and spièd me
> Behind a chest in lobby where I lay;
> And there against my will he dubbed me knight;
> Which was an eye-sore unto some men's sight.[1]

Throckmorton continued in favour when Northumberland succeeded Somerset, and he was promoted and granted estates. However, after Edward VI's death he apparently supported the attempt to crown Lady Jane Grey, and he was also involved in the Wyatt Rebellion against Mary's marriage to Philip II the following year. For this he was imprisoned in the Tower and charged with treason, but he defended himself effectively and was acquitted by a London jury in spite of his judges' evident determination to see him convicted. He was out of favour for the rest of Mary's reign, but was once more back in favour when Elizabeth came to the throne. The queen had known him when she was a young teenager in Catherine Parr's household and she always had a soft spot for him and listened to his advice. This was how he came to be chosen as ambassador to France in 1559. By this time he was married to Ann Carew, who was from a neighbouring gentry family. Unfortunately, Ann did not enjoy France. She excused herself from learning the language and in 1562 returned to England, where she was useful to her husband in collecting rents from tenants and borrowing money to meet the expenses of a resident ambassador. Nevertheless, in the long run Ann and Nicholas managed to produce six sons and a daughter, Elizabeth, who was to marry Sir Walter Raleigh.

From the start of his term in office Throckmorton was strongly in favour of Elizabeth's sending aid to the Huguenots in France. He was convinced that the only hope for the survival of Protestantism was support for the rebel lords in Scotland and also for the Huguenots. He suspected that Elizabeth's reluctance to help them stemmed from Cecil's cautious advice. Therefore, he gradually started to look towards Robert Dudley, another powerful courtier who had the queen's ear and who was fast becoming Cecil's rival. However, this did not mean that Throckmorton was not horrified when rumours reached him about Elizabeth's relationship with Dudley and the harm such rumours were doing to her reputation abroad. He poured out his feelings in a letter to his relative the Marquis of Northampton in a forthright style that the cautious Chaloner would never have used:

I wish that I were either dead or hence that I might not hear the dishonourable and naughty reports that are made here of the Queen, and the great joy in this court among the Princes here for the success they take it they are like to have in England, not letting to speak of the Queen and some others that which every hair of my head stareth at and my ears glow to hear. I am almost at my wits' end, and know not what to say. One laugheth at us, another threateneth, another revileth the Queen. Some let not to say, 'What religion is this that a subject shall kill his wife, and the Prince not only bear withal but marry with him?'[2] Rehearsing the father and grandfather. All the estimation the English had got is clean gone, and the infamy passes the same so far, and my heart bleeds to think upon the slanderous bruits I hear, which if they be not slaked, or if they prove true, their reputation is gone for ever, war follows, and utter subversion of the Queen and country. I beg you to help to slake these rumours. I pray that God will not suffer her to be *opprobrium hominum et abjectio plebis* [the contempt of men and disgrace of the people]. With weeping eyes I take my leave.[3]

At the same time Throckmorton wrote to Cecil urging him to do everything he could to prevent Elizabeth from marrying Dudley, adding, 'Remember your mistress is young, and subject to affections; you are her sworn councillor and in great credit with her … my duty to her, my good will to you, doth move me to speak plainly.'

While involving himself in the growing hostility between Catholics and Protestants throughout France, Throckmorton was given another, more personal task. Cecil asked him to look after his son Thomas, aged nineteen, whom he was planning to send to France for a year or two to learn French. Thomas would be accompanied by Cecil's secretary, Thomas Windebank, but Cecil needed Throckmorton's advice as to what the lad should do when in France. Cecil admitted that he was not particularly close to his son: 'Blame me not though I be long herein, for indeed to this hour I never showed any fatherly fancy to him but in teaching and correcting.'[4]

Throckmorton found Windebank, young Thomas and their horses a suitable house in Paris, but the visit did not go according to plan. It turned out that Thomas was not so much interested in learning French as in chasing French women:

Throckmorton to Cecil, 27 April 1562.
I desire you to send some letters to your son to check his inordinate affection with which he is transported towards a young gentlewoman abiding near Paris, which myself and Mr. Windebank by their admonition have tried to dissuade him from, but in vain.

She is a maid, and her friends will hardly bear the violating of her. I would have sent him hence to see other parts of France had it not been for the troubles here, which increase daily. The plague is very rife in Paris. You may recall your son upon the ground of the troubles here, and the plague, and I hope that you will judge of his passion as fathers do when they censure their sons' oversights, committed when most subject to folly and lost to reason; and that you will not measure your son by yourself, but repute him as other young men. If however you do not wish him home, then I think it would be best to send him into Flanders, where, when he has seen Antwerp, Bruges, Ghent, Brussels and other towns, he may reside at Louvain, and there exercise his French. I would request that you do not delay in this matter.⁵

Another episode seems to have involved Thomas seducing a young nun and promising to marry her if she left her convent, though the details are somewhat obscure:

Windebank to Throckmorton, 8 June 1562.
In my conversation with Mr. [Thomas] Cecil since his last coming from Paris I certainly gathered a promise of marriage to the nun, but whether it was made before witnesses he does not confess. I said it must be through his promise of marriage, which, if made without witnesses, was no matter; if made with them, the matter might be prevented if he would plainly tell it. Mr Cecil said it could not be remedied but by God's help. He also sayeth her younger brother knew of the matter, and consequently more of her friends, who determine to have her from the abbey; and sending to know if she was ready she sent word she could not, trusting to the promise Mr. Cecil had made to her. These things considered, I cannot see how he can stay in France, or any other country, except his own, lest the friends of the nun should seek the performance of his promise, and so put him in trouble by a suit. If he does not go to

England, Flanders will be the best place, so that at Louvain he may have the French language. It would be well to keep his going a secret, lest it should be known to her friends. I wish that his father would have him home. 8 June 1562.[6]

During all the time that Throckmorton was in Paris and Chaloner in Madrid, they corresponded with each other, having at the start, as Chaloner put it, 'proposed that we relieve each other's irked burden by mutual writing'. They passed on to each other any news they received from England, and in particular Chaloner told Throckmorton what he could glean about Philip's attitude to the hostilities in France, while Throckmorton responded with the latest events from France. For example:

Chaloner to Throckmorton, Madrid, 1 June 1562.
It is accounted here for certain that the King Catholic has resolved to send aid to the Guisians to the number of 10,000 footmen and 3,000 horsemen, part from Spain, Piedmont, and the Low countries. It will take some time before they are ready, for soldiers are not so soon levied in Spain, but it is intended; so the Protestants must prepare to resist. I understand that divers Italian and Spanish captains are already despatched to levy soldiers in Biscay and Navarre, as well as those in Catalonia. The Spanish will enter France by Perpignan, and join the Duke of Savoy's band. It being tedious for me to repeat these premises to Cecil, I write only a brief letter, referring you to the double of the two I sent to you, requesting you to send the same to Cecil accordingly. I desire you to inform me which faction the King and Queen Mother favour.[7]

Throckmorton to Chaloner, Paris, 14 June 1562.
The Queen Mother, and the King of Navarre, hath had some conference with the Prince of Condé of late betwixt Orleans, and

Estampes, with equal numbers for their garde, that is to say one hundred horsemen a piece. This colloquy was in the field and on horseback for fear of ambushes and treason, which they say was in practise at the first day assigned, and therefore the conference disappointed. In the end of this treaty with these great personages (whereof every man hoped some good issue) the matter is broken off uncompounded, and small hope left now for any composition, but such as the sword shall force. The King of Navarre, the Duke of Guise, the Constable and the Marshall of St André be encamped at this present three leagues beyond Estampes; they be noted in horsemen stronger then the Prince of Condé, but weak in footmen. The prince as yet hath not caused his camp to march from Orleans, but I think he will within this three or four days – the order of France is presently good cheap, for of late there was made nineteen new knights.

Other news I have none at this time worthy your advertisement, but do pray you to let me hear often from you. I will not tell you, for I am sure you know it better then I, that the bruit is in England that Sir Maurice Barklay shall marry Mistress Sands: You are too cold in your suites, and too far off to mind them. I pray you good my Lord Ambassador send me two pair of perfumed gloves, perfumed with orange flowers and jasmine, the one for my wife's hand, the other for my own; and wherein soever I can pleasure you with any thing in this country, you shall have it in recompense thereof, or else so much money as they shall cost you; provided always that they be of the best choice, wherein your judgement is inferior to none. I would be glad you would send them me by Mr. Henry Cobham, who I hear will be in these parts, or it be long; and, I would be glad to see him here before I depart, which I trust shall be before the end of July if these troubles grow to any end; for thereupon dependeth the coming forward of my successor. Thus I commit you to Almighty God.[8]

When, in July 1562, Condé made his offer of Le Havre in return for military help, Throckmorton urged Elizabeth to accept, which she finally did. This proved an expensive mistake, and at the Battle of Dreux he himself, along with Condé, was taken prisoner by the Catholics. After Le Havre fell Throckmorton was allowed to leave for England. He was sent back to France to help negotiate peace terms, but again found himself briefly imprisoned. Elizabeth then dispatched Sir Thomas Smith to Paris, where he was supposed to work with Throckmorton as a calming influence, but the two quarrelled and at one point, according to Smith, Throckmorton drew his dagger and threatened to kill him. It was by now becoming clear that while Smith was Cecil's man, Throckmorton was Dudley's. Eventually peace with the French was signed and Elizabeth's unsuccessful military intervention in the French civil wars was over.

Throckmorton was allowed to return home, but was soon sent off on another mission, this time to Scotland. He was instructed to try and persuade Mary Stuart to accept Elizabeth's offer of Dudley (now created Earl of Leicester) as a suitor, instead of the man Mary was threatening to marry – Henry, Lord Darnley. Oddly enough, Throckmorton had always got on well with Mary, even though they were totally opposed in their religious views. This plan, of course, failed, and Mary did marry Darnley. After Darnley's murder Mary found herself imprisoned by the Protestant Lords of the Congregation. Throckmorton's orders were now to try and mediate so as to obtain Mary's release. Here, again, he failed, and this time retired to his estates in England. The final episode in his turbulent career came in 1569 when he was sent to the Tower, accused of supporting a projected marriage of the Duke of Norfolk to Mary – a plan which was seen as a direct threat to Elizabeth's rule, and therefore treasonable. As Rowse comments, jealousy of Cecil and a sick man's temperament had warped Throckmorton's judgment, but his loyalty to Elizabeth was never in doubt.[9] He was released, and died not long afterwards when he was staying at the house of his patron, Robert Dudley. The ultimate verdict on Throckmorton must be that he was a man of great talents, but too enthusiastic and outspoken to be a useful diplomat in troubled times.

15

PROBLEMS OF AN AMBASSADOR
1562–1565

The office of resident ambassador was, for England at least, a relatively new feature of the diplomatic scene in the mid-sixteenth century. Special embassies were often sent when the need arose, but these were temporary. An example was Bishop Gardiner's magnificent embassy to the Diet of Ratisbon in 1540, in which Chaloner had played his part. A special embassy was an opportunity for an aspiring courtier to make his mark and perhaps further his career. They were also heavily subsidised so as to impress foreigners with their particular nation's wealth and significance. But to be appointed resident ambassador was a different matter. For various reasons such a posting was unlikely to be so attractive, and in fact might very well turn out to be a step backwards on the career ladder. The dispatches of practically all contemporary ambassadors are full of complaints about their role, and requests to be replaced as soon as possible. Sir Thomas Chamberlain, Chaloner's predecessor in Madrid, advised him to begin calling for his revocation as soon as he arrived.

A resident ambassador in the mid-sixteenth century had to play a very demanding role. Here one can hardly do better than to quote Miller's list of the requisite qualities and duties:

> An ambassador was expected to be a war correspondent, a linguist, the leader of a spy-ring, a man of dignity and presence, a snooper with a nose for news, a tactful and adroit diplomat, a snapper-up of pregnant hints, a purveyor of foreign trinkets and books, a man of courage and firm bearing, an amalgam of merchant, lawyer, scholar, and statesman, a servant of unswerving loyalty, and a leader of firm (but not uncompromising) principles – and all this on allowances so small and usually so tardy that it was necessary to have recourse to foreign money-lenders.[1]

One reason why life was difficult for Chaloner was expense. According to Garrett Mattingly, the only sixteenth-century resident ambassador who actually gained financially from his time in office was the 'shrewd and hard-fisted' Eustache Chapuys, Charles V's representative in England a decade earlier.[2] Otherwise, ambassadors of every nation found it difficult or impossible to live on their diets (i.e. the salaries they were paid for each day in office). While in service Chaloner received £3 6s 8d per day, from which he had to maintain his household in the kind of style expected of an ambassador, which included paying the wages of numerous servants, couriers and agents. In addition he might apply for 'extraordinaries', which were 'non-personal and unusual charges due solely to the requirements of his office', e.g. expenses involved with travel and correspondence.[3] These payments, which were supposed to be made quarterly, were barely adequate even if they had been delivered regularly, which they were not. Sir Richard Sackville, the Treasury official in London responsible for paying ambassadors, seems to have reckoned this duty very low in his list of priorities. In June 1563 Chaloner sent him an agonised appeal:

> It pulls away the courage of a well-willed horse to see his provender pinched at, and more miles by the day put to his task. If you were here as I am, in the extreme heat, sick of an ague, and in a house void of all fresh air, you would rather give a hundred pounds a week than continue here. I hope that you give order that my diets be paid at my pay day, without which I cannot abide here.[4]

Another explanation as to the non-arrival of Chaloner's salary was the possibility that it might have been stolen en route. In September 1562 he told Cuerton that he suspected 'two or three packets have been sent and intercepted. [I have] not received either the 1,600 ducats delivered for my use by a bill of exchange at the beginning of last May, nor the other 1,600 delivered for my use in England a month ago.'[5] That this was a real danger is evidenced by a letter from Cecil informing Chaloner that dispatches from Bishop Quadra, his Spanish counterpart in London, had been intercepted, and warning the same thing might happen to him.[6]

To prevent their regular messages to the queen or to William Cecil, her secretary of state, being opened and read illegally, ambassadors were expected to use cipher when conveying sensitive information. At first Chaloner operated a very simple code which involved substituting certain symbols for important names or phrases. In 1562, however, Cecil sent him a more demanding cipher in which, when composing an important phrase or sentence, every letter of the alphabet had its own symbol. Cecil warned him to use the cipher with discretion because 'the labour of deciphering is not small'. To use this particular code must have taken Chaloner, or perhaps his clerk, much time and effort, and added considerably to the burden of having to send regular reports home. This was also the experience of other contemporary ambassadors.[7] The basic trouble was that 'no cipher simple enough to be written rapidly and deciphered accurately could remain unbreakable when present in the bulk usual in long dispatches'.[8] However, they might still be useful in stopping a quick examination by, for instance, a dishonest embassy servant.

Yet another issue concerning communication was the problem of transferring money from England to Spain. It was one thing for a warrant in pounds sterling to be issued in London, but quite another for Chaloner in Madrid to actually receive the equivalent in Spanish currency. The transfer operated via bills of exchange, a device invented by medieval bankers. An agent based in Antwerp – in Chaloner's case a merchant banker named Richard Clough – would receive the warrant from London and, operating on the Antwerp bourse, have it transferred into a bill of exchange, which was an undertaking by a named merchant to pay an agreed sum by a certain day to whoever produced the bill. This document might then pass through several hands until finally it reached Chaloner, who would then have to look for someone who might accept it in return for paying him in Spanish money what he was owed.

Clearly, much could go wrong during this tortuous procedure, and many of Chaloner's letters are concerned with things that did go wrong. To take merely one example, he was sent a bill of exchange in the name of an Italian merchant named Stephano Leccario, only to discover that this gentleman had just fled from Spain and had all his property confiscated for illegally conveying money out of the realm hidden under legitimate cargo. Naturally, Chaloner found it impossible to find anyone who would pay him in return for being handed a bill of exchange in the name of

Leccario, and he had to apply to Clough in Antwerp to start the whole process again under a different name.

Chaloner, never a wealthy man, had somehow managed to find £1,300 to bring with him when he first arrived in Spain, but this was soon gone and he was forced to have recourse to moneylenders. In spite of his liveried servants and his status, it seems that in Madrid he was actually quite badly off. We find an ex-servant of his complaining that he had 'been given but 4l. for his long service, nor would he even give him a pair of hose, a vest, or cast livery'. Nor, he said, had Chaloner actually paid his latest wages, but had offered him a promise of future payment instead. And when it was time for Henry Cobham, the young gentleman who had accompanied Chaloner to Spain, to return home, there was another argument about money. Cobham wrote an angry letter in which he more or less accused Chaloner of being a miser because he had not given him enough to pay the embarkation charges at Bilbao: 'Although I told you how little money I had, yet you would not lay twenty crowns out of your purse, although it was in the Queen's service.' He went on, 'Although you think well of yourself, others do not think the same. Do not let your anger overcome you after reading this letter, but have patience and examine yourself.' Chaloner managed not to show the irritation he must have felt on receiving this message, and he produced a restrained reply. He explained that at the time he had been unable to give Cobham the money because he had none himself. He acknowledged that the younger man's words proceeded 'from such frankness as friends ought to use towards each other', and hoped 'that they may both forget that ever this little cloud came between them'.[9] Probably the affair was smoothed over, because both Henry Cobham's father and his mother wrote to thank Chaloner for looking after him in Spain.

In his letters home Chaloner constantly complained about the high cost of living in Spain. He wrote to Robert Dudley that 'if this outrageous dearth of things continue here I am sure to spend besides my diets, two or three thousand ducats every year out of my own purse'.[10] He tried to cut costs and thought of selling part of his estates back home, suggesting to Cecil complicated financial deals which he could make with Elizabeth:

> I pay to the Queen for the fee farm of Gisburgh 115l. per annum, and I would redeem either 100l. or else 80l. per annum, parcel of the same, by annuity during my life, and in recompense to pay the Queen five years' purchase. If she grant this suit I will give her for 80l. annuity at Gisburgh during my life, 500 marks ready money, and present her with two fair jennets from hence [i.e. small Spanish horses] that shall be worth 300 ducats apiece, or for 100l. per annum 400 marks ready money, and the said jennets. I have willed my brother Farnham to prosecute this matter.[11]

At one point he even considered branching out into commercial enterprise. He sent Cecil a present of painted leather hangings similar to the ones his predecessor, Chamberlain, had once bought, and asked whether he could be granted a monopoly to produce such hangings in England: 'I send your guardamezzilles. It is no small commodity for England to have the trade of these leather hangings, where sheep skins are so cheap. If the queen will grant me and my assigns a privilege for ten years to exercise the trade of these leather hangings, gilt, painted, or coloured, then I will bring two or three master workmen from hence at my own cost.' Apparently nothing came of this suggestion, or of the deal involving jennets. Nor did it of yet another proposal a few months later when he again asked Elizabeth whether he could have a licence to export some English beer to Spain, just as he had in 1559:

> I make suit for some *ayudo de costa* [aid in meeting his costs] to help me somewhat out of the briars here; some piece of a licence, if

money be scant, were it but for a certain quantity of beer free of all imposts and customs.

The seriousness of Chaloner's financial difficulties are shown here by the way he ignored the customary reluctance of gentlemen to engage in trade. Part of his problems no doubt stemmed from his dislike of Spanish food. He spent large sums buying commodities from England via his friend and agent John Cuerton. These included butter, cheese and salted or dried fish:

> Cuerton to Chaloner, Bilbao, 14 Nov. 1562
> Sends 165 pounds of salmon, sixty-nine couple of dried hake, and two Shropshire cheeses weighing nineteen pounds.

> Cuerton to Chaloner, Bilbao, 12 March 1563.
> By these bearers sends four barrels of herrings and two firkins of butter.[12]

Apart from finance, Chaloner's main difficulty in Spain was the lack of news from London. As ambassador he was expected to be able to justify his country's latest policies to Spanish grandees and to the king himself. Yet dispatches from England were often months out of date, or failed to arrive at all. The problem of lack of fresh news did not go away. In letter after letter Chaloner complained that he had been left without news from England for four, five or even six months at a time. In June 1563 he wrote to Cecil, 'Save that of the 1st of May, I have been six months without letters. What has passed in Parliament I know no more than the man in the moon.'[13]

Part of the difficulty was the sheer length of time it took for dispatches to travel between England and Spain, or vice versa.[14] There was also the issue of whether to post messages by sea or land. Theoretically, the sea route was faster, but here the season made a difference. In summer a voyage might take only eight days, but this depended on wind and weather. In winter the same voyage could last a month or more. Also, a message might have to wait at Bilbao for days or weeks until a suitable ship's captain was found who was willing to take a packet of letters. At least Chaloner had in John Cuerton an efficient agent with good contacts. But of course the letters had first to reach Cuerton in Bilbao from Madrid, carried either by one of Chaloner's servants or by someone who happened to be going there anyway, or, failing that, by a muleteer transporting merchandise on this fairly mountainous route.

The alternative was the land route across Spain and France. The Spanish postal service was second to none and Madrid was at the centre of six routes, one of which went north to the French frontier via Burgos and Irun. This royal service consisted of relays of posting centres with horses available for the needs of foreign ambassadors and other officials. There were also international links, one of which went on through France to Flanders, and Chaloner could certainly use this line if necessary. But again there were problems. For instance, he often used one of the royal couriers, named Gamboa, to send letters to Throckmorton in Paris or to Gresham in Antwerp. They would then forward his letters to London. Gamboa did not have a set schedule, however, and Chaloner sometimes suddenly heard he was about to leave and only had time to dash off a hastily scribbled message and hope he had not forgotten anything of importance. An even greater problem with the land route was that to send important letters across the whole length of France could be dangerous. During much of Chaloner's time as ambassador there was unrest in France, and the risk of interception was greater when open conflict took place between Catholics and Huguenots, as was the case during most of 1563. One way round all this was to make duplicates or even triplicates of his more important letters and send each by a different route.

It was the same for letters sent to him from England. Sometimes Chaloner had to wait several months for news from Cecil or Elizabeth, and then a packet might suddenly arrive which had been delayed for one reason or another, with letters composed at various dates. During his three and a half years in Spain no dispatch from London reached Madrid in less than a month; more generally it was two. As Phyllis Blazer says, uncertainty is the most descriptive word for sixteenth-century communications, and among those hardest hit by this uncertainty were foreign ambassadors. After all, their two main functions were to send home the latest news, and to explain to their hosts the current thinking of their respective monarchs. Both tasks were made more difficult when messages were delayed.

As well as the problems of finance, lack of news, etc., there were other difficulties for Chaloner which were particular to Spain. One was social isolation. His opposite number in England, Quadra, was constantly visited by Englishmen who were opposed to the religious changes brought about since the 1530s, and who still looked forward to the day when the old religion might one day be restored. Naturally, Quadra shared this hope and expectation. In fact he was so close to the English Catholic community that Cecil kept spies in his house so as to be up to date with any possible plots against the government. Chaloner, however, was not visited by disaffected Spaniards because there were none, or if there were, they were far too frightened of the Spanish Inquisition to risk contact with a heretical foreign ambassador. Consequently, the naturally gregarious Chaloner missed out on the social life he had been accustomed to in England, and even in Flanders.

The Spanish court tended to be secretive as compared with other European courts. Chaloner, as a Protestant, found it harder to make contacts with influential figures than did envoys from Catholic states. The Elizabethan court, in contrast, was far less formal. It regularly moved from place to place, often accepting the private hospitality of leading courtiers, and there were many days of entertainments and revels during the year which offered opportunities to outsiders to make new contacts. In Madrid, too, it was especially difficult for those like Chaloner to meet the king informally, and to obtain an official audience a convincing reason was always required. This is not to say that he found Philip cold or hostile when he did meet him. He was, according to Chaloner, 'a good and gentle Prince' and 'a lover of rest and quietness, delighting in hunting and retired solitariness with a few of his familiars'.[15] The difficulty was that Philip, although invariably gracious, was extremely cautious about committing himself. Typically, he would listen politely to what Chaloner had to say, accept any petitions or other documents he was handed, and then merely promise to consider them all carefully.

Then there was, overhanging the existence of all foreigners in Spain, including even ambassadors, the threatening presence of the Inquisition. Chaloner's predecessor, Sir Thomas Chamberlain, had been given written authorisation by the queen allowing him to 'use the ceremonies of the church in Spain' if he found himself in danger for not doing so. Presumably the same applied to Chaloner, although he never received such a specific permission. Yet Chamberlain still had his problems with the inquisitors, who once demanded that he send his cook to them for examination. He bravely refused, but he wrote to Elizabeth that he was himself afraid of the Inquisition, 'doubting lest they would charge me that in my own person I had not at Easter last followed their order'.[16]

Chaloner, too, was not immune from the attentions of the Inquisition. The affair of the broken chests when his luggage arrived at Bilbao has already been mentioned. There was also the crucial issue of whether a foreign diplomat should be allowed to hold Protestant services in his own house. The Spanish attitude was that this would merely encourage the spread of heresy.

Many of Chaloner's household servants were Spanish. Would the ambassador endanger their immortal souls by insisting that they participate in such dangerous rites? In London, Quadra was allowed to celebrate the Catholic Mass, and the English case was that it was only fair that a Protestant ambassador in Spain should be given the same freedom. However, the Spanish did not see it that way. They argued that in celebrating Mass their ambassadors were only doing what had been done for centuries, whereas the English had recently chosen to break away from the universal Church and were now making new and unacceptable demands. This was explained by the Count de Feria a few years later to Henry Cobham, who had by now himself become an ambassador:

> The Count asked him, Cobham, to recollect that we, the Spanish, never made any innovations or alteration in our religion, and did not ask them to do so. What we were yesterday we are today, as we have been the last ten, twenty, and a hundred years past, and should for ever be. He pointed out to him the calamities and misfortunes they, the English, had suffered since they had began to make these changes, which could not be justified by any law, human or divine.[17]

A related question was whether the ambassador should be expected to observe Spain's strict dietary rules during Lent, and also on Fridays. In England numerous households, both high and low, had been able to obtain exemption from having to stick to fish at these times. Chaloner's was one of these. Back in 1550 he had received permission for himself and his family to eat flesh and milk foods in Lent during his lifetime.[18] In Madrid he was prepared to conform to Catholic rules, but he still found it irritating. Madrid was far from the sea, and the quality of fish obtainable (and its high price, especially during Lent) did not please him. But he was diplomatic, and above all did not wish to get on the wrong side of the authorities. In a letter to his friend Sir John Mason he congratulated himself on managing to keep within the laws of both England and Spain:

> Chaloner to Sir John Mason, 27 June 1562.
> Concerning the eating of flesh; I am sure that I and my folks in this house keep more strait diet on prohibited days (fasting the Fridays and vigils), than the Spaniards themselves here do ... If you were here for judge of what has been reported you would soon perceive that, without offence of laws at home, I live here like no law breaker, nor accounted so here of king or court, which is a piece of mastery here.[19]

The underlying difficulty concerning all these religious issues was that at this date the position of a resident ambassador had not been sufficiently defined. It was therefore extremely difficult to steer a course that avoided falling foul either of the Spanish authorities or of the 'laws at home'. In another letter to Mason, who was a member of the Privy Council, Chaloner requested an official ruling on this vexed issue:

> Though I could conform myself to all tolerable things, reserving my opinion to myself, yet ye know our statute censures at home, of the which, as long as our lawyers be censors, if they say the camel hath horns, what remedy? I crave your opinion herein, if ye so vouchsafe; or rather, that ye procure I may have it from the Board.[20]

However, he never did get any specific instructions from the council as to how to behave, and only his caution and skilful diplomacy kept him out of trouble. It was not until many years later, in fact not until well on in the next century, that 'the curious fiction of extra-territoriality' was created, whereby it was assumed or pretended that an ambassador and his embassy stood 'as if on the soil of his homeland, subject only to its laws'.[21] For Chaloner there was no manual available to explain the role of a resident ambassador; he had to improvise.

The powerful Spanish Inquisition had its eye not only on Chaloner and his household but on every foreigner that set foot in Spain. As ambassador, one of Chaloner's most time-consuming and distressing duties was to try and help English men and women who had managed to fall into its clutches. There was, for instance, the sad case of Peter Frampton, a young merchant from Bristol who was imprisoned and tortured by the Inquisition.

The story starts before Chaloner's arrival in Spain, when another English shipmaster, Nicholas Burton, was arrested by the Inquisition in Seville, and all his ship's cargo, whose owners were various Bristol merchants, confiscated. Burton, 'having made no secret of the reformed faith in which he had been trained', was ultimately burned at the stake as fit punishment for an unrepentant heretic.[22] John Frampton went out to Cadiz as a trader in his own right but also with instructions to try and recover the value of the goods confiscated in Burton's case. He sailed from Bristol to Lisbon and then Cadiz, where he left his ship in order to ride to Malaga to buy wine. During his absence officials searched the ship and found in a chest a small book in English which they then confiscated. This was an English version of the *Distiches of Cato*, a Latin collection of proverbs much used for teaching schoolchildren morality as well as Latin. When asked, Frampton said he read it to pass the time on shipboard.

Frampton was arrested and taken chained up on the back of a mule to the castle of Triana near Seville, the headquarters of the Inquisition. There he spent many months in a dark cell being repeatedly questioned every twenty days as to his religious beliefs.

During one session he made the mistake of claiming to know the *Sancta Maria*, the prayer to Mary, which he then recited, except for the last sentence, 'Sancta Maria, Mater Dei, ora pro nobis peccatoribus', which he had never been taught as it had been deliberately left out of the Protestant version. Eventually his inquisitors decided to torture him to see what he was hiding and he was subject to the *strappado*, which involved hanging him by his arms from the ceiling with weights attached to his feet. He also suffered the *potro*, or rack. Apparently the Inquisition permitted the torture of suspected heretics provided no blood was spilt, hence the *strappado*, the *potro*, and the *toca*, or water torture. By this time Frampton was agreeing to everything his tormentors wanted, including to abjure his heresies. Later he was made to participate in an *auto da fé*, a public ceremony in which dozens of victims of the Inquisition were paraded in various costumes before receiving their punishments, some to be burnt, others imprisoned or sent to the galleys, etc. Frampton was sentenced to another year in prison, after which he was released, but instructed to remain in Spain for the rest of his life, and always to wear the *san benito*, the penitential garment, yellow in his case as a redeemed heretic.

All this we know because Frampton's own account of his experiences is included in the *Annals of the Reformation*, by the early eighteenth-century historian John Strype, who probably used records of the Court of Admiralty to which Frampton later appealed for compensation for what he had lost in Spain.[23] But long before that, just after his release from prison, he appealed first to Chaloner's predecessor, Chamberlain, and then to Chaloner himself for help. Frampton not only wanted back what had been confiscated by the Inquisition, he also wanted to prevent the Bristol merchants who had invested in his voyage to Spain from confiscating his personal possessions in Bristol until they got their money back. In April 1562 he wrote to Chaloner from Seville: 'I have been so ill used in England of such as were my creditors, that I have little joy to go home. I trust by your favour to have their goods here, and mine at liberty in England'.[24] Chaloner did what he could, appealing to King Philip on behalf of Frampton, but to little purpose. However, a few months later Frampton managed to escape from Spain and return to Bristol. It is interesting that he then gave up his career as a merchant and took up translating instead. Presumably he had acquired a good grasp of Spanish while he was in prison, and he translated several important books from Spanish into English. These included *The Most Noble and Famous Travels of Marco Polo*, and a book describing herbs that the Spanish had discovered in the New World, together with their medicinal uses.[25]

It might be appropriate to give one other, admittedly more trivial, example out of the several instances where Chaloner tried to help people who fell foul of the authorities, and especially of the Spanish Inquisition. This was the case involving Mrs Clarentius and her maid. Mrs Clarentius's maiden name was Susan White. She was born sometime before 1510 and in her twenties she was briefly married to a much older man, Thomas Tonge, who became Clarenceaux King of Arms – one with authority to grant (or withhold) a coat of arms to those seeking this mark of status. Throughout her life she kept the unusual name of Clarentius, derived from this office.

Mrs Clarentius became close to the young Princess Mary, and when Mary succeeded to the throne she was the leading gentlewoman of her privy chamber, holding the title of Mistress of the Robes. At crucial moments it was usually Mrs Clarentius to whom Mary turned. For instance, when Mary, on her knees, solemnly swore before the altar to marry Philip II there was no one else in the room except the Spanish ambassador and Mrs Clarentius. She also received many gifts from Mary, including lands in Essex, the home county of her family.

The death of Mary meant the sudden end of Mrs Clarentius's career as a courtier, but instead of retiring to the country, as did most of the Catholic courtiers surrounding Mary, she chose to become part of the household of Jane Dormer, another of Mary's gentlewomen, who had just married the Count de Feria. She accompanied her new mistress to France, where Jane gave birth to a son, and then on to Spain. This is where Chaloner's involvement with her and her 'poor maid' starts. The maid was an Englishwoman – unnamed in the state papers – who, in September 1562, travelled by ship from London to Bilbao together with a young man named Thomas, who was also to enter Mrs Clarentius's service. John Cuerton, Chaloner's agent in Bilbao, takes up the story:

> The Commissary of Porto Galleto [the port of Bilbao] having visited a ship which had come from London, found on board a chest which Mistress Clarencius' servant brought, in which was a book, in the calendar of which were blotted out the names of the Pope, and Saint Thomas of Canterbury. The chest and all it contained is stayed; and had it not been for myself, they would have been put in prison. I will not again interfere for those who will bring unlawful books. I send what they wrote about the books by the bearer, Mistress Clarencius' man [i.e. Thomas]. Bilbao, 22 Sept. 1562.[26]

Chaloner moved quickly on this case, and by mid-October was able to inform Cuerton that he had persuaded the Inquisitor Major, the Archbishop of Seville, to say he favoured the maid and would instruct the relevant local officials accordingly. Meanwhile Cuerton, in his capacity as a junior official of the Inquisition, had been permitted to take the girl into his own household. Chaloner now had some good news for him: 'As Mrs. Clarentius will next Monday ride with the Countess de Feria to Zafra, and not return till next spring, she has prayed you to look after this business during her absence, and likewise to keep her maid honestly there at her charge.'[27]

Unfortunately, as the habitual procrastination of Spanish officialdom took place, Mrs Clarentius changed her mind. She suggested the maid should 'get a service in Bilbao', in other words, find another employer, 'because she will be at no more charges with her'. Cuerton was incensed, especially as he now realised that it had been the young man, Thomas, who had put the offending book into her chest in the first place. His sympathies were with the maid, as were Chaloner's, who had to meet some of the ensuing expenses and wrote to Mrs Clarentius asking her to pay her share. Letters continued to flow between Cuerton, Chaloner and the Spanish authorities, until finally we hear that the maid had decided to go back to London and was 'just awaiting the first wind for her ship to depart'. As for Susan Clarentius, she died about two years later at the Ferias estate in Estremadura.

By the time he had been in Spain a few months Chaloner became fully aware that he was not playing the significant role that he had hoped for. He wrote to Mason asking bitterly why he was ever sent to Spain. Did he serve 'but to stop a hole'?[28] However, though he repeatedly pleaded to be recalled, this was not among the privy council's priorities. The problem was, firstly, the danger of offending Philip by withdrawing an ambassador accredited to his court, and, more important, the difficulty of finding his replacement. In view of the physical demands of the post, Chaloner wondered whether someone younger than he might not be more suitable. From his own experience he knew that the rigours of sixteenth century travel plus extreme changes in diet and climate could tax a man's physical constitution to the limit. But would a younger man have the status and experience required, not to mention the linguistic competence? He also once suggested to Elizabeth that the council could employ an Italian who, as a Catholic, might avoid problems with the Inquisition.

Nothing came of either suggestion, and in fact, when the time finally came to name his successor, what turned out to be a rather unfortunate decision was made. Dr John Man, Dean of Gloucester, was no younger than Chaloner had been when he was appointed, and had less diplomatic experience.[29]

During his first two years in Spain there was not much news of real substance for Chaloner to report. Scotland and France, where his colleague Nicholas Throckmorton was at the epicentre of the struggle between Catholics and Protestants, were the main theatres of action. Chaloner did his best to carry out what was seen as the principal task of an ambassador: to supply the queen and her council with the latest information from Spain. Consequently, he frequently filled up his reports back home with comparative trivialities – a 'strange and marvellous fire' on an island of the Azores, a small earthquake in Madrid in which no one was killed. Sometimes he heard of gossip from the Spanish court which he tried to make the most of. Much of this gossip concerned issues of precedence which were taken very seriously in the Spanish court:

> Yesterday at the King's chapel within the palace, the King being withdrawn in his travers[30] and the princes and *los grandes* according to fashion being set on a form at the travers side, it chanced the Prince of Parma to be set uppermost ere even the other of Florence came. Who, taking it for a touch to his degree, bade the Prince of Parma make more room to give him his place. Parma answered that the place where he sat was appointed to him by the king. Florence replied with some round speech, which altercation coming to the King's ears, he straight commanded them both to avoid the chapel and keep their houses till his pleasure were further known.[31]

Chaloner also reported as much as he could discover about Philip, particularly regarding his finances and the strength of the Spanish armed forces. Philip, it seemed, was very much in debt, not only to international bankers but also to the pope, Pius IV. He had to maintain garrisons in Flanders, and was also trying to build up his navy to counter the threat from the Turks in Constantinople and their allies the Barbary pirates. A few months before Chaloner had arrived in Madrid the Spanish galleons had suffered a major defeat at Djerba, an island off the Tunisian coast. Consequently, for months and years Philip organised a 'massive labour of naval construction from Palermo and Messina along the western coast of Italy and the whole Mediterranean coast of Spain'.[32]

16

DON CARLOS AND VESALIUS
1562–1563

At roughly the same time as the French war had started there was another event which, as well as affecting Philip personally, had international repercussions. Don Carlos was Philip II's only son. His mother, Maria of Portugal, had died soon after giving birth to him, and throughout his short life he showed signs of mental instability. This was probably the result of the inbreeding among the Hapsburgs over generations. For instance, Carlos possessed only six great-great-grandparents, instead of the normal complement of sixteen. However, in spite of his difficult and surly personality, he was still heir to Spain, so various suitable wives were considered for him. One was Mary Stuart, who eventually married Lord Darnley, and another was Elizabeth of Valois, who went on to marry his father.

When visiting a house in a suburb of Madrid in the spring of 1562, Carlos fell downstairs and wounded his head. Chaloner wrote long dispatches giving circumstantial reports of his condition and how the doctors were treating him. In the following account he explained how Philip, fearing his son might die, was already making plans for a possible alternative succession to the throne.

> Chaloner to the Queen, 11 May 1562.
>
> The case was strange; for on Sunday the 19th ult. the Prince, by occasion of play (others of them secretly saying in hasty following of a wench, daughter to the keeper of the house) making over much haste fell down a pair of stairs, broke his head, had two fits of an ague, which forced his physicians twice to let him blood, and for fear of apostumation[1] to make a larger incision for search, lest the scalp should be crazed. But now he is deemed quit of that danger, like as also of his quartan.[2]

Chaloner goes on to explain that Don Carlos's mental state now led Philip to consider alternative plans for the succession to the Spanish throne by inviting his young nephews from Germany to come and live in Madrid:

> Howbeit, the natural imbecility of the Prince (being of such a sprewlish body,) and thereto the tokens that he giveth by the manner of his curious questioning and solemness causeth the father (as I understand from some wise men) to conceive small hope of him, partly fearing lest hereafter he should somewhat take after the humours of the Emperor's mother.[3] So, whether this be so or not, the King is content to use some piece of the Prince's sickly constitution to another purpose. I have learned that ere long two of Maximilian's sons, Rudolph and Ernest, with his second daughter [Elizabeth], will be sent hither to be brought up with the Prince.[4] This King persuades with the Emperor of the constitution of the Prince of Spain, who if he should die without other issue of either of their bodies, the succession would devolve to the branch of Maximilian. In such an event, the King would be glad to have the

German manner of Maximilian's sons a little trained to know and be known of the Spaniards.

In a postscript to his report Chaloner added the latest rumours received. He himself, typically, thought that the weather was part of the problem:

> I understand that yesterday from Alcala, where the Prince lieth, came word in post to the King that the Prince the night before had sustained an evil fit of an ague, with much pain in his head. The news maketh all this court heavy, fearing lest the hurt in his head (which was counted past all danger) doth now aposthume inwards; which if it so fall out, your Highness may judge must needs be most perilous. Yesterday was nought but posting of lords and gentlemen to Alcala. This morning ere daylight the King himself in a coach rode post thither, and the greatest of his lords and council followed. I conjecture the danger to be great. Generally the air of Spain is evil for hurts on the head, and Alcala peculiarly noted for one of the worst places. It may be that for some incision to be made to search the hurt to the bottom, the medicins require the assistance of the King's presence. For brief, all folks here are pensive, and good cause why.[5]

In a dispatch the following day Chaloner told Cecil how the Spanish, despairing of doctors, were turning to superstitious solutions, including making the unfortunate prince spend a night in bed with 'the corpse of a dead friar'.

> Chaloner to Cecil, 12 May 1562.
> There is great fault in the persons about the Prince of Spain when he fell, and also in the negligent cure by his surgeons, who are to blame for beginning to heal the wound, it not having been searched to the bottom, whereupon this dangerous cure; afterwards accounted past

cure by all his troop of physicians jarring amongst themselves, which has hindered him the more, so if he escapes this accident, and falling down stairs (having been left twice for dead), it will be by men here accounted a miracle, and imputed to some saint. Here have been solemn processions of all religious orders, with images of our Lady and saints borne about; and amongst the rest an image of our Lady pertaining to a monastery of Black Friars, hereby accounted of great virtues for miracles which, after the procession done, was left all night for more devotion in the palace chapel. At Alcala, shepherds and Moors, which heal with oils, with clouts wetted in water, and with charms, have been admitted to the Prince's cure. Relics were applied to his wound, and lastly the corpse of a dead friar, now for his miracles accounted a saint, named Fray Diego de Alcala, was brought to the Prince and laid all night in bed by him; which friar that died many years since, as today I hear told, is counted a great miracle.[6]

A new factor now entered into the equation. Philip, from the prince's bedside, sent for the court physician, Andreas Vesalius, to join the Spanish doctors already in attendance. Vesalius possessed a European reputation. As a young man he had published his famous book *De humani corporis fabrica* ['On the structure of the human body'], which emphasised the importance of hands-on, direct observation by the physician rather than reliance on classical texts such as the works of Galen. He had come to Spain on the invitation of Charles V, and was now also in favour with his son, Philip. However, the Spanish medical establishment disliked him intensely. They were Galenists to a man and he threatened their conservative beliefs. Furthermore, he had been born and brought up in Brussels, and the Spanish tended to look down on the Flemish as an inferior breed. Chaloner's report to Cecil went on,

The surgeons in his father's presence made larger incision of the hurt place; the King brought Dr. Vesalius (not unknown for his excellent skill) from Madrid with him, whose better learning the Spanish medicins make not account of according to his worthiness, *quia figulus odit figulum.*[7] So he came *post festum,* when the other bunglers not searching the hurt deeply had promised all good hope to the King, and made untimely haste to the healing up of the incision, whereby the bone putrified, as at the second incision in the King's presence appeared. The hope all that day and the next was great of his recovery. [But then] the Prince waxed worse, and had that night a sore fit of an ague with a vehement flux, so as on Monday last in the morning when the surgeons came to dress him, they found his wound in very ill terms, promising great likelihood of his death. The said Monday in the afternoon he was in great pangs and peril, abandoned of all persons as drawing to his end.

After a month, and in spite of all the priests and the doctors did to him, Don Carlos got better. Chaloner wrote, 'The Prince of Spain has recovered, and has already voided from the bruise of his scalp a bone or scalp triangle, broader than a shilling.'[8] Mentally, however, having already shown signs of instability before the accident, he now became steadily worse. His behaviour became increasingly erratic and he made plain to everyone his hatred of his father. Finally, Philip decided to exclude him from the succession and have him locked up. Just before midnight on 17 January 1568, the king, in armour and with four councillors, entered Don Carlos's bedchamber, where they declared his arrest, seized his papers and weapons, and nailed up the windows.

Carlos remained in solitary confinement until his death six months later. It was later claimed by some that he had been poisoned on Philip's orders. This became part of the so-called black legend which in Protestant countries presented the Spanish nation and government as cruel, bigoted and self-righteous. Modern historians, however, think that Don Carlos probably died of natural causes. During his six months' imprisonment he had become very thin and he developed eating disorders, alternating self-starvation with heavy binges.

Don Carlos's life was unhappy and short, but his posthumous reputation has been considerable. The German dramatist Schiller made him into a romantic hero, and Verdi followed his example, turning Schiller's play into a well-known opera. According to Schiller, Carlos represents true love, democracy and freedom. He is presented as having fallen in love with his father's new young wife, Elizabeth of Valois, as well as planning to liberate the Netherlands from Philip's autocratic rule. When his plot is discovered he is executed. The drama is thus a travesty of the real facts and it is rather surprising that Schiller, who wrote his play in 1787, became shortly afterwards a history professor specialising in sixteenth-century Spain. No doubt the black legend had something to do with it.

Throughout the time he was in Spain Chaloner never felt entirely well, and his health problems became steadily worse as time went on. This no doubt reinforced the opinion he already had about Spain long before he was appointed ambassador. As early as June in his first year he summed up his feelings in a letter to Cecil – 'For dearth, manners, religion, and air Spain is least fitted for an Englishman.' – and that summer he was complaining of a 'tertian ague'[9] and blaming the climate. To his friend Mason he wrote, 'It has been extremely hot, during which time I have had a tertian, whereof some fits have held me from twelve to eighteen hours, but now they have left me; add thereto the lodgings so ill accommodated to the defence of the heat, with the stinking airs, and other annoyances of sick men, which in Madrid I cannot amend nor avoid, but tolerate.[10]

That winter he had a touch of rheumatism with pains in his stomach. He tended more and more to blame the climate, and especially the rapid variations between extreme heat and cold. The following summer the 'desperate heat' was affecting others as well as himself. His house was 'well nigh a hospital, with so many sick folks and visits of physicians'.[11]

From October 1563 until the following January the Cortes [i.e. Parliament] of Aragon was in session at Monzon, 300 miles from Madrid. Philip and his court, accompanied by Vesalius, attended the Cortes. Chaloner rented a house at Barbastro, a dozen miles north of Monzon, and it was from there he reported that he had been visited by the celebrated physician, who had recently been consulted over the case of Don Carlos:

Chaloner to the Queen, 23 Oct. 1563.
Complains of his sickness caused by calculus renium [i.e. kidney stone], whereof his father died. His long rest at Madrid with drinking these Spanish wines has increased it. Doctor Vesalius tells him that his reins [kidneys] are ulcerated with the fretting of the stone this journey. Rest and abstinence from all wine, and to drink only the decoction of liquorice and barley, must be a ground of his cure.[12]

Vesalius probably visited him several times because Chaloner wrote from Barbastro on 14 January that 'he wished Dr Vesalius would dine with him at Barbastro on Sunday or Monday'. He clearly agreed with the medical advice he was given, since he wrote to Cecil about the dangers of drinking Spanish white wines, 'which they mix with lime and other filthiness to make it look the whiter'.[13]

A few months after meeting Chaloner, Vesalius left Philip's employment to go on pilgrimage to the Holy Land. The reason why he left is not clear. According to one account it was because he was forced to leave in a hurry after a terrible mistake he made by starting to perform an autopsy on what he thought was a corpse:

On the second insertion of the knife she suddenly came to life, which thing struck such an admiration and horror into the hearts of all her friends that were present, that they accounted the physician, being before of good fame and report, as infamous, odious and detestable ... wherefore he thought there was no better way for him, if he would live safe, than to forsake the country.[14]

It is, however, more likely that Vesalius left Spain merely because he wanted to return to his research on the anatomy of the human body, which was almost impossible in the unscientific and heresy-hunting atmosphere of Spain. Also, he was no doubt tired of having to face the hostility of Spanish doctors. He did go to Jerusalem on pilgrimage, but died on the return journey and was buried on the island of Zakynthos, Greece. If he had been given more time he might have further revolutionised medical science. For instance, his work on the heart might well have uncovered the secret of the circulation of the blood, which in the event had to wait for Harvey a century and a half later. He has been described as the first man of modern science.

Shortly after Vesalius left Spain Chaloner learnt of another example of the dangers of trusting Spanish physicians. The following account is from the (possibly prejudiced because anti-Spanish) pen of the historian Froude, who quotes from Chaloner's letters home:

In August 1564, Philip's Queen (Elizabeth of France) miscarried of twins. Fever followed. They bled her in both arms; they bled her in both feet; and when spasms and paroxysms came on, they cupped her, and then gave up and left her to die. At the moment when Chaloner was writing to England 'she was lying abandoned of her physicians at the mercy of God. The palace gates were shut; the lamentations in the court both of men and women very tender and piteous; the chapel was filled with noblemen all praying on their knees for her; and great and unfeigned moans on all parts.'

Nature eventually proved too strong even for Spanish doctors. She rallied; and they flew at her once more. 'At last by means of a strong purgative of agaricum that made her have twenty-two stools, given at a venture in so desperate a case to purge those gross humours, she was ever since amended.'[15]

17

A POET IN SPAIN
1562–1565

During all the time he was in Madrid Chaloner spent many
of his leisure hours writing verse, either in English or Latin,
translating from others or creating his own poetry. He clearly
found relief in composing Latin verse after the daily stress of
being an ambassador in Spain. 'One cannot but wonder,' remarks
Clarence Miller, 'at the fortitudinous, almost outrageous, devotion
to learning and literature that made the composition of thousands
of Latin lines a distracting pastime and a comfort for the troubles
of diplomatic exile.'[1] But Chaloner, after years of schooling at
grammar school and university, was probably just as much at
home in Latin as in English. After all, students at Chaloner's
Oxford were not supposed to speak English in public, and all
the lectures had been in Latin. His readership was now that
elite who had been through a similar educational process and
could appreciate his verse. Latin, at this time, was the medium
through which educated men – very rarely women – of different
nationalities communicated with each other. Latin was more
precise, more sophisticated, and had a much larger vocabulary
than did pre-Shakespearian English. Through his work as an

author Chaloner enhanced his literary reputation even while his day job was proving less and less satisfactory.

There was not much point in showing an English poem to a Spaniard; very few outside England ever bothered to learn that language. There is evidence, however, that Chaloner's Latin verse was appreciated in Spain. For instance, members of the prestigious University of Alcalá, near Madrid, sent him their congratulations:

Edmund Tanere, chaplain, to Chaloner; Alcala, 14 June 1563.
I ask your pardon for detaining your verse, but I am not so culpable as the masters and licentiates of art and other learned men in this university. The praise that they have cannot be declared. Two young men send epigrams in praise of your poetry.[2]

Chaloner often sent his poetic efforts to friends and colleagues at home, such as Sir John Mason. He also tried the queen herself, not always with success. In December 1562 he sent Elizabeth a Latin epistle about her recovery from serious illness, only to be told by Mason that 'she bites not at that bait'. Nevertheless, two years later he tried again, composing an *Oratio pro reditu* ['Speech about revenue'] addressed to the queen, but this was never actually sent because, as he explained, it was very long and he had no copyist to make a fair transcript. He also sent Mason personally another lengthy Latin work, *Encomium Avaritiae* ['In praise of misers']. At the same time he added one of his habitual requests to be allowed to leave Spain and come home:

Chaloner to Mason, 30 Nov. 1564.
Asks him to help that he be no longer kept here. For his New Year's gift sends herewith a paradox which he dare not, considering the title, *Encomium Avaritiæ*, address to precise folks; also an epitaph on Lord Paget. Has finished his four books, *De Republica*, a work as big as Virgil's Aeneid; and has made to the Queen an *Orationem*

pro Reditu, but it is so long that he had not a meet man to write it forthwith, so in lieu thereof has made an elegy in verse to her, which he sends with an epistle, which he prays Mason to cause Croker to write in fair hand, and on New Year's Day present it himself to her. In case the Queen will give him no leave to come home altogether, prays him to help that he may be licensed to return for three or four months.[3]

It is not known whether Elizabeth actually got to read his elegy, but Mason did see, and apparently liked, the *Encomium Avaritiae*. This was a piece seemingly modelled on Erasmus's *In Praise of Folly*, which Chaloner had translated into English some years earlier. In his poem it appears that Venus, goddess of love, has another incarnation as 'Golden Venus' in which aspect she can be loved by the miser, with his hoard of gold coins. Chaloner clearly enjoyed extending his erotic comparison between misers and more conventional lovers:

The lover, I am told, is joyful when he takes possession of some passionate woman, when his sweet mistress has come into his warm embrace, when she has locked her arms about him, and pressed her body against his, and is ready for the pleasant mock-strife of the first encounter. If then the young man who has not been disappointed in his hopes of conquering his mistress is joyful, how would you describe the feelings of our miser, since to him Venus herself comes, placing at the disposal of the little old man breasts, not of milk, but of gold?

And the pleasures of the miser actually last longer than those of the lover:

When he tumbles about in his tawny gold and plays in it, would anyone say that he does not have his own private Venus? He kisses the yellow coins over and over again. Lord knows, such kisses lovers never have! ... You yourself will cloy your Dulcinea when you have become a tired lover, dragging back to the sheets the same old creaking hips and enervated belly. But your lover of the golden mistress always has a faithful wench to sleep with, and he prolongs their exchanges over many years.[4]

Many of Chaloner's poetic efforts have not survived, such as the Latin poem he wrote and sent to both Cecil and Mason about the French Wars of Religion, or his translation into English of a French poem by Mary Stuart (see below). But one Latin poem that has survived, and influenced other writers down the centuries, was his *Elegy on the untimely death of the most Protestant divine, Lady Jane Grey*. It is not certain when he wrote this, though it was certainly not in Mary's reign because the poem has a lot to say about 'pitiless Mary', who was responsible for the execution of the eighteen-year-old 'nine days queen'. Also, the wording seems to imply that Mary was already dead by the time it was finished, since towards the end he writes, 'Mary will be remembered with disgrace.' Chaloner must have written this poem either during 1560–61, when he was home in England, or sometime during his spell as ambassador in Spain. In any event, he kept it, and it was published in 1579 alongside his other Latin poetry.

The elegy is in heroic couplets, alternating hexameters and pentameters, and is a stylised and much-exaggerated paean of praise to Jane based on classical models of the elegiac format. Chaloner claims, for instance, that when she was arrested at the age of seventeen Jane was already highly educated (which is probably true) and knew seven languages, including Greek, Hebrew, Arabic and 'Chaldean' [i.e. Aramaic], which seems highly unlikely. Incidentally, it is not known whether Chaloner and Jane ever actually met, but certainly some of his friends, such as Walter Haddon and William Cecil, did meet her. I reproduce here a short extract translated from the Latin by J. Stephan Edwards, whose website is an invaluable source for anyone wanting to learn more about Jane.[5] This passage is about what happened to the privy councillors who sanctioned Jane's execution. It is a prime example of providentialism – the idea that nothing occurs by chance, and that justice will surely be dispensed, even in this life, to those who have done evil:

> And taking a dislike to the evil actions of the Privy Council, the god Nemesis punished many of them with long, painful illnesses before their own deaths.
>
> She inflicted one with dropsy, and another with painful kidney stones, Judge Morgan was driven mad, while others suffered similar punishments.
>
> So learn from this, you mortals: When the innocent are oppressed, God will always avenge them.
>
> And do not think that just because God does not immediately smite those who contradict His Will that He is therefore harmless.
>
> But let's move on from these things, since they are known to godly people, And they can be found in the holy Bible, which is like an eternal spring of truth.

An intriguing point in Chaloner's elegy is his claim that Jane was pregnant at the time of her execution. He writes that Mary, hard of heart, did not spare Jane, even though they were related by blood and Jane was 'heavy with child'.[6] This is perfectly possible seeing that both she and her young husband Guildford Dudley had been married for several weeks before they were separated from each other and both imprisoned in the Tower. We do not know whether they were allowed to visit each other during their imprisonment. However, it is also possible that Chaloner's assertion may have been merely an embellishment to Jane's sad history, so as to make it more of a love story and for Mary to appear even more stone-hearted.

By far Chaloner's longest Latin poem was *De republica Anglorum instauranda*, begun on Christmas Day 1562 and written during the long nights when he could not sleep because of the heat. Originally *De republica* was planned as two books, the first of which was finished by the following March and sent to Mason as 'a taste of his new work in hexameters'. By that August it was nearly finished, and would 'contain above 6,000 verses'. Probably, while he attended the Spanish court in Aragon he had little time to work on it, but when he returned to Madrid composition continued, until by November 1564 it was completed, in four books, and was 'as big as Virgil's Aeneid'. When it was finally printed in 1579 there were actually ten books, but this may have been due to William Malim's editing, since nowhere in his letters does Chaloner mention more than four.[7]

The *De republica* is impressive in its length, consisting of 8,000 lines in elegant Latin. It is an allegorical epic ostensibly about the condition of England at that time, and has been called a landmark in English humanism. However, to modern taste it seems vague, oblique and highly verbose. It is also an extremely demanding read, even for those like myself with a modicum of Latin. The ideas it offers are often expressed in terms of classical mythology, with long metaphors and much repetition. It starts off with Britannia personified, wounded by various iniquities and bemoaning her cruel fate. Later topics include education, farming and fishing, horses and siege engines, moneylenders, and taking pride in fighting for one's country. However, there is little precise contemporary reference or relevance. If one is looking for hard facts or even opinions about life or politics in Chaloner's day, one is likely to come away disappointed. The contemporary reader might tend to label as early modern clichés most of the views contained in the poem. Take, for example, a few of the points made – at considerable length – in book nine, which is all about women:

> The citizen needs a good wife; consider carefully the woman you hope to marry; don't marry a very young woman or her womb will not be big enough; marry an 18-year-old not a 12-year-old; a woman who has grown up in the city should not marry a farmer, or vice versa; your wife should spend her time in country tasks such as milking the cows, weaving and vegetable gardening; don't let your wife lead a life of idleness and luxury; when her husband is at home she should please him with elegant and chaste love; when he is away she should look after the house, servants, children – and run to meet him with a kiss; she should bring him food she herself has prepared; it is not good for a wife to be too learned because it makes her bold; it is not good if a girl is forced by her parents' desire for wealth to marry someone uncouth or an old man. She will complain to her parents and threaten suicide; be gentle and patient and forgiving to your wife and you will be happy.

In book three is discussed the need for a stable social hierarchy. The following passage applies to human society the well-known idea that a hierarchy, or chain of being, exists throughout the natural world. Just as stones do not try to become plants, and plants do not aspire to be animals, so those who find themselves in a lower social class should stay in their allotted place:

> Let the young people in the city and in the country drink in these verses, and also the great body of the ordinary people on the streets. Since it is their lot to live in subordination to the rule of their betters, and since Jupiter has made this irrevocable by the same nod with which he established eternal laws for the government of the universe, so that the different elements, each in its place, rest without strife, beautifully bound together by the

diversified chain of nature, so it is fitting that these people should
see to their own duties happily and contentedly … [Then] there will
be no reason for the lower classes to aspire to things above them,
or covet the management of things denied them.[8]

Here Chaloner may well have had in mind the popular risings
of 1549 which led to the fall of the Duke of Somerset. The
rebels were protesting against the enclosure of the land as well
as religious innovation. He goes on to explain how much happier
ordinary people are if they stick to the simple life and avoid too
much education:

O thrice blessed, if they only knew what was good for them,
are those men who have little sensibility and few intellectual
accomplishments, farmers, craftsmen, fullers, and all the ranks of
the common people who are excluded from the holy places of the
Muses! Deep anxieties do not enter their minds and trouble their
hearts. With their easy-going temperaments they are forgetful of
punishments and free from fear of evil threatening on the distant
horizon. They stretch out and snore peacefully in a deep sleep.

As he had done in the past, Chaloner continued to translate
Latin texts into their English equivalents. He translated one of
Ovid's *Epistolae Heroidum*, poems in which various women from
classical myths expressed themselves as if in letters. Helen, said to
be the most beautiful woman in the world, is wife to Menelaus,
King of Sparta. She is visited by Paris, a prince from Troy across
the sea, who expresses his love for her. Helen at first raises all
kinds of objections, but finally hints that she will give in and
accompany him back to Troy. Chaloner's version, *Helen to Paris*,
consists of 536 short lines. This extract is from the final stanzas:

Conclude that if I had the wit
Or spirit thereto I should

Thine ample proffers take,
As she, that wise is, would.
Or I perchance will take them to,
My shamefast fear up-cast,
And yield me to the time
That may me win at last:

Thus hitherto my pen that put
My secret mind in writing,
Since wearied in my hand,
Shall cease now from inditing:
The rest hereof by Clemenee
And Ethra thou shalt know,
My privy damsels both,
And councillors also.[9]

Perhaps the most successful of Chaloner's various verse translations from Latin were the nine he made from *The Consolation of Philosophy* by the sixth-century poet and philosopher Boethius. Since Boethius wrote these verses when in prison awaiting execution, Chaloner, exiled in a country he had come to hate, perhaps sympathised with him. The following poem seems to me to show that Chaloner had a certain gift for English lyric poetry. Here the poet is addressing the moon, which controls not only the movement of all the stars but also life on earth:

O maker of the starry sky,
That sitting on thy steady seat above;
Incessantly
Dost swiftly weld the Heaven round:
And makst the stars that by a law they move, to order bound:
Thou, while the chilly winter blast hath spoiled the trees,
Dost make the drowsy day the shorter last,

And thou, when summer hath begun his pleasant warmth,
Hast bid the night away the swifter run.

Why, the poet asks, when the moon has such power over nature, does she not also control the fortunes of men, and impose some justice where none now exists?[10]

So nothing breaks thy statutes old,
But in the work thou hast them tasked to,
Their order hold.
Thus ruling all the certain end,
Save only men: thou lettest what they do
Unbridled wend.

For why hath Fortune thus her will
In turning things now up, now down,
So oft withouten skill?
The pain that for offence besits [fits],
The guiltless have: and wickedness aloft in honour sits.
And harmless folk with most unright
Are by the guilty trodden under foot,
And virtue bright
Is hoodwinked under darkness halt.
And laid is on the just, withowten boote [without recourse],
The wickeds' fault.

The poem ends with a request to the moon to extend her just laws, which seem to apply to the rest of the universe, to human affairs also:

O! now the wretched earth behold,
What ere thou be that things ylinked hast
In league so old:

No mean part of thy workmanship, we men
With fortunes' waves are tossed
And cast in steerless ship.

Be steersman, and these floods allay:
And as thou guidest all the Heaven wide
In such a stay:
Vouchsafe into that league to tie
This earth also, that here may order bide with certainty.[11]

Another translation project of Chaloner's concerned Mary Stuart. In the summer of 1562 Mary and Elizabeth planned to meet in northern England, and Mary sent Elizabeth a diamond together with some French verses spoken as if by the diamond itself. Sir Henry Killigrew, a prominent diplomat, sent these verses to Chaloner to be translated into English and Latin. Killigrew liked Chaloner's versions and showed them to Mary. Killigrew, it appears, generally had a high opinion of Chaloner's English poetry, since he told him that he was 'desirous to recover some of your doings in English rhyme, and among others those out of Ariosto'. So far as is known, no translation of Ariosto from Chaloner's pen has survived.[12]

Apart from literature, there was another form of relaxation which took Chaloner away from the stresses of ambassadorship, and that was music. While in Spain he continued his interest in the lute, at one point buying '25 dozen lute string minikins' from Flanders.[13] He also wrote to Robert Dudley about the internationally renowned Neapolitan lutist Fabrizio Dentice. One passage shows he had invited Fabrizio to perform in his house, and also that he himself played the lute:

The young man Fabricio, a gentleman Neapolitan of a seemly personage, was with me in my lodging. I heard him both play and sing; his play for clean handling and deep music and parts withal

and excellent fingering in time and place, is incomparable of any
that ever I heard. A lute in his hand speaketh other language than
ever I yet heard, and pardee [by God!] I can somewhat play and
have skill of lute play myself.[14]

To conclude this chapter I have transcribed a letter from Chaloner
to Elizabeth which he sent together with a Latin book for her to
read. The letter reveals something about Chaloner's relationship
with the queen. Firstly, he emphasises what a rare and fascinating
book this is. Secondly, he flatters her by explaining that whereas
he (a forty-three-year-old scholar) is quite incapable of judging
the merits of the book, she, with her 'high wisdom', will be able
to do so. And thirdly, he says that when he returns to England he
will tell her more about the book. In other words, the letter and
the book seem to be intended as a kind of bait to speed his recall.

I send unto your Majesty a written book concerning the doctrine of
Frater [brother] Georgio Siculo. Of this book I suppose there is not
six copies extant anywhere. I came by it at the hands of an Italian in
this Court who, being a disciple of the said Siculo, brought it hither
covertly with him as his manual. But being constrained to depart
for Italy, and fearing the dangers of the passage for the Inquisition,
left it with me upon solemn commission to save it for him if I could.
The circumstances what this Siculo was, be long to recite, which on
my return I shall more fully detail unto your Highness.

Now (as appearing by so much of his work as I have read), his
doctrine, which he affirmeth to have received by special revelation,
seems in divers points to differ both from the Papist and Protestant
assertions. I dare not pronounce how far his doctrine is sound,
but sure his manner of writing is in a high trade, and alleging
authorities out of Scripture for every point.

I thought it not amiss (as I kept the book for your Majesty to
have a sight of) to send it to the same by this bearer. With the

humble protestation that, as I neither dare approve nor yet disapprove his doctrine, so me thought it meet for your Majesty to peruse, whose high wisdom can judge more rightly what it doth import. And as my return (which with your gracious leave I look for now ere long time past), in case the book be sound and legible, I will be so bold to demand it, or the copy thereof, again at your Majesty's hands. Seeing I also for my part am curious of such rare things to be had.

Almighty God preserve your Majesty and send the same good life and long. From Madrid the last of August 1563.[15]

18

COLLEAGUES AND FRIENDS

Thomas Chaloner was a gregarious gentleman who had a wide range of friends and acquaintances. There were, of course, those he acquired during his diplomatic activities, such as Sir Nicholas Throckmorton and the Count de Feria, both of whom I discussed earlier. Another who falls into this category is Sir John Mason, whose career paralleled Chaloner's except that he was seventeen years older and rose higher up the ladder. He had been to Oxford, studied in Paris, and then commenced his diplomatic career. Mason spent many months on missions abroad, and so could be expected to sympathise with Chaloner's longing to come home. He had been (the elder) Sir Thomas Wyatt's secretary and close friend when the latter was ambassador in Spain, and, along with Wyatt, had been accused of treason for communicating with Catholic opponents of Henry VIII.[1] While Chaloner was languishing in Spain Mason had become an influential member of Elizabeth's council. The two exchanged many letters, and Chaloner's show that he considered Mason a real friend. One of his letters concludes,

My four books *de Repub: angl:* are almost finished, they will contain above 6,000 verses. I suppose you will not mislike them.

God send me, once at home, to walk with you a turn or two at
Gonnolsbury or under your short alley in your London garden.[2]

Mason was to be one of the small group of friends who oversaw
the requests in Chaloner's will. He died a few months after
Chaloner himself.

Another less reputable friend was the Reverend Thomas
Thurland, to whom Chaloner wrote affectionately, 'I have sundry
times in this vehement state here wished for your cold hall to play
at slyde grote, and much more for a jug full of your cold nappy
beer, but what booteth wishing, where if wishing might serve, more
than this had passed already.' He ends this letter in humorous style,
hoping Thurland will find the time to write to him: 'When you have
said over your service and holy meditations, and dined with a good
piece of beef and a jug of claret wine, I pray you in the afternoon to
put off your tippet and long robe and bestir yourself a little in your
damask jacket. Farewell good parson and dearest friend.'[3]

Thurland was master of the Savoy Hospital. This was an
institution founded in pre-Reformation times by Henry VII. It
was well endowed with lands and functioned as a night shelter
for up to a hundred poor and homeless people. The master
managed the hospital's property and had under him a large staff,
including four chaplains, two priests, four altarists to assist in the
services in the chapel, a clerk of the kitchen, a butler, a cook, an
under cook, a doorkeeper and an under-doorkeeper, a gardener, a
matron, and twelve other women. Unfortunately, according to the
Victoria County History of London, Thurland was not an ideal
master: 'The foundation was almost ruined by Thomas Thurland,
the master, who was removed in 1570, but not before he had
burdened the hospital with his private debts by a misuse of the
common seal, granted unprofitable leases, taken away the beds,
and disposed of jewels and other treasures of the house. He
was also accused of not being resident, of going very seldom to

church, and spending his time in playing bowls and gambling, of maintaining his relations at the expense of the hospital, etc.'[4] It seems that most of the money Thurland took from the hospital went on his obsession, which was trying to discover gold and copper in obscure parts of Cumberland. He employed hundreds of miners, including specialists from Germany, but found very little.

There was also the group of literary colleagues whom Chaloner may have got to know either when he was involved in the court revels of 1551–2 or a few years later during Mary's reign as collaborators in *The Mirror for Magistrates*. This chapter looks at them and their connections with Chaloner, so far as the evidence allows us to go. Typically for the age, all of them were involved, to a greater or lesser extent, in political life as well as in literature. All attended either Oxford or Cambridge, and Chaloner may well have known some of them at university.[5]

William Baldwin

The first of these, William Baldwin, is the one whose life we know least about, although his literary works were popular at the time. We do know that he worked for many years with a well-known London printer. He was the editor of the first edition of *The Mirror* which was suppressed in 1555 but saw the light of day after Elizabeth's accession. Chaloner, of course, was one of Baldwin's team, and he would certainly have known the books Baldwin wrote earlier. One of these, *A Treatise of Moral Philosophy* (1547), was very similar in aim to what Chaloner himself was trying to do with his translations from Latin. It sought to introduce classical learning to a wider public, and also, in the style of Erasmus, to harmonise classical philosophy with Christian belief.

Another of Baldwin's books is entitled *Beware the Cat*.[6] This was completed by 1555 though, like the *Mirror*, was not published during Mary's reign, in this case because its satire attacked the

Catholic Church. It is set at the time of the court revels of 1552 and takes the form of an argument between Baldwin himself, George Ferrers and others as to whether or not animals such as cats can think and talk like human beings. Baldwin's real purpose here was to expose and ridicule various aspects of society in the same way as Erasmus, More and Rabelais did before him.

We have no way of knowing whether Baldwin and Chaloner continued to meet or correspond after 1555. It seems that Baldwin became a vicar and gave up the printing trade. He wrote in the 1563 *Mirror* that he had been 'called to an other trade of life' in 1559, and he is probably the William Baldwin who was ordained deacon by Archbishop Grindal in that year. Stowe mentions a Baldwin preaching at Paul's Cross in September 1563 who died a week later of the plague, and this was very likely him.[7]

George Ferrers

George Ferrers was about ten years older than Chaloner, but the links between them stretched over at least quarter of a century. He trained as a lawyer and started his literary career by producing legal texts, the most important being the first translation into English of *Magna Carta*. By 1538 he was a member of Thomas Cromwell's extended household, as also was Chaloner. Over the next few years Ferrers became a prominent courtier and Member of Parliament, married the first of his three wives, and even received a small legacy from the will of Henry VIII. In 1547 he was made commissioner for transport during the Duke of Somerset's campaign in Scotland which culminated in the Battle of Pinkie Cleugh. At this point he, again like Chaloner, was seen as 'a gentleman of my lord Protector's'.[8]

Perhaps the high point in Ferrers' career came when he was appointed Lord of Misrule, in charge of organising the court revels in 1551. He proved a great success, producing and writing several of the dramatic pieces that were much appreciated by the court, and especially by the thirteen-year-old Edward VI. According to the seventeenth-century critic George Puttenham, he wrote 'in Comedy or Interlude, wherein he gave the king so much good recreation, as he had thereby many good rewards'.[9] He was reappointed the following year when the revels were even more ambitious – most likely to divert Londoners from the impending execution of Somerset.[10] His role as Lord of Misrule over three years netted him various grants of money and property.

Ferrers seems to have had no difficulty in switching his allegiance to serve the Catholic Mary after Edward's death; in fact he took an active part in helping to suppress the Wyatt Rebellion in 1554. A year later there was a curious episode in which he accused the young Princess Elizabeth, together with the famous magus Dr John Dee, of using 'enchantments' against Mary and her husband Philip. In a contemporary letter it was alleged that Dee evidently retaliated with more magic since 'Ferys, one of their accusers, had, immediately upon the accusation, both his children stricken, the one with present death, the other with blindness'.[11]

Not unexpectedly, after this event Ferrers did not hold any important offices under Queen Elizabeth, but he was by now a wealthy man and could retire to his estates in Hertfordshire with his third wife. His last contact with Chaloner, so far as we know, was the letter he wrote to him in early 1563 advising him to give his consent to the marriage of Chaloner's sister Ellen to Francis Saunders.[12] Ferrers wrote that Saunders was a good lawyer and also happened to be a relative by marriage of Chaloner's friend Walter Haddon. Ferrers died within a few months of sending this letter.

Thomas Phaer

Phaer was perhaps the nearest thing to a Renaissance polymath among Chaloner's friends. He went to Oxford and then became a lawyer, writing two well-received textbooks on aspects of the law.

He was appointed solicitor to the council of the Welsh Marches, and settled in Pembrokeshire, marrying the wealthy widow of a Welsh merchant. He then embarked on a second career as a medical man, later obtaining a doctorate from Oxford, and publishing several books on aspects of medicine, including one on the plague.

The most innovative of his medical works was *The Boke of Chyldren*, the first treatise ever published by an Englishman on the diseases of childhood. This book was also one of the first treatises to make a distinction between children and adults. Phaer discussed possible remedies for various conditions affecting children, including 'apostume of the brain' (meningitis), 'terrible dreams and fear in the sleep' and 'pissing in the bed'. He counselled against unnecessary treatments for childhood diseases such as smallpox or measles ('the best and most sure help in this case is not to meddle with any kind of medicines, but to let nature work her operation'). He also condemned the tendency of medical practitioners to obscure their meaning by using Latin, and the consequent confusion for the patient: 'How long would they have the people ignorant? Why grudge they physic to come forth in English? Would they have no man to know but only they?'

As well as practising as a lawyer and then a doctor, Phaer was also writing poetry. He was one of the four authors whom we know contributed to the 1555 edition of the *Mirror*, the verses about the Welsh hero Owen Glendower being almost certainly by him. He produced many other poems in English, his magnum opus being a translation of Virgil's long poem the *Aeneid*, which he had almost finished when he died. His version was popular with contemporaries, and Puttenham rated him highly, writing, 'In Queen Mary's time flourished above any other [poet] Doctor Phaer.'

Phaer was keen to uphold the worthiness of the English language on patriotic grounds. He claimed to have undertaken his translation of the *Aeneid* in part 'for defence of my country's language (which I have heard discommended of many, and esteemed of some to be more than barbarous)'. Very likely Baldwin and Ferrers would have agreed with this, as would Chaloner, the translator of Gilbert Cousin and Erasmus. All of them were acquainted with Phaer throughout his career. Baldwin must have known him before the *Mirror* since most of Phaer's earlier books were produced by Edward Whitchurch, the publisher for whom Baldwin worked. Ferrers was certainly a close friend. When, in 1558, Phaer made a will, he requested 'a stone upon my grave with such Scripture thereupon, graven in brass, as shall be devised by my friend Mr. George Ferrers'.[13] And when Phaer died, Chaloner wrote an epitaph for him.

Thomas Sackville

Sackville was much younger than the other members of Chaloner's literary coterie, and he was also the one who was to rise highest in the hierarchy of court and government. He started life with considerable advantages, as both his mother and father came from affluent families with a tradition of government service. Also, his father was first cousin to Anne Boleyn, so Sackville could claim to be a kinsman of Elizabeth.

When Chaloner knew him, Sackville had already acquired a reputation as a poet and playwright. In 1561 his best-known work, the tragedy of *Gorboduc*, was put on before the court as part of their Christmas revels. It was set in ancient Britain and concerned an imaginary episode in which the divided succession to the throne led to civil war. It may have been written partly as veiled advice to Elizabeth to marry, or at least to name her successor. Two years later Sackville contributed to the second edition of *The Mirror for Magistrates*, though it is quite likely he actually composed his contribution – the two poems *Induction* and *The Complaint of Henry, Duke of Buckingham* – in 1554–5 along with Baldwin and the others.[14] In 1562 he was one of the group of friends and relatives who gathered in Chaloner's house in Clerkenwell to keep company with his sister Ellen after the death of her husband.[15]

In about 1566 Sackville composed another poem, *Sacvyles Olde Age*, which represents his farewell to poetry, as he had now decided to devote his life to government service. At this time Elizabeth is said to have described him as 'a scholar, and a traveller and a courtier of special estimation' whose discourse was 'judicious but yet witty and delightful'. His political career now took off; he soon became a peer, and was granted one office after another, culminating in his succeeding Lord Burleigh (William Cecil) as Lord Treasurer of England. He survived well into the reign of James I.

Of course there must have been other literary friends of Chaloner about whom we know little. For instance, there was Drue Drury, another of those invited to Chaloner's house in Clerkenwell by his sister Ellen 'to make her merry' after the death of her husband. A decade earlier Drury had performed with Chaloner at the court revels at Greenwich. There was also the young poet Barnaby Googe, who, in the spring of 1562, visited Chaloner in Madrid. After this visit Chaloner detailed one of his own servants to accompany Googe back to England.[16] He certainly knew Walter Haddon, who was related to Francis Saunders, the young lawyer who became the second husband of Chaloner's sister Ellen. Haddon was famous for his Latin verse. 'There is no better Latin man within England, except Gualter Haddon the lawyer,' wrote Thomas Wilson in *The Arte of Rhetorique*, 1553. It was Haddon who was to compose the Latin inscription which was attached to Chaloner's tomb.[17] One of the saddest aspects of Chaloner's posting to Spain was that he was cut off from all those he had known in the 1550s who appreciated and shared his humanist and literary tastes.

19

FAMILY AND MARRIAGE

Unlike, for instance, Nicholas Throckmorton, Chaloner had no wife who might have controlled his affairs in England while he was in Spain. Consequently, he had to look to others to manage his estates, collect his rents and also to maintain his London house. For all this he relied on two people especially: his younger brother Francis, and his trusted agent Robert Farnham, most likely a relation of his brother-in-law Thomas Farnham, who was married to his sister Ellen. Francis was trained as a lawyer and seems to have spent much of his energy engaged in personal litigation. He had acquired certain properties through his marriage to the illegitimate daughter of Sir William Bowyer, an ex-mayor of London, and he was continuously busy trying to protect his rights to these properties or in disputes with his tenants. The line of demarcation between Farnham and Francis was vague. For example, in October 1564 one of Chaloner's tenants wrote that he was withholding his rents until it was made clear to which of the two he should pay them. A few months earlier Francis wrote that another tenant, a Mrs Penne, who apparently thought she was owed money by Chaloner, had applied to the courts to be granted part of Chaloner's diets, i.e. his income as ambassador:

Francis Chaloner to Sir Thomas Chaloner, 18 Dec. 1563.
As for your rents of Gisburne and Steeple Claydon, they are appointed by Farnham to pay Mrs Penne and others; for she made suit to have part of your diets stayed for her debt, and if she be not paid shortly the penalty will be taken.[1]

So far as we can judge, Robert Farnham was an excellent and reliable agent. He collected rents, received and passed on letters and reports, and even made the long journey to Spain more than once. But could the same be said about the litigious and argumentative Francis, who seemed to enjoy picking quarrels and making enemies? For instance, he took against the Percivals who were employed by Chaloner to look after his house in Clerkenwell. Percival was supposedly 'a knave not to be kept, for divers causes', and Francis also accused Mrs Percival of having sold or pawned the Spanish wall hangings that were supposed to have been sent to the home of the previous ambassador, Sir Thomas Chamberlain. He alleged that he, Francis, had found it too dangerous to enter Chaloner's house and check what had happened to the wall hangings. This, he claimed, was because Mrs Percival had infected the house with the plague, one of her children having fallen sick with it.[2] In the same letter Francis even warned Chaloner against William Cecil, 'that he had no cause to make any great account of Mr Secretary's friendship, for he examined his men strictly of his [Chaloner's] behaviour there and at home in time past, [and] intercepted some of his letters'.

Not long after this Chaloner received a letter from another long-standing servant of his, William Brackenbury, whom he had sent from Madrid to London with messages for various friends. Francis had accused Brackenbury of showing to Cecil all the private letters he had been entrusted with.[3] Now Brackenbury retaliated. 'Everyone knows here,' he wrote sarcastically, 'that wise Mr Francis has nothing to do but invent lies'. Faced with this tangle of accusation and counter-accusation, Chaloner must hardly have known which way to turn or whom to trust. Small wonder he wrote to a friend, 'All my things at home run to manifest wrack. My receivers in the country keep my rents, and I am eaten up by interest.'

We hear little of Chaloner's other brother, John, who was now spending most of his time in Ireland, where he had been made Secretary of State for Ireland – a role not as important as it sounded, and which he did not fully exploit. John wrote to Sir Thomas in August 1564 that he wanted to resign his office, and in the same letter he gave his brother a convoluted explanation of why he had been unable to send him the 'brace of lean greyhounds' that he had earlier promised him.[4] John Chaloner's real interest lay in mining, and he hoped to quit his political career and devote himself to the search for Irish minerals, particularly in Lambay, an island near Dublin which he was convinced was rich in alum. Whether he was still married at this stage in his life is not known, but his two teenage children, Thomas and Bessie, were staying with his sister Ellen. In 1563 Ellen told Sir Thomas she was tired of having to look after them, especially as John never wrote and thanked her. Also, she did not approve of a recent attachment Bessie had made. She wrote, 'The wench has lost my favour by reason of the love betwixt her and William Raven; and the boy cannot learn here so well as in some good school.'[5] Overall, one has a (perhaps unfair) impression of John as well meaning but somewhat ineffectual in both his public and his private life.

Ellen herself had just become a young widow. In September 1562 Chaloner received the sad news. She wrote that it had pleased God to punish her by taking away her dear husband and youngest child, both within two days. Also, she had made so bold as to come and live in his house in Clerkenwell, because after her husband's decease the house they had lived in had to be sold. She reported that her cousin Beaumont, Drue Drury, Thomas Sackville, her brother-in-law John Farnham, and her brother Francis and his wife, all of whom she found in his house, were now supping with her 'to make her merry'.[6]

As soon as he heard about the death of Ellen's husband Chaloner wrote back, saying that of course she must 'use his house as her own'. He also later wrote that if she wanted to remarry he hoped she would not do so without his advice. Not long afterwards she did decide to Mary Francis Saunders, a young lawyer, and Chaloner approved, particularly as two of his closest literary friends had asked him to give his consent. George Ferrers wrote listing Saunders' qualifications, not the least of which was that he was related to Walter Haddon, being the brother of Haddon's wife.[7] Haddon, Ferrers and Sackville had been leading contributors to *The Mirror for Magistrates*, and now all three were clearly part of Chaloner's intimate circle, though of course he was unable to join them. The knowledge that they were all meeting regularly in his house no doubt increased his loneliness, and the dissatisfaction he felt with his role in Spain.

Meanwhile, his niece Bessie and her chosen partner, William Raven, were determined to marry. Raven had been employed by Thomas Farnham, Ellen's recently deceased first husband, who had apparently encouraged the match and had promised to give Raven the tellership of the Exchequer, a post which Chaloner himself had originally held and then passed on to Farnham. In a letter dated January 1563 Raven requested Chaloner's assistance in writing a letter of commendation to Bessie's father in Ireland, John Chaloner, whom he also criticised as being 'unnatural' as 'he seemeth to give but small regard of his children'. Raven refers to Bessie as 'your poor kinswoman'. In the same letter he asked whether Chaloner would grant him a lease to the parsonage at Steeple Claydon, promising that 'he would gladly be his farmer for years, either for a yearly rent or money in hand'.[8] As far as we know these suggestions were accepted. Raven did become Chaloner's tenant and married his niece Bessie, but unfortunately nothing more is known about the couple.

A friend and frequent correspondent of Chaloner was Elizabeth Parr, Marchioness of Northampton. This lady had followed a highly chequered career under four Tudor monarchs. In the court of Henry VIII her beauty and vivacity had made her much admired. However, she incurred scandal by openly becoming the mistress of William Parr, a married man, and the brother of Catherine, who was to become Henry's last wife. A few years later, when Parr's close friend the Duke of Northumberland became regent to the young Edward VI, Parr's fortunes changed. He was permitted to annul his marriage and take on Elizabeth as his official wife. He was also created Marquis of Northampton and Elizabeth became his marchioness. However, in 1553 she, together with her father, Lord Cobham, became involved in the plot to set Lady Jane Grey instead of Mary on the throne. Now everything changed again. William Parr lost all his lands and title and was forced by Mary to return to his former wife. Then, with the death of Mary, all changed for the third time. William and Elizabeth became close to Queen Elizabeth and were able to recover their former wealth and to set up house together at the prestigious Winchester Palace in Southwark. This, then, was the politically experienced and broad-minded lady whose younger brother Henry Cobham had accompanied Chaloner to Spain to start his apprenticeship as a diplomat,[9] and who now became the recipient of Chaloner's personal and financial worries.

In one letter Chaloner wrote that he had received her thanks for looking after young Henry, adding that he was charmed 'to be visited with so courteous a letter from such a lady's hand, which I will keep amongst my dearest papers'. He went on to bemoan his lack of social contact in Madrid, 'for few will take pity on a wifeless wanderer, and since my years now are such as having no child to inherit that living which God hath sent me, it were time for me now to wed (my next brother's children being not such as he or I make great account upon)'. Here he was, isolated in Spain, and deprived of 'all the dearest pleasures of my life'. Clearly Chaloner was hoping that the marchioness would suggest some possible brides in England for his consideration.[11]

Another letter to the marchioness, transcribed from the original in the British Library, gives us a further example of Chaloner's somewhat elaborate style. Here he thanks God for her recovery from a recent illness, and acknowledges that her brother might not have altogether enjoyed his time in Madrid. The letter ends with his usual request to any of his friends whom he thought might have some influence, to press his case for permission to return home.

Good Madam

It is daily said that an ill news cometh sooner than a good. What grief the report hither written of your dangerous sickness did minister here to me and Mr Henry Cobham your brother I shall not need to enlarge. I mourned for the loss of so good a lady and friend, he with extreme passions cried out on his hard fortune to be deprived of so dear and worthily beloved sister whose ... [subsequent recovery?] I assure you madam he did celebrate with tears at large. After all the sorrows, when the next letter brought us better tidings, it needeth not to recite our thanks to God and glad congratulations, whereupon he thought meet to put himself in immediate order to return, and see, I trust with his own eyes, your desired amendment, which after by his letters I look he will participate unto me that I may recognise the more fully.

Now as for this time that he has taken part and borne his cross in my company, if he hath not found things here to his contentment, this might also have fallen forth in any other country than Spain. I trust it hath wrought this good unto him by trial of hardness to know the better what pleasures of home is worth.

For my part in respect of the vowed good will that I have always borne toward your ladyship I could have extended [his visit] further. I would have been and will be glad at all times to show so much I am yours.

Requiring the same for that special confidence which I put in your friendship as well to help with your word that I may have leave to come home this next spring to put order in my divided things. Come Easter next it shall rest a year and a half since I last departed forth of England, where unto adding other xi months confined in Flanders, it will be two years and a half the time spent in the ambassade, besides so many years spent in former service. And of very reason considering my case as it standeth, her Highness ought to give me leave to return, as well to take a wife for children as to pay my debts and stock my grounds, which to my great loss for want of money afore hand, consumed ever in service of the Prince, I am fain to leave unfurnished. The damage whereof hath been greater to me than a great reward will recompense. But of these matters it were surplus here to entreat further.

Most humbly recommending my self and my case to your honoured friendship and beseeching the same to make my dearest commendations to my good Lord Marquis. And wishing to your brother all glad and good things.

Madrid the 13 October 1562.[12]

Chaloner believed in marriage. He once made the following sententious observation (in a letter to Cecil): 'Marriage and the fruit thereof is a sure pawn to bind all men's hearts; time gained to put our things in order and settle things begun but not achieved; with a thousand other accidents that the time itself would discover for occasion to take hold upon, do draw one down to that side.'[13] A large part of his ambition to get married was clearly his desire for a male heir, and this was one reason why he was especially anxious to return to England so as 'to woo for myself ere ever my beard wax grey, for these fair women that are young will bid have away the old man'.[14] There was one particular lady he seems to have singled out for the honour of becoming his wife. This was a certain Elizabeth Sands, one of Queen Elizabeth's gentlewomen.[15] Unfortunately, news arrived that she had chosen another suitor, Sir Maurice Berkeley, an ambitious and successful courtier. To make matters worse, Berkeley was even older than Chaloner himself. He was piqued: 'It should appear she loves ancient ware, with a house full of other folks' children.[16] God send her well to brook her choice hereafter, and myself to consider better what match I make hereafter.'[17] He told the marchioness that he blamed his brother Francis for putting off the lady by 'making a direct proposal' when he had only been given authority to 'feel the inclination of a certain gentlewoman'. Then Chaloner said that he had actually foreseen Mrs Sands's refusal. In fact, even before he knew about it he had had a certain dream which seemed to predict it. He proceeded to recount the dream:

For methought I saw the party [i.e. Elizabeth Sands] going from the privy chamber towards the chapel very fair trimmed, with a great number of ladies following her; and that I also was very trim apparelled, but all in tawny, and that Sir Jacques Granado and one or two more of my friends, now dead, told me that they never saw garments better become me; whereat I rejoiced, and thought no more of her that went to church. This dream I write for that it was so notable; and write it to you, Madam, to the end ye may see how well my tawny garments pleased me. And now to tell you my fantasy; in all such wooing cases, perchance I have more often refused than been refused; and being refused, I count my halfpenny none the worse silver, for women's likings (as men's also), are but private to themselves, where twenty to one perchance would not choose the like.[18]

After he had seen Vesalius in the autumn of 1563, Chaloner wrote to Mason that he was feeling somewhat better.[19] This may just possibly have been connected with a visit from another English lady, Audrey Frodsham, whom he was later to marry, and whom also he presumably knew well before he became ambassador in Spain. She was the daughter of Edward Frodsham, Esq., of Elton, Cheshire. Audrey's name is sometimes given its Latin equivalent, Etheldreda. She was born in 1529, which would make her about thirty-three when she travelled to meet Chaloner. We do not know exactly when she arrived, but it was very likely that December when Chaloner had left Madrid and ensconced himself in lodgings in the small town of Barbastro, a few miles from Monzon where the king was meeting the Cortes of Aragon. No doubt it would have been easier here than in the ambassador's residence in Madrid to seclude Audrey and her retinue from prying eyes. It was a suitable house in which to receive a gentlewoman:

> William Phayre to Chaloner, 20 Dec. 1563.
> Has prepared a lodging for him and stable for ten horses, a handsome kitchen, three fair pieces without hangings or bedding; all things else shall be in good case.[20]

Robert Turton mentions a letter which Chaloner received at Barbastro in January 'containing commendations to Mistress Audrey', but I have been unable to trace his reference.[21] We do know, however, when the lady re-embarked for England, due to some brief mentions in the state papers. The first of these is when Chaloner, who had just returned to Madrid after six months at Barbastro, wrote to John Cuerton in Bilbao to say that Robert Farnham, his agent, was about to join him, and asking whether Audrey had already sailed:

> Chaloner to Cuerton, 22 June, 1564.
> 1. Sends this foot post after his servant, Rob. Farnham, with letters, which he requires Cuerton to deliver him when Farnham comes to

Bilbao, for which he departed hence yesternight.—Madrid, 21 June
1564.
2. P.S.—Have Awdry's and my folks embarked?

A fortnight later Cuerton replied that Audrey had sailed,
accompanied by Farnham. (Portugalete was the port of Bilbao.)

Cuerton to Chaloner, 11 July, 1564.
On the 6th inst. James Conant sailed from Portugallette and
Mistress Adrea and the rest that came with her, and Farnham and
Harvy went with them.

Audrey's departure was then confirmed by a letter to Chaloner
from another English merchant living in Balboa.[22]
There is a further piece of indirect evidence about Audrey's
visit contained in the letter to Chaloner from his servant
Brackenbury, which is mentioned above. This letter, of July 1564,
mostly consists of an attack on Chaloner's brother Francis, and
it includes the following passage: 'I will prove he [Francis] hath
made more to do for your woman than any other, and of the
usage of your house, to the hearing of all that lists, as he feareth
she should be his hindrance.' The implication here is that Francis
was frightened that he would be disinherited if Chaloner went
ahead and married his 'woman'. And towards the end of the letter
the author disassociates himself from Francis's attitude: 'I never
have evil spoken of you for having her.'[23]
Audrey's visit is important because it probably means that
when she left Spain she was pregnant with Chaloner's son,
Thomas. There has been some debate about whether Thomas
Chaloner junior was actually Chaloner's son, or rather his
stepson. Clarence Miller was sure it was the latter because,
not being aware of Audrey's visit, he argued that there was no
possibility of Chaloner being the father since he was continuously

living in Spain from 1561 until 1565. Miller therefore deduced that Thomas junior must have been Audrey's son by a former marriage. However, Chaloner's brother Francis did later describe this son as a 'bastard', although, according to Miller, the word need not be taken literally.[24] Furthermore, in the documents we hear nothing of Audrey's married name, if indeed she had been married earlier (on all this, see also chapter 21).

The instigator of Audrey's visit was undoubtedly Chaloner himself. His earlier courtship activities and his concern to leave behind him an heir have already been mentioned, and recent illnesses would have helped to reinforce a keen sense of his own mortality. No doubt he planned to marry Audrey as soon as he got back to England and could arrange the wedding in a Protestant church. In fact, this is just what he did. There is no direct evidence of the wedding, but on the basis of a letter in the state papers one might conclude that it took place in October 1565. This letter, dated 20 November 1565, was from Richard Clough in Antwerp to William Phayre in Madrid, and states, 'Sir Thomas Chaloner [has] changed his life, being one month married.'[25]

There then arises the question of when the younger Thomas was born. Miller suggests 1561, but this is contradicted by the various dates of milestones in his life, such as his entry into grammar school and into Magdalen College, Oxford. In particular, the monument to him in the chancel of Chiswick church where he is buried states that 'the aforesaid Sir Thomas Chaloner died the 18th day of November 1615, being of the age of 51 years'. It is therefore likely that he was born towards the end of 1564, about a year before his father's death in October 1565.

20

SAILORS AND PIRATES
1563–1565

In the summer of 1563 a new crisis loomed up which was to engage much of Chaloner's time and energy. It was about the rivalry between Spain and England on the high seas, and it caused the unfortunate ambassador great stress until, a sick man, he eventually obtained his recall home. The crisis involved disputes over the Flanders trade as well as numerous aggressive incidents in which English freebooters attacked Spanish merchant shipping. This was labelled sheer wicked piracy by the Spanish and other nations, although later nationalistic British historians saw it in a different light. According to Froude, writing in the heyday of the empire, the attacks were

the first movements of the struggle which transferred from Spain to England the sovereignty of the seas; the first beginnings of that proud power which, rising out of the heart of the people, has planted the saplings of the English race in every quarter of the globe, has covered the ocean with its merchant fleets, and flaunts its flag in easy supremacy among the nations of the earth ... Piracy would be the very source and seed vessel from which the naval power of England was about to rise.[1]

During the summer and autumn of 1563, Chaloner received messages describing such events from his various contacts and agents:

Tipton to Chaloner, Seville, 26 June 1563.

Four days past came in a ship from the Indies from Puerto Rico, which at Cape St Vincent met with two small ships, who killed two or three of her men, and hurt divers, and robbed them of 3,000 pieces of money, ten chests of sugar, 200 great hides, and all their ordnance, cables, and anchors. The mariners say they were Englishmen, for that they shot so many arrows that they were not able to look out. They carried away the pilot of the Spanish ship. If they do more hurt, all the English goods here will be embargoed. I told them that they were Scots and Frenchmen, and some Englishmen amongst them, a sort of thieves gathered together to go a robbing.[2]

Cuerton to Chaloner, Bilbao, 15 Dec 1563.

All the country cry out upon the English men-of-war, for they have done great hurt to Spaniards. I know that within these three months they have taken, first, a French ship laden with linen cloth, most of the goods Spanish, to the value of 12,000 ducats, which should have come to this town; a French ship of war worth 7,000 ducats, with all Spanish goods; and two French ships which Stuckley took out of a port in Galicia, laden with Spanish goods worth 30,000 ducats. On this coast an English met a Spanish ship and hurt nine of her men. Here in Santander was one Phetipas with two ships of war; there came in a Spaniard laden with iron and rosin, which he took, and with seven or eight of his men went to sea with her and has been no more heard of.[3]

Stukeley and Phetipace were two of the more notorious 'pirates' and hate figures for the Spanish authorities and merchants. Thomas Stukeley, from a Devon gentry family, was a violent, untrustworthy and slippery egoist who had already carved out for himself a career as a mercenary soldier, happy to fight for the highest bidder. In June 1563 he told anyone who would listen, including the queen, that he intended to set up a colony in Florida. To advertise his project he staged a massive naval pageant on the Thames before enthusiastic crowds and the royal barge. There was a mock sea battle with 'infidels' in elaborate costumes, copious pyrotechnics, swordplay and buckets of phony blood. In spite of all this he did not get the financial backing he wanted, so he went to see the Spanish ambassador, Quadra, and hinted that he was thinking of transferring his allegiance to Spain. Quadra was sceptical and reported to Philip that 'he is not much to be trusted'. Eventually Stukeley did get some backing, including the loan of a ship from Elizabeth. He set sail for Florida from Plymouth with much fanfare, but actually proceeded to Ireland, where he set up a base for his piratical activities over the next two years. These were so successful that his name became notorious throughout Europe.[4]

The trouble was that during the civil war in France, in which Elizabeth had involved England, enterprising English sea captains could obtain from the government 'Letters of Marque' which gave them a legal right to attack any ships bearing a French flag, and some of them felt it unnecessary to distinguish carefully between different foreign nationalities. As Chaloner later tried to explain to an angry Philip, 'with more than 400 sail of adventurers serving during these wars at their own charges, which could not contain less than 20,000 or 30,000 mariners and soldiers, it was scarce possible among so many (what order soever the Queen took to the contrary) but some would in such a scope of the seas abroad play some lewd parts'.[5] Chaloner himself, of course, thoroughly disapproved of all such 'lewd' behaviour, which only made his job more difficult. Commenting on Stukeley in particular, he wrote to Cecil, 'Stuckley's activities are much railed at here, and I hang down my head in shame.'[6]

The Spanish authorities retaliated harshly against all English merchants trading with Spain. The king issued a proclamation prohibiting exports and imports to and from England. He also gave a strong incentive to informers and local corregidors[7] by awarding them a percentage of the value of any English ships and goods seized. In January 1564 Chaloner informed Elizabeth that 'a thousand mariners and others of our nation, with above thirty ships and goods, are arrested'.[8] It fell mainly to him to try and get justice for merchants who had lost everything, and for sailors experiencing intolerable conditions in Spanish gaols. He received information from his contacts up and down Spain, as well as numerous pathetic requests from shipowners and the prisoners themselves, and he pulled every string he could think of which might help them. As mentioned, he had an audience with the king, and he also tried to involve anyone influential that he knew, including the Count and Countess de Feria. But everywhere he came up against the delays and obfuscations of Spanish bureaucracy. Officials were never in a hurry to help, especially over issues that involved 'heretics'.

One particular case pushed Chaloner's patience to the limit, although it did turn out to be a rare success for him. It concerned a powerful Spanish nobleman, Alvaro de Bazan, who was himself a shipowner and naval commander.

Tipton to Chaloner, Seville, 8 Dec. 1563.
On the 15th Nov. eight English ships laden with wines, raisins, and almonds, &c., in the port of Gibraltar were ready to depart, when there came in a French ship of 100 tons, well armed and with many men, with all her banners and flags spread. One of the small English

ships laid her aboard, and they fought together, so that men were slain on both parts. The other ships (by reason of the much artillery shot off in the castle of Gibraltar) could not come to help their companion, and so the eight ships went out of the haven and there tarried for a wind, and the Frenchmen remained still in the port. In the meantime came Don Alvaro de Bazan with his galleys from Cadiz to take the English ships, and they obeyed him without resistance; and so he brought them to Cadiz, and put all the masters and part of the mariners into the galleys in chains, and handled them very evil, and put other men on board the ships, and took the English banners and hanged them out at the stern of the galleys, dragging them along in the water, as though they had taken their enemies; and all because they fought with the Frenchmen within the port; and the Frenchmen they did not meddle with. With this there goes a testimonial, taken by the merchants in Gibraltar. I desire that you speak to the King in their behalf; and if he will not put them at liberty, that he will name some Alcade de Corte in Seville who may be judge in this cause.[9]

Chaloner did his best for the sailors seized at Gibraltar even though he felt they were partly to blame by their rash actions. He wrote to them, 'Ye served some angry saint so inadvisedly to take such an enterprise in hand in these parts where our nation findeth so short courtesy; and ye played the part of wavering inconstant heads, having once begun a matter to suffer yourselves so vilely to be taken, which if ye had held together I think ye needed not.'

By the following June over forty of these sailors out of the 240 originally imprisoned were said to have died through 'evil treatment' in prison. The main cause of death was disease, largely brought on by lack of food. It seems that foreigners in Spanish prisons received a diet exclusively composed of bread and water. However, largely through Chaloner's efforts, it was eventually reported that by order of Philip's leading minister, the Duke of Alva, the sailors were to be released. After seven months they were free, though 'most of them came forth in that sort that if they had tarried but eight days longer half of them would have followed their fellows'.[10]

This was only one case among several that Chaloner had to deal with. He spent hours and days communicating with those arrested, badgering members of Philip's court and forwarding depositions, pleas, and statements of evidence to Philip's secretary Erazzo. He also managed to secure two audiences with the king himself, neither of which got him very far. At the first Philip was non-committal, merely promising that his council 'would peruse' the Gibraltar case and that it was to be remitted to a judge in Seville to deal with. At the second meeting he took the offensive, saying that 'having been informed of the spoils committed upon them [the Spanish] by the English on the sea during the wars with France, he has been moved to proceed to this arrest by way of reprisal'.[11]

Chaloner sent Elizabeth and Cecil regular reports about what he was trying to do, but received back little support or even comment. In these matters he was on his own. He clearly took this aspect of his job very seriously, because at one point he was given permission to quit Spain and return home but decided he could not leave with so many unresolved issues pending. In fact, he had hoped to embark from Bilbao with Audrey Frodsham in July 1564, but as it turned out she had to leave without him.

Chaloner's response to this crisis was remarkable considering the state of his health and the obstacles put in his way. The ambassador who succeeded him, Dr John Man, was less troubled about the fate of imprisoned sailors, and there are few records in the state papers about him trying to help them. Maritime disputes between Spain and England, of course, did not disappear. In fact they became steadily worse. Many of the English pirates were now starting to turn their attention to the New World, and one of them was John Hawkins, who got in touch with Chaloner shortly after his first voyage to the Caribbean. Hawkins had managed to acquire 300 slaves in Sierra Leone and then sell them to the Spanish merchants of Santo Domingo. He then invested his profits in a return cargo of hides which he instructed his second-in-command, Thomas Hampton, to try and sell in Cadiz. However, when Philip heard about Hawkins' voyage he ordered the cargo be seized. Chaloner, in the midst of trying to deal with Spanish bureaucracy, was asked to intervene, but refused, telling Hawkins that 'it was an ill time for obtaining any suit' due to the strong feelings in Spain against English adventurers, especially in what was considered Spanish territory. He also wrote to Elizabeth, 'Our folks must be narrowly looked to, and specially that they enterprise no trade or voyage to the Indies or islands of this king's navigation; which if they do, as already they have intelligence of some that do propose it, surely it will breed occasion of much matter of pique.'[12]

Long after Chaloner's death it was the activities of Hawkins and Francis Drake which, among other causes, finally led to open war with Spain and the defeat of the Spanish Armada.

21

RETIREMENT AND AN HEIR
1565

A few months after Audrey Frodsham's departure from Spain, rumours of her visit had clearly reached some of Chaloner's friends in England. One of them wrote reprovingly, 'I can be content you use the company of Eve now and then, but take heed of gluttony.'[1] However, the warning was quite superfluous because Chaloner, now back in Madrid, was more ill than ever and in no condition to seek the consolations of Eve. He wrote to Jane, Countess de Feria, whom he had planned to visit, 'I am now a confirmed invalid and cannot visit you at Zafra,' and to another friend, 'I am so weak I cannot ride.'[2]

He continued to send letters begging for his recall:

I have been three years in Spain and am so sickly that I can scarce put pen to paper. It is a great oversight of my Lords at home to have no young men trained up under the older to serve the state. Next Christmas shall be the sixth I am abroad and I have never had one letter of thanks from the Queen. She should in any case revoke me on account of my sickness.[3]

Evidently at the height of depression, Chaloner also wrote to Sir Ambrose Cave, an old friend who was related to Cecil. He clearly hoped that Cave, with his powerful connections at court, might put in a word for him:

> Surely I have had great wrong, but it is the old wont of our court never to think upon the training of a new servant till the old be worn to the stump. It is each man's part to serve their prince; but there is a just distributing, if subjects durst plead with kings. I have not much more to hope, having twenty years served four kings, now further from wealth or that staff of age which youth doth travail for, than I was eighteen years agone. Methinks I became a retrograde crab, and yet would gladly be at home with that that yet resteth, to pay my debts and live the rest of my life perhaps contentedly enough.[4]

As mentioned above, he did eventually receive permission to quit his post and return home, but this was at the height of his battle to save the hundreds of sailors and others who were in Spanish prisons or who, having been released from prison, had no money and no means of getting home. Chaloner felt he could not abandon them and he stayed out of compassion; Audrey Frodsham had to leave without him. This was perhaps his most generous deed during the course of a long career in government service.

By the autumn of 1564 he had achieved the promised release of at least some of the imprisoned sailors, but his health had deteriorated still further. He renewed his pleas for immediate recall and it was at this stage that he added the queen's favourite Sir Robert Dudley to the list of influential people who might possibly help him. He wrote Dudley a rather fulsome, fawning letter reminding him of 'that Noble Duke your father's favour towards me'[5] and adding that 'your noble gentleness has won of me a determinate mind to desire the continuance of my bond from the father to the son'. He begged in conclusion, 'Your rider is ready to depart, set in your hand and favour that I be kept here no longer.' It seems that this plea, or others, finally worked, and once again Chaloner was sent his revocation. This time there was no hesitation; he took leave of Philip on 26 February and said goodbye to Madrid on 2 March, leaving William Phayre in charge. In a letter to Elizabeth, Philip praised the retiring ambassador 'for his skill in conducting affairs'. It was also reported that he gave Chaloner, as a parting gift, a horse (which he would never ride), as well as a licence to take out of the country four horses for himself and twelve for the queen.[6]

Exhausted and ill, Chaloner 'embarked from St Sebastian in a ship of Lyme' on 28 April. He was accompanied by an old steward of his, Roger Hooker, who had come out from England to bring him home. They arrived after an exceptionally quick passage of four days, and Hooker took him to stay in his home at Exeter to recover from the journey. They then proceeded to London by easy stages, arriving at Chaloner's Clerkenwell home to be greeted by Audrey and her six-month-old son, Thomas.

When he returned to his house Chaloner must have known he had not long to live. One of the first things he did was to make a new will. When he heard about this, his brother Francis was very angry. Robert Turton takes up the story:

Francis was wild at the thought that the possessions to which, or at least to part of which, he expected to succeed, should slip from his grasp. In a scurrilous letter actuated by his disappointment at the frustration of his hopes he described the hasty summoning of a scrivener on the morning of Saturday, 25th July, and the execution of a will devising all Sir Thomas' lands to the 'bastard' only, and bequeathing all his goods to the 'danderly', by which opprobrious terms he referred to the younger Sir Thomas and Lady Chaloner respectively.[7]

Over the next couple of months Chaloner felt able to conduct a little business, probably from his bed. We know, for instance, that he helped his other brother, John, obtain a lease of mining rights in Ireland – a project John had been pursuing for several years.[8] At last, most likely in mid-October, there took place the long-anticipated marriage between Audrey Frodsham and Sir Thomas Chaloner. It seems that one of his friends in particular, John Jewel, Bishop of Salisbury, had been instrumental in urging him to marry before it was too late. There is no official record of this marriage. As Chaloner was then on his death bed it was most probably granted under licence from the Archbishop of Canterbury, but the relevant records for that year are missing. As mentioned above, the only evidence as to when he married is in the letter from Clough in Antwerp to Phayre.[9]

Since the legal situation regarding Audrey and her son had now altered, and because there was the strong possibility that Francis might start litigation against the July will, it was now thought necessary to make a new settlement which could not be challenged in the courts. This involved two indentures made on 11 October between Chaloner and a group of seven of his closest friends, headed by Sir William Cecil and including Sir William Petre and Sir John Mason. The indentures made over all Chaloner's lands and property to these men as trustees, and gave them directions as to how to proceed after his death. The lengthy will itself, which has been transcribed in full by Miller, repeats and forms 'a sort of appendix' to these earlier indentures.[10]

This settlement was much the same as the July will which had so angered Francis. It made plentiful provision for Audrey during her lifetime, including the house in Clerkenwell, and it left most of Chaloner's estate to the baby Thomas when he should come of age. Audrey was given full charge of her son up to the age of six, but after that Cecil was to play the major role in decisions about the boy's education, for which money was set aside. There were numerous bequests to servants, the largest being to Roger Hooker, who had brought Sir Thomas home from Spain, and to Chaloner's chief agent, Robert Farnham. A striking feature of the will, however, was that there was no mention at all of his two brothers, John and Francis, although there were small bequests to John's son, Thomas, and to Francis's wife, Agnes.

No legal challenge to these arrangements arose afterwards since Francis was fully occupied in a long-drawn-out lawsuit involving the heirs of his father-in-law, Sir William Bowyer. In the event, Francis died within a few months of his brother, no doubt much to the relief of Cecil and the other trustees.

Chaloner died the day after signing his will. We might well ask, what was the actual cause of his death? Any medical pronouncement must of course be supposition, but from the few phrases he wrote about the nature of his illnesses when he was in Spain it is possible to suggest a tentative diagnosis. He referred more than once to 'quartans' or 'tertian agues'. These would have been intense periods of fever, involving shaking and high sweat, suffered at regular intervals, each attack lasting perhaps a day or two. They were a clear symptom of malaria. At some time in his life Chaloner must have been bitten by an *Anopheles* mosquito which injected the malarial parasite into his bloodstream. Mosquitoes do not usually breed in the British Isles, so this was probably when he was abroad in a hotter climate. It could have been when he was aged twenty-one and took part in Charles V's disastrous expedition against the pirates of Algiers. However, because he does not mention any such feverish attacks in letters written before he went to Spain, it is more likely he contracted the disease in that country.

Malaria, however, while highly debilitating, is unlikely to kill. The most obvious cause of his death, therefore, is renal failure brought on by stones in the kidneys. This was Vesalius's diagnosis, although his remedy, a 'decoction of liquorice and barley', would hardly have been effective. Kidney stones are normally the result of an excess of calcium carbonate which builds up in the kidneys, and this in turn might be due to environmental factors such as drinking water (or wine) containing large amounts of calcium. There may, too, have been a genetic predisposition in Chaloner's case since his father is also said to have died of 'calculus renium'. Today renal failure is dealt with by regular dialysis, which removes waste products from the blood, and in extreme cases by kidney transplant, but in the sixteenth century no effective cure was known.[11]

In his will Chaloner left the disposal of his body to his executors, with the proviso that the funeral arrangements should have 'due regard of my estate and calling'. He did receive a sumptuous funeral with Cecil as chief mourner, and he was buried in St Paul's Cathedral. On his monument was erected a brass plate with a Latin inscription by his friend Walter Haddon. Unfortunately, the monument was destroyed in the Great Fire of London a century later, and the brass plate has disappeared. However, the inscription has survived and is reproduced in Chaloner's *De republica Anglorum*:

Natura Thomas Chalonerus, & arte valebat,
Vtilis & patriae vir fuit ille suae.
Publica cum magna suscepit munera laude,
Laude pari libros scripserat ille domi.
Sic patriae vixit magno, dum vixit, honore,
Sic patriae magno concidit ille malo.[12]

Audrey did not remain a widow for long, marrying Edward Brockett of Wheathampstead, Hertfordshire, by whom she had seven children. She died in 1605. Cecil conscientiously undertook the duties with which his friend had entrusted him. He sent Thomas junior to St Paul's School and, in due course, when Thomas was about fifteen, secured a place for him at Magdalen College, Oxford.[13] Cecil also engaged a well-known scholar, William Malim, to edit and publish all Chaloner's extant Latin poems, including his magnum opus, *De republica Anglorum*. Malim had earlier been a rather severe headmaster of Eton College, and he had become high master of St Paul's at the time Thomas junior was a pupil there.

Thomas Chaloner junior went on to have a career just as successful as his father's. He gravitated towards the court faction of Sir Robert Dudley, now the Earl of Leicester, even though it was opposed to that of his guardian, William Cecil. When Leicester was appointed governor-general of the Netherlands by Elizabeth, Thomas went with him, and this was the start of much travelling abroad, especially in Italy. He fought at the siege of Rouen and was rewarded with a knighthood by the King of France, Henry IV. At a later point he worked as a foreign agent for the Earl of Essex, sending him information from Florence. However, when Essex fell from power and was tried and executed for rebellion, Thomas avoided being implicated. Here he proved himself the worthy son of a father who had managed to survive through the stormy politics of four reigns.

A particular achievement of the second Sir Thomas Chaloner was to become close to James VI of Scotland even before James inherited the throne of England on the death of Elizabeth. This led to the new king entrusting him with the guardianship of his elder son, Prince Henry. Thomas was in charge of the prince's large and expensive household, which became virtually a new court in its own right. By the time of his unexpected death at the age of eighteen, in 1612, Henry, supported by Thomas, was showing himself to be a young man of energy and taste, interested in a wide range of topics, from exploration to Italian art.

Henry's death was the end of Thomas's career as an administrator and courtier, and he retired to the Steeple Claydon estate in Buckinghamshire that he had inherited from his father. He now had time to develop another interest – one which he hoped would make him rich. This was to set up an alum mine and refinery on his Guisborough estate in North Yorkshire. The potential of local alum shale deposits in this area had probably first been noticed by his cousin Thomas from Ireland, the son of John Chaloner, and in about 1607 Thomas Chaloner junior went into partnership with neighbouring landowners, securing a thirty-one-year monopoly of alum manufacture in the north of England. However, the venture was not particularly successful, and eventually Thomas and his partners were bought out by the Crown in return for annuities which in fact were never fully paid.[14]

Thomas married twice, producing in total some eighteen children. Like his father before him, he was beset by money problems towards the end of his life. He sold his property at St Bees, but his eldest son, William, who was created a baronet, inherited Guisborough and also Steeple Claydon. Sir William died without an heir, and it is from the next brother, Edward, that the Chaloners of Guisborough are descended.[15]

22

THE NEW AMBASSADOR

For a year after Chaloner's departure, English diplomacy in Spain was managed by William Phayre as *chargé d'affaires* until another ambassador could be found. Phayre, who spoke Spanish fluently and was probably a Catholic, was a long-standing member of the English community in Spain. He had already helped Chaloner, for instance, by finding him a suitable house when he travelled from Madrid to join Philip's court at Monzon in Aragon. The other certain fact we know about Phayre is that many years later, when he was living in England, he was charged with treason for being part of some kind of conspiracy against the queen. In the calendar of state papers there is a summary of a pathetic letter from him admitting guilt and begging for his life:

Wm Phayre (A prisoner in the Tower) to Lord Burghley, 25 Nov. 1577.

Details his intrigues with the Spaniards, for which he is now justly lying under sentence of death. Begs, however, that his life may be spared in order that he may henceforth devote it to the promotion of her Majesty's interests. His qualifications for so doing are as follows: credit with the Spanish nation – none better of an Englishman; the like with papists within the land; sufficient experience to practise according to any of his lordship's instructions; acquaintance with the humours and conditions of the Spaniards, Italians, and Frenchmen; languages; not ignorant in the liberal sciences; with other virtues of the mind which he would use with all fidelity and diligence. Little can his death profit, which is his great grief, whereas if it were his lordship's pleasure that he might be employed and live, both his spirit and his heart promise to his country good service.[1]

Phayre's plea was unsuccessful, and he was executed shortly afterwards.

In April 1566 a new ambassador finally arrived at Madrid to take up his duties. John Man has been a controversial figure, both for his contemporaries and for modern historians. Garrett Mattingley had this to say about him: 'Among English ambassadors perhaps the outstanding example of the emissary of bad-will was Dr John Man, Dean of Gloucester. Just why Elizabeth and Cecil thought that a bigoted Protestant divine, without tact or breeding, would prove a successful representative at that ticklish point in Anglo-Spanish relations is a mystery ... No other English diplomat gave quite as effective a demonstration of sturdy prejudice as Dr Man.'[2] More recently, however, Dr Man's reputation has been partly vindicated. Gary Bell has researched his background and his time as ambassador. His conclusion is that in fact Man was a suitable choice, and that whatever went wrong during his three years in office was on the whole not his fault.[3]

In the first place, Man was exceptionally well educated. He had an MA from New College, Oxford, and had lectured on Greek at Oxford. He had also translated and published at least one Latin text into English. In other words, he was a fully qualified humanist scholar. He was also a fluent speaker of Italian and had most likely studied in that country as a young man. Before arriving in Spain – at the age of fifty-four – he had pursued a fairly successful career in government service which had been rewarded with various lands and sinecures. For patronage he looked to Matthew Parker, Elizabeth's first Archbishop of Canterbury, and it was probably Parker who recommended him to Cecil as a suitable ambassador. Just previous to his appointment he had been made Dean of Gloucester Cathedral, so that he had an adequate income for the likely extra expenses of the new post.

The problem was that Dr Man was neither a courtier nor a knight. The Spanish court was excessively status-conscious, and in their eyes Man did not match up to his predecessors, Chamberlain and Chaloner. For Spaniards, academic achievement was an inadequate substitute for social standing. William Phayre, who seems to have taken against Man early on, described him in a letter to Cecil as not 'de la qualidad de los passados'.[4] Also, it was rumoured that he was a married priest, a status that Catholics found abhorrent. Actually, in spite of being a dean he had never taken holy orders. It was true that he was, or had been, married, and he brought his young son to Madrid with him.

Man seems to have started off his stint as ambassador quite well. He was cautious not to offend his hosts' religious feelings. For instance, it was noted by the papal legate that he was very respectful when a religious procession bearing the holy sacrament passed by his house. Apparently, too, he became a good friend of Philip's French wife, Elizabeth of Valois. However, he made two mistakes which led to important people becoming his enemies. The Count de Feria, because he had lived for many years in England and had an English wife, was seen as the patron of the English expatriate community. Feria had got on well with Chaloner, but during Man's first year an issue arose concerning the relatives that Jane, Feria's wife, had left in England. The count felt they were not being treated with respect and he blamed Elizabeth and also Dr Man for their lack of support. The new ambassador's second mistake was that he did not employ as agents certain members of the English community, such as William Phayre and a certain Robert Hogan, who were accustomed to being paid for their advice on Spanish affairs. The net result was a concerted campaign to undermine Man. He was said to be socially awkward and uncouth, to employ too few servants, and not to know how to treat the guests who came to his house. According to Gary Bell, historians have misjudged Man because they have been too reliant on Hogan's vitriolic attacks. For example:

> Robert Hogan to William Phayre, 20 Feb. 1568.
> Wishes Mr. Man were called hence; he doth but dishonour the Queen and shame the country. There is no ambassador in so little estimation as he is since he misbehaved himself unto the Count de Feria, who always was a faithful friend to all Englishmen, and at this day the King remits all matters of England to him. Man is taken to be meeter to sow sedition than to maintain amity, he is of so simple a judgement and small understanding.[5]

Philip II, too, fully accepted this view of Dr Man. At this time the king was becoming more and more preoccupied with the growth of Protestant opposition to his rule in Flanders, and he was inclining to the view that heresy was a dangerous and contagious disease that threatened the health of nations and governments as well as the Church universal. Consequently, he was prepared to listen to those who told him that heretics, whoever they were, should be isolated so as not to contaminate others. As regards the English ambassador, Philip first gave orders that he was not to be allowed to hold Protestant services at the embassy and that all his servants must attend the local Catholic church. He followed this up by banning Man from Madrid and insisting that he live in a small village some way outside the city. This of course meant that he could not pursue his diplomatic functions and attend the Spanish court. When Elizabeth heard about his treatment she saw it as an insult to her honour and recalled him to England. He fell ill during the journey and had to be brought by litter to Windsor for an audience with the queen. She exonerated him from any blame and wrote to Philip to say that her ambassador was a 'very learned and worthy individual' who had been unfairly libelled by the English exiles in Madrid.[6]

During Man's three years in office relations between England and Spain deteriorated steadily. This was partly owing to continued disputes over trade and piracy, and partly because Philip was facing new demands by his Dutch subjects for independence. This, coupled with a revolt of the Moriscos[7] in Granada, meant that the king felt himself increasingly threatened by the growth of heresy throughout his dominions, and he blamed Elizabeth in particular for fomenting unrest in the Netherlands. In 1567 another event occurred which brought England and Spain closer to open war. This was the arrival of Philip's leading general, the Duke of Alva, in Brussels with an army of 10,000. It was seen by Elizabeth and Cecil as a major threat, since once Alva had pacified the Netherlands there was little to stop him turning his attention to England, the land from which the heresy was thought to originate. Alva's arrival has been called 'one of the turning points of western European history'[8] because it led directly to the revolt of the Netherlands, and ultimately to the collapse of Spain as a major European power. The episode involving the unfortunate Dr Man merely contributed to the growing international tension. After 1568 no more resident ambassadors were sent from England to Spain until the following century.

CONCLUSION

A SUPPLICATION

FORGET not yet the tried intent
Of such a truth as I have meant,
My great travail so gladly spent,
  Forget not yet!

Forget not yet when first began
The weary life ye know, since whan
The suit, the service none can tell;
  Forget not yet!

Forget not yet the great assays,
The cruel wrong, the scornful ways,
The painful patience in delays,
  Forget not yet!

Forget not! O, forget not this,
How long ago hath been, and is

The mind that never meant amiss –
> Forget not yet!

Forget not thine own approved
The which so long hath thee so loved,
Whose steadfast faith yet never moved –
> Forget not this!

These verses are by Sir Thomas Wyatt, the most celebrated poet of the age of Sir Thomas Chaloner. But the narrator of the poem could well have been Chaloner himself as his years of devoted service to his queen, and also his life, drew towards their close. 'Scornful ways' and 'painful delays' were just what he experienced during his years of 'great travail' while serving his country as Elizabeth's resident ambassador in Spain. Truly Chaloner's motto might well have been what he once wrote in a letter to Cecil: *'non nobis nati sumus sed patriae.'*[1] Although Wyatt was considerably older than Chaloner, the two had much in common. Both were at one time clients of Thomas Cromwell, both once served as ambassadors in Spain, and both were prolific and experimental poets. When Wyatt died in 1542, Chaloner, then aged twenty-two, wrote an elegy for him.

Sir Thomas Chaloner's life was short by modern standards, but extremely active. His career might perhaps be divided into two parts: first, his rapid rise to an important position in the Tudor courtly and diplomatic hierarchy; second, his years as an ambassador at the court of Philip II, in Flanders and then in Spain.

Not long after university the young Chaloner achieved a position of considerable status (though not the very highest). This was initially due to help from his father, but then to his own hard work and talents. His employers found him to be reliable, cautious and conscientious, and his humanistic and literary qualities were highly valued in the milieu to which he aspired. Also, his command of modern languages qualified him above many others. Once he gained the coveted position of secretary to the Privy Council there was no stopping him. He was increasingly entrusted with important and delicate missions, especially in Scotland and France.

In his introduction to *The Mirror for Magistrates*, William Baldwin seems to imply that there was considerable luck involved in how some had successful careers while others fell by the wayside. He referred to the 'slippery deceits' of Fortune, that 'wavering Lady'. One has a mental picture of ambitious politicians crowded together, all trying to maintain their balance on Fortune's whirling wheel, the unlucky ones falling off while others held their position. This image is particularly appropriate for the twists and turns of policy that took place in the four reigns during which Chaloner succeeded in keeping his footing.

There was, however, one aspect of this slippery contest which Baldwin fails to mention. Those who fell off the wheel did not merely slip – they had to be pushed. To succeed at the highest level in Tudor times one had to show ruthless determination, even if this meant abandoning former friends and patrons. It was Stephen Gardiner who headed the 1540 legation in which the young Chaloner was given the chance of his first experience of foreign diplomacy, but Chaloner was among those who subsequently testified against Gardiner at his trial for treason. It was the Protector Somerset who knighted Chaloner after the Battle of Pinkie Cleugh, as a result of which he was able to marry a wealthy heiress, become a Member of Parliament and start to acquire landed estates. However, we later hear of Chaloner reading out to Londoners a proclamation concerning 'the very truth of the Duke of Somerset's evil government'. Not so long afterwards, Somerset was executed for treason. Chaloner, it seems, did not lack the ruthlessness needed for survival in this world. In Tudor times this was a crucial quality for those anywhere near the top of the tree. How many whom Chaloner knew personally ended their lives on the block? A quick survey has to include

Thomas Cromwell, Henry Norris, John Fisher, John Cheke, Thomas Seymour, possibly Jane Grey, and the dukes of Somerset and Northumberland.

In this context it should also be remembered that Chaloner did not allow his own beliefs to prevent him from serving the Catholic Queen Mary, as he had previously served the ultra-Protestant Somerset and the more moderate Protestant Northumberland. Actually, there are few indications of Chaloner's personal religious beliefs, which he knew how to keep to himself. No doubt the traumatic changes that took place in Henry VIII's reign while he was growing up taught him to be careful about that. It is, however, fair to assume that as an adult he inclined towards Protestantism, or he would hardly have supported in print Henry's dissolution of the monasteries or published a eulogy on Lady Jane Grey. However, he made sure both these works only saw the light of day after the death of Mary.[2] Five years later, in a comment on the Catholics in France, he wrote to Cecil, 'For these thirty years I never was so weary of this preposterous religion as now.'[3] It is interesting, too, that the authors whose Latin works were picked by Chaloner to translate into English – Erasmus, Cousin, Boethius, Chrysostom – had all been seen by many during their lifetimes as rebels or heretics. Perhaps Chaloner himself would like to have been a rebel against all established religion, but of course he was far too cautious.

From 1559 onwards Chaloner was a resident ambassador at the court of Philip II, first in Flanders and then for three and a half years in Spain. His reports and letters during this period show his growing disillusionment with his role, and also with the conditions under which he served. He made numerous complaints, ranging from the weather and the cost of living in Madrid to the lack of contact with England, the irregularity of his diets and the difficulty of dealing with the inflexible Spanish bureaucracy. Miller describes many of his letters as containing 'a sort of stylized whine',[4] which seems to have been typical of resident ambassadors in general, both English and foreign, at this time. But this is not to say that Chaloner's complaints were unjustified. It appears he was not very well treated by William Cecil, his superior in London and his friend from university days or soon after. Cecil kept him short of the latest news, and for a long time failed to listen when he begged to be allowed to come home.

The main trouble was, however, that resident ambassadors were relatively new arrivals on the diplomatic scene, and the rules for their conduct were not yet generally agreed between the nations. There was, for instance, no clear concept of diplomatic immunity, and this was particularly awkward when it came to relations between England and Spain with their mutually hostile ideologies. Chaloner was undoubtedly the right man for the job, and he played his part with restraint and tolerance. Yet the stresses he encountered ultimately took their toll, especially in view of his increasing sickness. This, too, was a constant theme of his letters. It might be easy to label him a hypochondriac, except that his death within months of coming home contradicts that verdict.

Yet, in spite of all his troubles, Chaloner was a successful ambassador. One has only to compare him with the three other ambassadors discussed in this book. There was Throckmorton, who was imprisoned by the French authorities; de Quadra, suspected of plotting against his hosts and humiliated by being turned out of his residence; and Man, who got on the wrong side of Philip II and was forced to quit his Madrid embassy. Chaloner, however, managed to remain on good terms with both Philip and Elizabeth. There is little doubt that if he had not been bedridden on his final return home he would have been invited to court to be congratulated, and perhaps promoted.

It remains to mention again his writing, which his literary friends probably saw as his chief claim to fame. Chaloner was pre-eminently a Christian humanist in the tradition of Erasmus,

Ascham and Cheke, and as a young adult he spent much of his leisure translating from Latin into English. His proclaimed aim here was the admirable one of gaining a wider readership for works he considered important. Although steeped in the classics, he avoided using terms derived from Latin when he could find an Anglo-Saxon equivalent. However, he was also a man who was clearly in love with words, not to mention the occasional extravagant metaphor. When it came to writing letters to his humanist friends his style is often elaborate and sometimes opaque, with a scattering of Latin phrases. In this context I cannot resist finally quoting an excerpt from a letter to Cecil about a shipwreck that drowned numbers of French soldiers en route to Scotland. It makes one wonder whether even Cecil always fully grasped what Chaloner was trying to say:

> The Spaniards at Brussels be sorry for the news. The loss is esteemed of no less moment than an overthrow by land. If hope might allow men to sit idle, we might suppose the French undertake this enterprise *diis malis* [on evil days]. Nevertheless let us provide as if every Frenchman were two; so the best will save itself: and trust we none but God and ourselves. For if I were God, I would swear by myself that I believe our trust is in God's defence only, and by Him, in our foresight; so our professed enemies and faint friends instead of cartels of defiance will send us solemn letters of congratulation. – Otherwise *vae victis* [woe to the conquered]. Stick not at money where life and liberty hangeth in the balance; England well used were a better cow to give milk than all Italy.[5]

As regards the Latin verse Chaloner composed later when he was in Spain, I am unfortunately, as I mentioned before, hardly the person to judge its merits. Given that Latin is such a difficult language, it might seem strange to us that he found the composition of Latin verses a relaxation from his duties as ambassador. But Latin in Chaloner's day was the medium in which educated people from different nations throughout the western world communicated with each other. His major Latin work, *De republica Anglorum*, has to this day never been translated into English, but when it was eventually published it impressed the small elite who read it, many of whom had probably been his friends or acquaintances.[6] It was William Cecil, now Lord Burghley, who organised the publication of this work several years after Chaloner's death, and who also composed a moving tribute to his friend, the former ambassador, as a foreword:

TO OUR DESCENDANTS IN LONG HEREAFTER AGES

WILLIAM LORD BURGHLEY, TREASURER OF ENGLAND,
TO THE MEMORY OF SIR THOMAS CHALONER,
on his return from his Embassy in Spain, and departure to the
celestial shores of the blessèd.

Just causes have I to cherish you in loving memory though now gone from our sight: aye, weighty reasons! That friendship betwixt us from our green youth, when first the Royal Court united us; those questions of State, that pressure of public care, those duties of Ambassador which you performed abroad while I at home kept watch over this Kingdom's course.

Since such have been the bonds between us, 'tis very just that when you mounted to the stars you should have entrusted to our good faith your wife, your son, and servants, and all of yours to be protected. Thus rightly upon me had lain the due fulfilment of your prayer.

Now your last born child – offspring of genius, fruit of deep thought when public affairs were tempered by the studious Muses – is at last to be led upon the Stage of Life.

When Death, envious of the great, cast jealous glance upon your glory, my undimmed love has moved me to commit to the care of

Malim that dear work, in eloquence more polished and than gold more precious.

And so your friends may willingly welcome this memorial of your genius; and the whole world may look upon these pledges, wherein shines the sacred glory of our English race. By this let the world discern that you were worthy of a command at the wars, worthy to serve your Princes, worthy of a name that shall overcome Time; let it recognise you as deserving of the threefold preferments. [i.e. as soldier, ambassador and poet.]

These few verses have I made as proof, never to be forgotten, that in my mind you yet live; witnesses that our attachments shall for ever endure.

Thus to our descendants, who shall flourish in long hereafter ages, to whosoever amongst them values conscientiousness, foresight, and true manliness, will I testify that all such graces, divided by others, were united in Chaloner.[7]

Appendix I
SIR THOMAS CHALONER'S ESTATES

As mentioned in chapter 15, Chaloner, as compared with many
of his courtly and diplomatic contemporaries, was never a
rich man. True, he owned many acres of land and was paid
rent and various fees by numerous tenants up and down the
country. But while he was abroad he found it difficult to look
after his estates. In particular, he could not profit directly from
his land by stocking it with sheep or cattle but had to rent it
out to others instead. Furthermore, his estates at St Bees and
Guisborough were held of the Crown in fee farm, which meant
a considerable portion of his annual income from rents went to
the Exchequer. At his death this tax amounted to £259 11s 6d
annually out of a total income of £482 8s 10¼d for these two
estates. He paid no fee for Steeple Claydon, which appears to
have been freehold, but for all his estates he had also, especially
when he was abroad, to pay the salaries of rent collectors,
bailiffs and agents. Taking all this into consideration, his total
clear annual income from land at his death in 1565 came to
£352 12s 6¼d[1] Little wonder that he tried more than once to

persuade Cecil and Elizabeth to reduce his fees to the Exchequer, although with little effect.[2]

Between 1559 and 1565, when Chaloner was mostly living abroad, there were many disputes between his various tenants and agents which must have caused him considerable stress as he was not on the spot to deal with them. Here are two examples, the first from his Guisborough agent:

John Rudyard to Chaloner, 28 August 1563.
Whereas you did direct me not to suffer John Martin and others to have anything to do or come with any carriage within your ground of Carlinghow, the said John, on the 28th inst., came, aided with eight of your tenants, to carry away the tithe as well as the rent corn, which he said he had bought of Robert Farnham. I, however, resisted them. I now desire that you will direct your servants and tenants to aid me; and also that Farnham shall not let Martin have any interest in the said rent corn.[3]

The second example is clearly part of a long-running and complicated dispute. The letter is from Chaloner's agent in St Bees, James Grindal, who is described as 'clerk'. He was very likely the vicar of St Bees, and the brother of Edmund Grindal, who was born in that parish and was later Archbishop of Canterbury. The letter is interesting as it mentions two important local products: coal and also salt, which was either mined or evaporated from seawater using nearby coal deposits.

James Gryndall, clerk to Chaloner. 5 April 1564.
1. I have sent a letter to your factors concerning your business at St Bees, and willed them to show it you at your coming home. I caution you to give no credence to Lacy, who causes you to spend much money. Because I would not suffer him to have all the coals within your lordship of St Bees, (for which he said he should pay

no rent), by counsel of James Skelton he took your old friend Henry Curwen to be first in commission, but I, having a friend in the same commission that would not consent to Curwen's doings, he has given over to call the commissioners to sit.

2. I have got a grove in the brode whynes which will serve me for long time, and I got eleven score sceppes of coylles [measures of coal] for my pans when there was never a coylle to be gotten in all the lordship for them; and there are in the garner by estimation 200 straks of salt that came of the said coals. When Lacy saw that I had gotten such a grove he sued me to York before the Council, trusting to get it into his possession ere you came home, but he failed.[4]

St Oswalds

The descent of this ex-monastic property was as follows. It was granted to Sir Thomas Leigh as a reward for his participation in the Dissolution. On his death in 1544 he left the estate to his nephew and namesake, Thomas Leigh, who sold it in 1555 back to Sir Thomas Leigh's widow, Joan, who by this date was married to Chaloner. On Joan's death a few months later, it passed to her daughter, Katherine, who subsequently married James, Lord Mountjoy. Always short of capital for his unsuccessful mining projects, Mountjoy first mortgaged the property and then sold it to his wife's uncle by marriage, Sir Thomas Gargrave. From him it ultimately passed to the Winn family. In 1733 Sir Rowland Winn commissioned a Palladian house near the site of the old priory. The estate, now named Nostell Priory, is presently owned by the National Trust.[5]

Guisborough

Chaloner acquired his estate in and around Guisborough in three stages. Firstly, in 1547, he was given a long lease of various lands previously belonging to Guisborough Priory at a rent of £49 per annum to the Crown. Then, in 1550, he was allowed to buy the same lands for £998, a sum which he paid off over the next eight years. Finally, in 1558, he was granted the manor of Guisborough with further lands. Unfortunately, however, this last grant involved a large annual payment. The manor and lands were to be held '*in capite*, by the service of the fortieth part of one knight's fee, and by paying therefore yearly to us [and] the heirs and successors of us the aforementioned Queen [Mary], a hundred and thirty-five pounds, fifteen shillings, four pence and one farthing'.[6]

Chaloner visited Guisborough rarely – perhaps only once in his life. He did visit in May 1552, when his accounts show that he travelled to York from Carlisle, went shopping, and then moved on to Guisborough. On this occasion he probably stayed several nights because, as shown in his accounts, he paid out gratuities to two different households for his keep:

> given at Gisburgh to Sir Edmund Carter's wife for my table
> there in reward xx s., to her maids iii s. iiii d., to Anthony
> Wycleffes maids vi s. viii d.   xxx s.

Sir Thomas Chaloner junior must certainly have visited Guisborough regularly in connection with his alum project, and may even have resided there after he retired from court life following the death of Prince Henry in 1612. However, it was not until after the Restoration that a descendant, the Edward Chaloner mentioned below, built himself a house in the vicinity of the town and came to settle there with his family. Richard Chaloner, Baron Gisborough, is today his successor.

Steeple Claydon

The manor and lands of Steeple Claydon near Aylesbury, Bucks, were bought from the Crown by Chaloner in 1557. He paid £2,100 for them, and the annual income from rents and fines was then said to be £100.[7] In 1559 Cecil also arranged separately for Chaloner to buy the rectory of Steeple Claydon:

> Chaloner to Cecil, 27 Aug. 1559.
>
> Thanks Cecil for the stay, by his goodness, of the parsonage of Steeple Claydon. The whole of it is worth but 14l. per ann., the glebe lands (which mostly he seeks), being interlaced with his own ground, are not above twenty nobles or 7l. per ann. Prays that when his brother, Farnham, returns to London, he may have Cecil's aid for the transaction of the purchase to his use.[8]

When Chaloner died the income from the manor was said to be £137 4s 0d, and from the rectory, £36 17s 10d After his death the Chaloner family remained at Steeple Claydon until the mid-seventeenth century, after which they moved to Guisborough.[9] The *Victoria County History of Buckinghamshire* explains the descent of the manor and property:

> In 1557 the reversion of the manor was granted in fee to Sir Thomas Chaloner. He died in October 1565, leaving a son and heir Thomas, afterwards Sir Thomas Chaloner, kt., who was in possession in 1585. On his second marriage in 1604 he made a settlement in tail-male on his sons William, Edward, Thomas and James. William Chaloner succeeded in 1615, and became a baronet in 1620. He settled his estates in 1634 on his surviving brothers Thomas and James in trust for his heir Edward Chaloner (son of the second brother, Edward), who was still a minor in 1644. Thomas and James Chaloner appear to have renewed the trust of Steeple Claydon Manor to the use of Edward in 1647. At the Restoration, since both had signed the death warrant of King Charles, Thomas the survivor was attainted, and died soon afterwards. In 1661 Charles II granted Steeple Claydon Manor to Sir Richard Lane, who had helped him to escape after Worcester,

but Edward Chaloner bought it from the grantee in 1662, and his son William had succeeded him before 1683. He made a declaration of his title in 1701, and conveyed the manor in 1704 to John Verney, Viscount Fermanagh. It has since descended with Middle Claydon, and Sir Harry Calvert Verney, bart. is the present owner.[10]

St Bees

St Bees is situated on the Cumberland coast, south of Whitehaven. The lands belonging to the Benedictine priory of St Bees passed to the Crown after the dissolution of the monasteries. As reward for his work in Scotland, the Duke of Northumberland arranged for Chaloner and his wife Joan to acquire from the Crown a miscellaneous collection of lands in Cumberland and Yorkshire, including the manor of St Bees:

> June 16, 1553
> The manor, rectory, and cell of St Bees in Cowpland, Cumberland; the site of this cell and the lands attached to it formerly leased to Thomas and Joan Chaloner; the manor of Syntall, Yorkshire; and other lands formerly held by the monasteries of Jervaux and Monkbretton and the priory of Worksop.[11]

The total yearly income was £175 13s 9½d, for which Chaloner had to pay fees of £143 16s 2½d per year to the Exchequer. In 1561 he arranged an exchange with the queen whereby he gave up certain of his lands in Cumberland to the Crown, receiving instead two 'parsonages', those of East Haddon and Cold Ashby, both in Northamptonshire.[12]

Both coal and salt may have increased the value of lands in the parish of St Bees,[13] but, as mentioned above, there were disputes with tenants, and overall this estate was probably more trouble than it was worth, especially as, like Guisborough, it was held in fee farm. At Chaloner's death the net income from St Bees was only £21 2s 1½d The properties in Cumberland seem to have passed directly to his son, but Sir Thomas junior sold them off towards the end of his life when his debts were mounting.

Appendix II
TIMETABLE

Year	Events concerning Sir Thomas Chaloner	National events
c. 1520	born	
1525		Tyndall translates New Testament
c. 1528	to grammar school	
1531		Henry VIII proclaimed head of the church
1533		Henry marries Anne Boleyn
c. 1535	to Cambridge	execution of Fisher and More
1536		execution of Anne Boleyn
1536–40		dissolution of the monasteries
1538	joins household of Thomas Cromwell	

Year	Events concerning Sir Thomas Chaloner	National events
1540	present at Diet of Ratisbon	fall of Cromwell
1541	shipwrecked off Algerian coast	
1542		execution of Catherine Howard
1543	translates *Of the Office of Servants*	
1544	translates Chrysostom's *Homilies*	
1545	appointed clerk to privy council	
1546	marries Joan Leigh	
1547	present at battle of Pinkie Cleugh; knighted by Somerset	death of Henry; Edward VI succeeds; Somerset becomes Lord Protector
1549	translates *The Praise of Folly*	popular risings against enclosure, etc.; trial of Somerset
1550	death of Roger Chaloner	Northumberland succeeds Somerset
1551	treats with Scots at Norham	
1552	New Year court revels; conference on Debatable Lands	
1553	briefly appointed ambassador in France; recalled by Mary	death of Edward VI; Lady Jane Grey replaced by Mary I
1554		Mary marries Philip II; Wyatt's rebellion
1555	co-author of *Mirror for Magistrates*	

Year	Events concerning Sir Thomas Chaloner	National events
1556		Charles V resigns Spain to Philip
1557	death of Joan	battle of St Quentin against France
1558	meets Emperor Ferdinand	death of Mary; Elizabeth I succeeds; William Cecil appointed secretary of state
1559–60	resident ambassador in Flanders	Elizabethan religious settlement; Treaty of Cateau Cambrésis
c. 1560	builds Clerkenwell house	Treaty of Edinburgh with France
1561	to Spain as ambassador	
1562–4	composes long Latin poem *De republica Anglorum*	(1562) start of Huguenot wars; English ships seized in Spanish ports
1565	returns to England; marries Audrey Frodsham; death; death of Francis Chaloner	
1579	poems published	

NOTES

Abbreviations

The following abbreviations are used in the notes:

APC	Acts of the Privy Council of England
Blazer	Phyllis Gene Blazer, *The Life of Sir Thomas Chaloner*, unpublished PhD dissertation submitted to the University of New York at Buffalo, 1978
BL	British Library
Campbell	Lily B. Campbell, *The Mirror for Magistrates*, Cambridge, 1938
CPR	Calendar of Patent Rolls
CSP Dom.	Calendar of State Papers, Domestic, Edward, Mary & Elizabeth
CSP For.	Calendar of State Papers, Foreign
CSP Scot.	Calendar of State Papers, Scotland
CSP Spain.	Calendar of State Papers, Spain (Simancas)
EEBO	Early English Books Online
EETS	Early English Text Society

Froude	James Anthony Froude, *The Reign of Elizabeth*, 1872 (Everyman edn, 4 vols, 1911; vols I & II)
HMC	Historical Manuscripts Commission
Hoak	D. L. Hoak, *The King's Council in the reign of Edward VI*, Cambridge, 1976
LP Henry VIII	Letters and Papers of Henry VIII
Mattingly	Garrett Mattingly, *Renaissance Diplomacy*, 1955
Miller	Vol. II of Clarence Harvey Miller, 'Sir Thomas Chaloner's Translation of *The Praise of Folly*', unpublished PhD thesis presented to the Department of English, Harvard University, 2 vols, 1955
NA	National Archives, Kew
ODNB	*Oxford Dictionary of National Biography*, 2004
OED	*Oxford English Dictionary*
STC	Short Title Catalogue
Read	Conyers Read, *Mr Secretary Cecil and Queen Elizabeth*, 1955
Rowse	A. L. Rowse, *Ralegh and the Throckmortons*, 1962
Turton	R. B. Turton, *The Alum Farm*, Whitby, 1938

Preface

1. To access the state papers I have used two websites: www.british-history.ac.uk/ and gale.cengage.co.uk/state-papers-online-15091714.aspx/. Unfortunately the latter is at present only available through subscribing institutions.

Introduction

1. Sir Thomas Elyot, *A Preservative against Death*, 1545, quoted by James Mervyn, *Society, Politics and Culture*, 1986, p. 378.
2. W. K. Jordan, *Edward VI: The Young King*, 1968, p. 232.
3. BL Cotton Vesp. CVII (13 Oct. 1562).
4. Miller, pp. 213 & 303.

1 *Roger Chaloner, 1493–1550*

1. John Graves, *The History of Cleveland*, Carlisle, 1808, p. 416.
2. LP Henry VIII, II, pt. II, no. 2923.
3. LP Henry VIII, XIX, no. 527 (30), quoted in Miller, p. 183.
4. NA C1/889/19–21. I would like to thank Yvette Erskine for this reference.
5. I have no idea what a jebitt was. It is not in the OED.
6. Roger and Dorothy were granted a lease of Abbot's Inn in 1534, and a freehold grant of the property the following year: LP Henry VIII, XIX, pt. I, no. 80 (5), & pt. 2, no. 846 (93).
7. For a description of the house, see http://challonerfamilyireland. wordpress.com/roger-challoner-of-london/.
8. See 'The London Inn of the Abbots of Waltham: a revised reconstruction of a medieval town house in Lovat Lane', Derek Gadd, *Transactions of the London and Middlesex Archaeological Society*, vol. 35, 1984.
9. This was *The Supplication against the Beggars*, renamed *The Supplication against the Ordinaries*; see David Starkey, *Six Wives: the Queens of Henry VIII*, 2003, p. 449. Starkey dates this incident to 1532 rather than earlier, as previous historians have thought.
10. CSP For. 1563, no. 1337.
11. His will has been transcribed by Miller, pp. 316–20.

2 *Education, 1527–1538*

1. There is some uncertainty about his exact birth year. Clarence Miller, the leading authority on Chaloner, wrote in the *ODNB* in 2004 that it was 1521. Yet in his PhD thesis (Harvard, 1955), as well as in his edition of Chaloner's *The Praise of Folly* (1965), he argued for 1520.
2. The statutes of St Paul's School are printed in Howard Staunton, *The Great Schools of England*, 1865, pp. 179–185. They are available online at https://archive.org/.
3. Starkey, p. 490.
4. LP Henry VIII, VI, no. 396.
5. LP Henry VIII, VI, no. 601.
6. N. Jones, *The English Reformation; religion and cultural adaptation*, Oxford, 2002, p. 202.
7. This is not entirely certain. Anthony Wood (*Athenae Oxonienses*, 1813) says he was a student at both universities, but Miller says he could find no reference to him in the records of either (Miller, 188). The only evidence that he was at Cambridge comes from the statement by William Malim (see chapter 3).
8. J. & J. A. Venn, *Alumni Cantabrienses*, pt. I, Cambridge 1924, p. 236; Blazer, p. 598.

9. LP Henry VIII, III, pt. 2, no. 357.
10. Fisher and Lady Margaret Beaufort, mother of Henry VII, were co-founders of St John's College.
11. This letter was written in 1540; J. A. Giles (ed.), *The whole works of Roger Ascham*, 1854–5, vol. 2, p. 37.
12. Quoted by Miller, pp. 188–9.
13. See p. 86.
14. C. H. Cooper, *Annals of Cambridge*, Cambridge, 1842, vol. 1, pp. 374–5.
15. In 1935 Fisher, along with Thomas More who had been executed the same year, was canonised by Pope Pius XI.
16. Jones, p. 93.
17. Blazer, p. 35. For Richard Cecil, see Read, pp. 19–22.
18. Miller, p. 190.
19. Read, p. 33.
20. Apparently Cecil was nearly killed in this battle. His death might have altered the course of English history. The chronicler William Patten states, 'Where he was like to have been slain, but [was] miraculously saved by one that putting forth his arm to thrust Mr. Cecil out of the level of the cannon, had his arm stricken off': Read, p. 471.
21. LP Henry VIII, XIII, pt. 2, no. 1184.
22. LP Henry VIII, XV, no. 776.
23. Susan Brigden, *Thomas Wyatt. The Heart's Forest*, 2012, pp. 310 & 322–3.

3 *Travel and Danger, 1540–1541*

1. This is the only reliable evidence we have that Chaloner went to Cambridge.
2. *De republica Anglorum instauranda*, 1579, STC 4938. This translation is published in William Hakluyt, *The Principal Navigations, Voyages, Traffiques and Discoveries of the English Nation*, 1599, vol. 2, p. 99.
3. LP Henry VIII, XVI, no. 269.
4. Miller, p. 193.
5. Miller, pp. 193–5, quoting Foxe: *The Acts and Monuments of John Foxe*, New York, 1965, vol. 6, pp. 165–8.
6. Henry's calming order makes it quite possible that Gardiner was communicating with the Pope under the king's specific, but secret, instructions: see J. A. Muller, *Stephen Gardiner and the Tudor Reaction*, New York, 1926, pp. 96–7.
7. LP Henry VIII, XVII, no. 84.

8. For details of Charles V's expedition to Algiers see Vandenesse, *The Itinerary of the Emperor Charles V*, in R. Bentley, *Correspondence of the Emperor Charles V*, 1850, pt. 2, cited by Blazer.

4 *Literature and Employment, 1542–1547*

1. See the account of Catherine's life by Retha M. Warnicke in the ODNB.
2. It was treasonable to have known of the queen's adultery and not reported it.
3. Miller, p. 342.
4. This was in addition to the post of teller of the receipt of the Exchequer, which he already held in partnership with his father.
5. LP Henry VIII, XX, pt. 2, no. 1068 (38).
6. Hoak, pp. 274–5.
7. Hoak, p. 332.
8. Hoak, p. 163.
9. APC, vol. 1, p. 275 (26 Nov. 1545).
10. The following paragraphs are based on the introduction to, and translation of, Chaloner's poem by John B. Gabel & Carl C. Schlam: *Thomas Chaloner's 'In Laudem Henrici Octavi'*, Kansas, 1979.
11. Edited and published by William Malim in 1579. See chapter 17.
12. Blazer, p. 81.
13. See Family Trees.
14. For St Oswalds, see appendix I. For the Hospital of St Giles, see the *Survey of London*, 1914, vol. 5, pt. 2, 'St Giles-in-the-fields', pp. 117–126.

5 *In Praise of Folly, 1547–1550*

1. William Patten, *The expedicion into Scotland*, 1548, printed in A. F. Pollard, *Tudor Tracts*, 1903, pp. 110 & 149.
2. David Lloyd, *The States-men and Favourites of England Since the Reformation*, 1665, pp. 343–5.
3. CPR, Edward VI, vol. 4, no. 141, & vol. 5, no. 356.
4. APC, vol. 2, nos. pp. 166–7 (31 Jan. 1547–8).
5. CSP Dom. 1547–80, vol. 8, no. 4.
6. C. Wriothesley, *A Chronicle of England ... from 1485 to 1559*, vol. 2, Camden Soc., 1877, p. 26.
7. See chapter 3.
8. APC, vol. 2, p. 270 (27 March 1549); CSP Dom. 1547–1580, vol. 14, no. 12.
9. See www.kateemersonhistoricals.com/TudorWomen/.

10. APC, vol. 3, p. 427 (23 Nov. 1551). Gargrave was Chaloner's brother-in-law, having married his wife's sister.
11. See Clarence H. Miller (ed.), *Sir Thomas Chaloner, The Praise of Folie*, Oxford, 1965. In the following paragraphs I have borrowed extensively from this book and also from Miller's Harvard doctoral thesis.
12. This stated aim means that Chaloner's translations have a part to play in the so-called inkhorn controversy which involved contemporary disputes about how best to extend the vocabulary of the English language.
13. White Kennet, *Moriae Encomium: or the Praise of Folly* (1683), 5th edn, 1735, p. 357.
14. Miller, p. 375.
15. Roger's will is transcribed in Miller, pp. 316–20. For Chaloner's siblings, see chapters 7 & 19.

6 *Scotland, 1551–1552*

1. CSP For. 1551–53, no. 318.
2. CSP Scotland 1547–63, no. 372 (May 1551).
3. CSP For. 1551–53, no. 348; NA SP 68/7 f. 28. Blazer correctly guessed the solution to this mystery, though she did not see the manuscript of the letter.
4. CSP Scotland 1547–63 (May 1551), no. 372.
5. Richard Grafton, *A Chronicle at Large*, 1568, p. 1317, quoted in Campbell, pp. 27–8.
6. Grafton, p. 1317.
7. Albert Feuillerat (ed.), *The Loseley Manuscripts*, Louvain, 1914, p. 278 (taken from www.archive.org/). Jacques Granado, Drue Drury and Thomas Cobham were all friends of Chaloner.
8. APC, vol. 3, 1550–52, pp. 491–3 (28 Feb. 1551/52).
9. NA MPF 1/257.

7 *Accounts, 1551–1554*

1. Or at least no one seems to have published a transcription, or benefited much from the information contained in them.
2. Neither is his previous trip to Scotland in the summer of 1551 (to negotiate the Treaty of Norham) mentioned, since the accounts only start in September of that year.
3. In Mary's reign he was also granted an estate at Steeple Claydon, Bucks. For more about these estates, see Appendix I.
4. As to his clerkship, this agrees with the figure given by Hoak, p. 271. The two salaries would cease to be paid on Mary's accession.

5. *Inquisitions post mortem*, 38 Henry VIII, no. 146.
6. *Survey of London*, vol. 8: Shoreditch, 1922, pp. 40–47.
7. CPR, vol. 3, pt. 5, no. 305.
8. William Brackenbury was still a servant of Chaloner ten years later when they were both in Spain.
9. Ian Mortimer, *The Time Traveller's Guide to Elizabethan England*, 2013, p. 200.
10. A rich silk cloth, much in use at this period.
11. Mortimer, p. 158.
12. Lace or cord for attaching the hose to the doublet.
13. Rodiginus (1469–1525) was a Venetian scholar who produced commentaries on classical Roman writers. Alessandro Alessandri (1461–1523) was an Italian jurist and philologist. The others were classical Roman authors.
14. See p. 30
15. A viol was an instrument with more strings than a violin or a viola.
16. Could this be the card game today known as Irish switch?
17. 'White money' meant silver; 'pistolets' were foreign gold coins.
18. The property can be traced to 1557, when it was sold as '2 messuages, 2 gardens, 2 orchards, 40 acres of land and 60 acres of pasture in Hoxton by Francis Chaloner, Agnes, his wife, daughter of Bowyer, and John Turner, alias Bowyer, to John Thomas and others'. (*Feet of Fines*, Middlesex, 4–5 Philip & Mary).
19. For John Chaloner's career see Turton, pp. 9–17.
20. Turton, p. 11.
21. A play entitled *Self Love*, perhaps by Nicholas Udall, was performed at court in 1553, either to celebrate the coronation of Mary or at Christmas that year: Alice Hunt, *The Drama of Coronation*, Cambridge, 2008, p. 135.

8 Queen Mary and The Mirror for Magistrates, 1553–1558

1. CSP For. 1547–53, nos 643, 645.
2. The constable was the highest official in France under the king. Anne de Montmorency was the (male) holder of this office.
3. The future King Francis II.
4. CSP For. 1547–53, no. 672 (1 May 1553).
5. HMC, Cecil papers, vol. 1 (16 May 1553).
6. Andrew Kippis, *Biographia Britannica*, 2nd edn, 1784, vol. 3, p. 417.
7. For Steeple Claydon: CPR, Philip & Mary, vol. 4, no. 146; for Guisborough: John Walker Ord, *The History and Antiquities of*

Cleveland, Stokesley & London 1846, pp. 580–91. See also Appendix I.

8. Published in 1579 along with his *De republica Anglorum instauranda*. J. Stephan Edwards has translated Chaloner's elegy on Jane and kindly allowed me to quote from his version. See his website: www.somegreymatter.com/chalonerelegy.htm/. For this poem see also chapter 17.

9. CSP For. 1561–2, no. 878: Chaloner to Sir John Mason, 9 Feb., 1562.

10. CPR, Philip & Mary, vol. 1, no. 410.

11. The Hanaper was that part of the Exchequer where fees were collected for enrolling and sealing deeds.

12. Wyatt was the son of the poet Sir Thomas Wyatt.

13. Lacey Baldwin Smith, *This Realm of England*, 1966, p. 148.

14. The following paragraphs are based on Campbell. For more on members of the group see chapter 18.

15. Campbell, p. 21.

16. Richard Grafton, *A Chronicle at Large*, 1568, vol. 2, p. 1339.

17. See Eveline I. Feasey, 'William Baldwin', *Modern Language Review*, 20 (1925), pp. 407–18.

18. *The Diary of Henry Machyn: Citizen and Merchant-Taylor of London* (1550–1563), 1848, p. 123.

19. A name applied indiscriminately to both iron and copper pyrites.

20. For Mountjoy's career, see Turton, pp. 35–49.

21. CSP Scotland 1547–63 (Feb. 1556), no. 15.

22. APC, vol. 6, p. 260 (Feb. 1557).

23. CSP Dom. 1547–80, vol. 12, no. 693.

9 Elizabeth – The Marriage Question, 1558–1559

1. Quoted in Read, p. 124.

2. Froude, vol. 1, p. 25.

3. Details on Eric of Sweden are from Norman Jones, *The Birth of the Elizabethan Age*, 1993, pp. 123–4.

4. CSP Spain, vol. 1, 1558–67, no. 2 (25 Nov 1558).

5. For more about Philippine Welser and her morganatic marriage to Ferdinand, see the German Wikipedia entry about her, and its references.

6. Froude, vol. 1, p. 141.

7. CSP Spain, vol. 1, no. 27 (18 April 1559).

8. Francis Russell, 2nd Earl of Bedford, was a privy councillor. In the Royal Collection there is a Holbein drawing of him as a boy, but from this it is difficult to tell whether his head was unusually large or not.

9. Froude, vol. 1, p. 68.

10. CSP Spain, vol. 1, no. 27.
11. Froude, vol. 1, p. 100.
12. Froude, vol. 1, p. 143.
13. Froude, vol. 1, pp. 197–8.
14. A sterile marriage.
15. A lustful marriage begun in exuberance and ending in mourning.

10 *Flanders, 1559–1560*

1. Froude, vol. 1, p. 86.
2. i.e. a retort equal to its provocation, a blow for a blow.
3. CSP For. 1559–60, no. 225.
4. CSP For. 1559–60, nos. 1091 & 1114.
5. CSP For. 1559–60, no. 1116.
6. NA SP 70/6 f. 15.
7. CSP For. 1558–59, no. 1341.
8. CSP For. 1559–60, no. 1091.
9. M. Lettenhove, *Relations Politiques des Pays-Bas et de l'Angleterre*, 1882, vol. 2, p. 463 (taken from https://archive.org/).
10. CSP For. 1558–9, no. 1384.
11. CSP For. 1559–60, no. 1258.
12. NA SP 70/9 f. 21.
13. CSP For. 1558–59, no. 1393.
14. HMC Salisbury, 19, 9/1 (6 Dec. 1559).
15. NA SP 70/6 f. 29.
16. NA SP 70/10 f. 41.
17. CSP For. 1559–60, no. 279.
18. CSP For. 1559–60, no. 354.

11 *Alvaro de Quadra, 1559–1564*

1. CSP Spain, vol. 1, no. 155 (14 March 1562.
2. CSP Spain, vol. 1, no. 81 (27 July 1559 to Feria) & no. 52 (27 Dec. 1559 to Philip).
3. Quoted by Froude, vol. 1, pp. 199–200.
4. CSP For. 1559, 411.
5. Froude, vol. 1, pp. 278–9.
6. CSP For. 1563, no. 545.

12 *Journey to Madrid, 1561–1562*

1. *Survey of London*, 2008, vol. 46, 'South and East Clerkenwell'.
2. CSP Dom. 1547–80, vol. 22, no. 23.
3. For more on both of these ladies see chapter 19.
4. For Elizabeth Parr, see chapter 19.
5. For more on this lively character, see chapter 14.

6. CSP For. 1561–62, no. 682. Charles IX died in 1574 at the age of twenty-three.
7. BL Lansdowne, 111/54 & 112/57.
8. This incident concerned Mrs Clarentius's maid. See chapter 15.
9. CSP For. 1561–62, no. 916.
10. CSP For. 1561–62, no. 877. At this time a ducat was worth about six shillings.
11. Gary M. Bell, 'Sir Thomas Chaloner's Diplomatic Expenses in Spain', *Historical Research*, vol. 53, issue 127 (May 1980), pp. 118–24.
12. Bell, p. 120.
13. BL Lansdowne, 112/57 (16 Feb. 1562).
14. 34 maravedis (m.) = 1 real (R.); 11 reales = 1 ducat. According to Bell, at this date 1 real was worth about 6½d.
15. The old Alcazar palace was a medieval Moorish castle converted to a royal palace by Charles V when he moved the Spanish capital from Toledo to Madrid.
16. Guadamazilles were painted and gilded leather hangings, manufactured in panels and assembled for covering walls as an alternative to tapestry. The technique came to Spain from North Africa.
17. CSP For. 1563, no. 578.

13 Mary Stuart and War in France, 1562–1563

1. Two years later Elizabeth sent Throckmorton to Edinburgh to try and persuade Mary to accept Robert Dudley as a suitor for her hand.
2. For Don Carlos see chapter 16.
3. CSP For. 1562, no. 277. Comines's opinion was that when two princes meet face to face, the outcome is always uncertain.
4. Froude, vol. 1, p. 274.
5. CSP For. 1561–62, no. 943.
6. CSP For. 1562, no. 170.
7. CSP For. 1562, no. 514.
8. Froude, vol. 1, p. 358.

14 Sir Nicholas Throckmorton, 1515–1571

1. Rowse, p. 13.
2. It is most unlikely that Robert Dudley had anything to do with Amy Robsart's death. However, just this situation did occur in Scotland a few years later when Mary Stuart married Bothwell who had been involved in the murder of her previous husband, Darnley.
3. CSP For. 1558–9, no. 623.
4. For Thomas Cecil's visit to France, see Read, pp. 212–17.

5. CSP For. 1561–62, no. 1059.
6. CSP For. 1562, no. 169.
7. CSP For. 1562, no.139.
8. CSP For. 1562 no. 188. For Mistress Sands see chapter 19.
9. Rowse, p. 52.

15 *Problems of an Ambassador, 1562–1565*

1. Miller, p. 239.
2. Mattingly, p. 225.
3. Bell, p. 121.
4. CSP For. 1563, no. 263.
5. CSP For. 1562, no. 640.
6. CSP For. 1562, no. 170.
7. See Tracy Sowerby, 'The role of the ambassador and the use of ciphers', *State Papers Online*, at www.british-history.ac.uk/.
8. Mattingly, p. 238.
9. CSP For. 1562, nos. 925 & 1055.
10. CSP For. 1562–63, no. 17.
11. CSP For. 1563, no. 545.
12. CSP For. 1562, no. 1054; 1563, no. 440.
13. CSP For. 1563, no. 903.
14. The following paragraphs about sending letters are based on Blazer, pp. 383–7.
15. CSP For. 1561–2, no. 804.
16. CSP For. 1559–60, no. 629; 1560–61, no. 719.
17. CSP Spain, vol. 2, no. 256.
18. CPR Edward VI, vol. 3, no. 305.
19. CSP For. 1562, no. 262.
20. CSP For. 1562, no. 878.
21. Mattingly, p. 259.
22. Blazer, 396, quoting Henry Charles Lea, *A History of the Inquisition in Spain*, vol. 3, p. 446.
23. John Strype, *Annals of the Reformation*, 1824 edn, vol. 1, pp. 228–35.
24. CSP For. 1562, no. 983.
25. Donald Beecher, 'John Frampton of Bristol, Trader and Translater', in Carmine Di Biase (ed.), *Travel and Translation in the Early Modern Period*, 2006.
26. CSP For. 1562, no. 684.
27. CSP For. 1562, no. 866.
28. CSP For. 1562, no. 557.
29. For Dr Man see chapter 22.
30. Traverse: a curtain or screen drawn across a room (OED).

31. BL Cotton Vesp. CVII, 8 Nov. 1562.
32. Fernand Braudel, *The Mediterranean and the Mediterranean World in the Age of Philip II*, New York, 1973, vol. 2, p. 986.

16 *Don Carlos and Vesalius, 1562–1563*

1. A gathering of purulent matter; an abscess (OED).
2. A quartain ague meant an attack of fever likely to recur every few days.
3. i.e. Joanna 'the Mad', mother of Charles V and the Emperor Ferdinand, and grandmother of Philip. See the Hapsburg tree in Family Trees.
4. Ferdinand, Charles V's brother, was Emperor until his death in 1564. He was succeeded by his son Maximilian II.
5. CSP For. 1562, no. 46.
6. CSP For. 1562, no. 52.
7. A Roman proverb: 'A potter hates [other] potters.'
8. CSP For. 1562, no. 171. The fragment of bone was actually removed by a trepanation of the skull performed by Vesalius.
9. These regular feverish shaking fits are associated today with malaria.
10. CSP For. 1562, no. 262.
11. CSP For. 1563, no. 1037.
12. CSP For. 1563, no. 1337.
13. CSP For. 1563, no. 1338; 1564–5, no. 467.
14. J. B. Saunders & Charles O'Malley (eds), *The Illustrations from the Works of Andreas Vesalius of Brussels*, 1973, p. 39.
15. Froude, vol. 2, p. 205. Elizabeth survived, but died four years later after giving birth to a daughter.

17 *A Poet in Spain, 1562–1565*

1. Miller, p. 286.
2. CSP For. 1563, no. 893.
3. CSP For. 1563, no. 547.
4. Translated by Miller, pp. 36–9.
5. www.somegreymatter.com/.
6. '... *nec dura pepercit/Nec consanguineae (tam pia) nec gravidae*'.
7. Miller, p. 289.
8. Miller, pp. 13–14.
9. Published in Sir John Harington, *Nugae Antiquae*, 1804 edn, vol. 2, pp. 372–89.
10. A plea which seems to contradict Chaloner's seeming confidence in the justice of providence, as shown in his elegy on the death of Lady Jane Grey.

11. *Queen Elizabeth's Englishings of Boethius*, EETS, original series 113, 1899; taken from http://en.calameo.com/.
12. Miller, p. 292. Ludovico Ariosto was an early sixteenth-century Italian poet, best known as the author of *Orlando Furioso* (1516).
13. CSP For. 1562, no. 845. Minikins were gut strings used for the treble string of the lute.
14. T. Crawford, 'Lute counterpoint from Naples', *Early Music*, vol. 34, no. 1 (Feb. 2006). I owe this reference to Yvette Erskine.
15. NA SP 70/62 f. 200; Siculo was a Benedictine monk and author who was executed for heresy by the Inquisition in 1551.

18 Colleagues and Friends

1. Susan Brigden, *Thomas Wyatt: The Heart's Forest*, 2012, especially chapters 11 & 13. It is possible that the young Chaloner himself was also in Spain with Wyatt and Mason (see page 34).
2. NA SP 70/62 f. 97. Gunnersbury was Mason's country estate in Middlesex.
3. NA SP 70/40 f. 235.
4. *Victoria County History of London*, 1909, vol. 1, pp. 546–8.
5. The following paragraphs rely on the relevant articles in the ODNB and on Campbell, pp. 20–39.
6. For the full text of *Beware the Cat* see www.presscom.co.uk/.
7. For Baldwin see the article by John N. King in the ODNB.
8. W. Patten, *The Late Expedicion in Scotlande*, 1548.
9. G. Puttenham, *The Arte of English Poesie*, 1936 edn, p. 60.
10. See chapter 6.
11. Quoted in Campbell, pp. 29–30.
12. See the next chapter.
13. Campbell, p. 32.
14. Jacobus Swart, *Thomas Sackville: A Study in Sixteenth-Century Poetry*, Gronigen, 1948.
15. See the next chapter.
16. CSP For. 1562, no. 19.
17. See chapter 21.

19 Family and Marriage

1. CSP For. 1563, no. 1500 & 1564–65, no. 721.
2. Very likely Chaloner did not believe these allegations, since in his will he left to 'Richarde Percevall my Servaunte' an annuity of fifty-three shillings.
3. CSP For. 1563, no. 1500 & 1564–65, no. 541. This accusation must have reminded Chaloner of the passage about the servant who

betrays his master's secrets in the book *Of the Office of Servants*, which he had translated twenty years earlier. See chapter 4.

4. CSP For. 1563, no. 139
5. CSP For. 1563, no. 1196.
6. CSP For. 1562, no. 706.
7. CSP For. 1563, no. 136.
8. NA SP 70/63 f. 14.
9. Henry Cobham (1537–92) was later appointed resident ambassador in Paris.
10. i.e. Thomas and Bessie, whom sister Ellen was reluctantly looking after.
11. CSP For. 1562, no. 509.
12. BL Add. MS 35831 f. 82.
13. CSP For. 1559–60, no. 354.
14. CSP For. 1562, no. 257.
15. She was the daughter of Anthony Sands of Throwley, Kent.
16. This is a reference to the fact that Berkeley, whose first wife was recently dead, had been left with a brood of three sons and five daughters. See www.tudorplace.com.ar/Bios/ MauriceBerkeleyofBruton/.
17. CSP For. 1562, no. 266.
18. CSP For. 1562, no. 257.
19. CSP For. 1563, no. 1332.
20. CSP For. 1563, no. 1521.
21. Turton, p. 24.
22. CSP For. 1564–65, nos 513, 552, 562.
23. NA SP 70/73 f. 2.
24. Miller, p. 301.
25. CSP For. 1564–65, no. 1680.

20 *Sailors and Pirates, 1563–1565*

1. Froude, vol. 2, p. 433.
2. CSP For. 1563, no. 944.
3. CSP For. 1563, no. 1487.
4. For the colourful career of Thomas Stukeley, see the article by Comer Plummer in www.militaryhistoryonline.com/.
5. CSP For. 1564–5, no. 466.
6. CSP For. 1564–5, no. 879.
7. These were powerful local officials who had a free hand to sit in judgement and decide punishments for all kinds of crime.
8. CSP For. 1564–5, no. 67.
9. CSP For. 1563, no. 1465.
10. CSP For. 1564–5, nos 454 & 576.

11. CSP For. 1564–65, no. 86.
12. NA SP 70/72 f. 100.

21 *Retirement and an Heir, 1565*
1. CSP For. 1564, no. 791.
2. CSP For. 1564, no. 856 & 1565, no. 987.
3. HMC, Pepys MSS, f. 35 (30 Nov. 1564).
4. NA SP 70/72 f. 112.
5. HMC Pepys MSS, f. 33 (7 June 1564). It was John Dudley, Duke of Northumberland, who had appointed Chaloner a commissioner to negotiate the Treaty of Norham with the Scots; see chapter 6.
6. CSP For. 1564–65, no. 1007; HMC, Pepys MSS, f. 54.
7. Turton, p. 25. See also CSP Dom. Eliz. vol. 36, no. 1 (7 Aug. 1565).
8. Turton, pp. 9 & 13.
9. CSP For. 1564–65, no. 1680.
10. Miller, pp. 299–300 & 305–316; Turton, pp. 25–6.
11. For these suggestions about Chaloner's illness and death I am indebted to Dr Tom Duncan, FRCS.
12. Nature and art in Chaloner combined / And for his country form'd the Patriot's mind. / With praise deserved his public posts he filled; / And equal fame his learned labours yield. / While yet he lived, he lived his country's pride, / And first his country injured when he died. (English translation from Charles & Thompson Cooper, *Athenae Cantabrienses*, Cambridge, 1858, vol. 1, p. 237.)
13. In the following paragraphs I have relied on the article about Thomas Chaloner junior by Simon Healy in Andrew Thrush and John P. Ferris (eds), *The History of Parliament: the House of Commons, 1604–1629*, p. 2010.
14. This might have been one reason why one of Sir Thomas Chaloner's grandsons – yet another Thomas – joined the Parliamentarian side in the Civil War. Thomas the third was one of the 'regicides' who signed the death certificate of Charles I.
15. B. J. D. Harrison & G. Dixon, *Guisborough before 1900*, Guisborough, 1981, p. 121.

22 *The New Ambassador*
1. CSP For. 1577–78, no. 487.
2. Mattingly, pp. 191–2.
3. In the following paragraphs I have used Bell's work: Gary M. Bell, 'John Man: the Last Elizabethan Resident Ambassador in Spain', *Sixteenth Century Journal*, VII, p. 2 (Oct. 1976).
4. CSP For. 1566–68, no. 245.
5. CSP For. 1566–68, no. 2018.
6. CSP For. 1566–68, no. 2523.

7. Moriscos were former Muslims who converted, or were coerced into converting, to Christianity.
8. R. B. Wernham, *Before the Armada*, 1966, p. 290.

Conclusion

1. 'We are not born for ourselves, but rather for our country', an adaptation of a phrase from Cicero.
2. For his poem about Henry VIII, see chapter 4; for the one on Lady Jane Grey, chapter 17.
3. CSP For. 1562, no. 859.
4. Miller, p. 292.
5. CSP For. 1559–60, no. 580, quoted in Froude, vol. 1, p. 129.
6. STC 4938 (See EEBO).
7. Translated by the Revd W. Stanhope-Lovell, librarian at Hatfield House.

Appendix I: Sir Thomas Chaloner's Estates

1. These figures are derived from the valuation of Chaloner's property made after his death, which is among the Chaloner papers held at the North Yorkshire Record Office in Northallerton: NYRO ZFM 56B.
2. The fee for Guisborough was reduced by £20 as part of the 1561 property exchange mentioned below.
3. CSP For. 1563, no. 1183.
4. CSP For. 1564–65, no. 290.
5. Turton, pp. 35–37; William Jackson, 'Papers and Pedigrees Mainly Relating to Cumberland and Westmorland', *Publications of the Cumberland and Westmorland Antiquarian and Archaeology Society*, vol. 2, 1892, pp. 7–8.
6. These grants are printed verbatim in John Walker Ord, *The History and Antiquities of Cleveland*, Stokesley & London, 1846, pp. 576–91.
7. CPR, Philip & Mary, vol. 4, no. 146.
8. CSP For. 1558–59, no. 1258.
9. B. J. D. Harrison & G. Dixon (eds), *Guisborough before 1900*, Guisborough, 1981, p. 121.
10. *Victoria County History of Buckinghamshire*, 1927, vol. 4, pp. 226–9. See also John Broad, 'Contesting the Restoration Land Settlement? The Battle for Regicide Lands in Steeple Claydon', *Records of Buckinghamshire*, vol. 47, pt. I (2007).
11. Quoted by Miller, p. 326, citing CPR, Edward VI, vol. 5, nos. 14–15.
12. NA E211/177; CPR, Eliz., vol. 2, 102.
13. CSP For. 1561–2, no. 765.

INDEX

riding time: South Yorkshire to London : four days   p 78

(& cf p. 274 , n.9)

←